Brazil in the Geopolitics of Amazonia and Antarctica

Brazil in the Geopolitics of Amazonia and Antarctica

Edited by

Fábio Albergaria de Queiroz,
Guilherme Lopes da Cunha, and
Ana Flávia Barros-Platiau

LEXINGTON BOOKS
Lanham • Boulder • New York • London

Published by Lexington Books
An imprint of The Rowman & Littlefield Publishing Group, Inc.
4501 Forbes Boulevard, Suite 200, Lanham, Maryland 20706
www.rowman.com

86-90 Paul Street, London EC2A 4NE

British Library Cataloguing in Publication Information Available

Library of Congress Cataloging-in-Publication Data

Names: 1 Queiroz, Fábio Albergaria de, edi | 1 Cunha, Guilherme Lopes
   da, 1981- edi | 1 Platiau, Ana Flávia Barros, edi
Title: Brazil in the geopolitics of Amazonia and Antarctica / edited by
   Fábio Albergaria de Queiroz, Guilherme Lopes da Cunha, and Ana Flávia
   Barros-Plat
Description: 1 Lanham, Maryland: Lexington Books, 2 | Includes
   bibliographical references and in | Summary: "From a pioneering
   perspective, the book contributes to the state-of-the-art contemporary
   Geopolitics by bringing together Amazonia and Antarctica in a single
   interdisciplinary volume. Three key issues are 1) the interconnectedness
   between these vital regions, 2) non-linearity, because they may lead to
   unpredictable effects on the Earth system, and; 3) emergence, which
   means the varied interactions between Amazonia and Antarctica may lead
   to unique results"-- Provided by publis
Identifiers: LCCN 2023013894 (print) | LCCN 202301 (ebook) | ISBN
   9781666902686 (cloth) | ISBN 9781666902693 (epub)
Subjects:
Classification: LCC F2523 .B726 2023 (print) | LCC F2523 (ebook) | DDC
   320.1/20981--dc23/eng/20230503
LC record available at https://lccn.loc.gov/2023013894
LC ebook record available at https://lccn.loc.gov/2023013895

Contents

Acknowledgments

As Amazonia and Antarctica are, directly or indirectly, linked to long-term issues that may affect geopolitical and scientific-technological scenarios, this book contributes to the project Prospective for Security and Defense (Prospectiva para Segurança e Defesa), grant number 88887.387694/2019-00, in the context of the Academic Cooperation Program in National Defense (PROCAD-DEFESA), supported by Brazil's Ministry of Defence and Ministry of Education. The editors and authors appreciate the financial support granted for the manuscript's proofreading.

Introduction

Fábio Albergaria de Queiroz, Guilherme Lopes da Cunha, Ana Flávia Barros-Platiau, and Paulo E. A. S. Câmara

As properly pointed out by Richard Haass (2017), we have entered a new international system. It is the so-called World Order 2.0, where little stays local and just about anyone and anything can reach almost anywhere, thus establishing intense relations of interdependence marked by complexity and disruptive challenges, some of them unprecedented.

In this context, prone to multiple connections of varied order, where the destinies of both the traditional nation-states and nonstate actors are interwoven in different ways, we are led to think about all these aspects as variables capable of potentially posing threats that gain emphasis in the current *geopolitical environment* as overlapping and interdependent layers. Accordingly, we have managed significant and complex challenges, among them increasing concerns about the future of what the renowned Brazilian geographer Bertha Becker (2005, 77) labeled as the "El Dorados of the 21st century": Amazonia[1] and Antarctica.

Amazonia and Antarctica together! Initially, it seems an odd correlation. So, what could both possibly have in common? Separated by thousands of kilometers, they are two of the main domains where nature's great stocks are located, and both play distinct but vital and complementary roles in Earth's dynamics. They are essential in climate and the biosphere balances and equally suffer from a lack of understanding of their relevance in preventing a catastrophic collapse with multiple implications: from economics to politics, from the military sector to the environmental sector.

Consequently, both face serious threats of irreversible damage and tipping cascades. Thus, Amazonia and Antarctica are not only El Dorados because they are sources of wealth that are still largely unexplored, they are also "Earth's Achilles' heels" because their condition may engender impacts on a global scale. Therefore, both of them are "tipping elements," identified

1

as such in 2007, the same as other "vital organs of the planet": the Arctic summer sea ice, the Greenland ice sheet, the El Niño Southern Oscillation, the Atlantic thermohaline circulation, the Indian monsoon, the West Africa monsoon, and the boreal forest (Lenton et al., 2007). Consequently, human-kind faces a difficult choice: exploring the El Dorados to respond to acceler-ated market demand for food and minerals or adopting a more science-led approach to prevent catastrophes as the "outcome of the interaction between political, financial, social, technical and natural circumstances." as Kron (2013, 1381) puts it.

In the past, in their own time, Amazonia and Antarctica represented the last frontiers to be conquered—in essence, both still are. Indigenous communities inhabited the Amazonia region, and it was first visited by Europeans in the sixteenth century when Francisco de Orellana (1511–1546) first arrived there. Although endowed with extraordinary resources, the forest was too dense and dangerous to be explored. As a result, the region has never been fully explored, and some of its areas are still pristine. Antarctica has a similar his-tory, allegedly having been discovered in the seventeenth century by a Maori sailor, according to Percy Smith (1899). Mainstream narratives acknowledge that European whalers and sealers arrived there much later, in the nineteenth century. Unfortunately, to avoid trade competition, they did not record their locations and dates in their logbooks.

As a result, it is impossible to be sure who arrived first in Antarctica, but the laurels usually go to the Russian sailor Fabian Bellingshausen (1778–1852). Some years earlier, the famous British explorer and navigator Captain James Cook (1728–1779), in one of his exploring expeditions on February 6, 1775, registered in his manuscripts that "the risk that one runs in exploring a coast in these unknown and icy seas is so very great, that I can be bold to say, that no man will ever venture further than I have done, and that the lands which by to the south will never be explored."[2] The South Pole itself was attained only in 1911 by Roald Amundsen (1872–1928), and today there still are several places (like Amazonia) where no humans have set foot yet. Also, the weather and associated dangers still pose a significant risk for people who visit the region.

Figure 0.1. Captain James Cook's Manuscripts on February 6, 1775. The National Library of Australia offers public access to the Captain James Cook's Manuscripts, which registered his journey in the South Pole on February 6, 1775. See: Cook (1775).

From a climate and weather perspective, both play a crucial role in planetary cycles. While Amazonia is a great humidifier, Antarctica acts like a big cooler. By cooling down the sea currents, Antarctica also cools regions further away from it and, at the same time, plays a vital role in frontogenesis, which is very important in keeping the rainy seasons in the south and southeast portions of Brazil, where important crops are concentrated. On the other hand, in the country's northern regions, the Amazon rainforest is responsible for these rains and ensuring economically important crops.

Interestingly enough, the central part of Brazil receives influence from both areas. When the wet and warmer Amazonia influence is more significant than the Antarctic one, we have the rainy season. Likewise, when the dry and colder Antarctic weather influence is stronger than Amazonia's, we have the dry season. This alternation between only two seasons, a wet one and a dry one, instead of four seasons, is only familiar to those living in the heart of Brazil. However, it is also pivotal for balancing the main biome in central Brazil: the Cerrado (a large region with savannah-like vegetation).[3] Since some plants only flower in the dry season, whereas others only bloom when it rains, insects and pollinators depend on the changes between dry and wet seasons. Consequently, we can infer that it is not an exaggeration that this unique ecosystem (i.e., the Cerrado) depends on both Amazonia and Antarctica for its healthy functioning as a biome.

Both Amazonia and Antarctica also hold significant differences, such as human influence and effects. For example, the Amazonia forest has been home to Indigenous people for thousands of years, whereas autochthonous humans have never occupied Antarctica. In addition, Antarctica is the last place on Earth where sovereignty claims were postponed for some point in the future, while the Amazonia rainforest is part of several countries' territories.

On the other hand, the pressure to use its economic resources is increasing in Amazonia, as it faces deforestation and somehow uncontrolled exploration of its natural resources. Ashes from burned Amazonian trees can be found even in Antarctic ice. For now, such exploration of natural resources in Antarctica is forbidden, but that may change soon, as tourism activities tend to soar, for example.

The increase in population and its associated need for natural resources already pose considerable challenges for Amazonia and Antarctica. Therefore, deepening knowledge of both regions and their connections is paramount. Moreover, it makes it feasible to deal with upcoming changes and challenges. Furthermore, with a collective effort to gather contributions from different ontologies and epistemologies for a better understanding of the complexity of the Earth system, it will be possible to make rational and balanced decisions that guarantee the governance of strategic spaces such as Amazonia and Antarctica.

THE BOOK

This book is a pioneer, as it may be the only publication bringing together Amazonia and Antarctica in a single, interdisciplinary volume from a Brazilian standpoint. Thus, it may provide an innovative analysis capable of contributing to the state-of-the-art concerning these two vital regions of the planet.

In the midst of different (re)interpretations of what geopolitics is, in this book we start with a comprehensive definition, notwithstanding quite simple. Most of the analysis produced derives from the epistemological contributions of great exponents such as Friedrich Ratzel (1844–1904), Rudolph Kjellén (1864–1922), Karl Haushofer (1869–1946), Halford J. Mackinder (1861–1947), Nicholas J. Spykman (1893–1943) Yves Lacoste (1929), or more recently, Saul Bernard Cohen (1925–2021).

In this sense, from our perspective, being cautious to avoid the risk of conceptual stretching,[4] we depart from the understanding of contemporary geopolitics as being the outcome of multiple and complex interactions between geographical settings and world politics. We conceive, in this equation, objective and ideational variables: technology patterns, availability of natural resources, beliefs, identities, material capabilities, and distribution/perception of power.

On that account, the book aims at providing a unique geopolitical perspective reflecting on some key issues: 1) the *interconnectedness* between Amazonia and Antarctica, 2) *nonlinearity*, meaning that even minor events regarding both issues may constitute tipping points that bring about significant effects to the Earth system and, 3) *emergence*, which means that the varied interactions between Amazonia- and Antarctica-related issues may lead to unique and unpredictable results.

Therefore, in ten chapters, the authors bring together contributions from different theoretical perspectives to respond to the following guiding questions: What were, are, and will be the epistemological contributions of Brazilian thought on these two themes in the scope of geopolitics? From this intellectual exercise, how do we interpret the role of Antarctica and Amazonia in shaping the current asymmetrical, transnational architecture of power?

At the same time, the inferences achieved draw attention to possible anthropic externalities to the so-called planetary boundaries. These are limits that, if overstepped, have the potential to put at risk the stability and resilience of the Earth system (Rockström et al., 2009). Among them, for our purposes, some "core boundaries" stand out as processes by which a myriad of stake-holders engages in a wide range of activities: framing, communicating, contesting, and negotiating their interests about Amazonia and/or Antarctica, such as loss of biosphere integrity (biodiversity loss and extinctions), climate change, and the global hydrological cycle. Consequently, the main takeaway argument is that the time has come for each country to revisit geopolitical priorities based on scientific evidence and take new responsibilities for the interest of humankind.

To adequately address these pragmatic points, the book is divided into three parts. The first part, consisting of five chapters, analyzes a broad picture of the Brazilian geopolitical perceptions of Amazonia. Subsequently, the second part brings together three chapters through which it is possible to verify how Antarctica gradually takes part in Brazilian strategic thinking in multiple dimensions. The third part of the book proposes possible connections between the El Dorados. The last two chapters highlight the role of Amazonia and Antarctic in the context of scientific diplomacy as a path to a more stable geopolitical order to, then, explore similarities and differences between the heritage of these strategic spaces and their impact on the construction of historical narratives. Last but not least, we invite all readers to join us on this challenging geopolitical journey.

NOTES

1. It is worth mentioning that both spellings, "Amazonia" and "the Amazon," are used in the book to designate the same object of analysis. The choice is purely a stylistic matter up to each author. This way, while the first one seeks to value Portuguese semantics, the second one, as is well-known, is widely used in international literature.

2. James Cook, *Journal of Captain James Cook kept on HMS Resolution on his second voyage to the Pacific*. Volume 2 1772–1775 Series, p.202. The National Library of Australia, Online Historic Collection Section, (as filmed by the AJCP) [microform]: [M722]. Consulted November 25, 2022. https://nla.gov.au/nla.obj -1402274252/view.

3. Covering nearly two million km² or 23 percent of the Brazilian territory, the Cerrado is the second largest Brazilian biome, just after the Amazonia. It has been considered the world's second most important savannah in terms of biodiversity, with an estimated flora and fauna composed of between 80,000 and 160,000 species. Many of these species are endemic, meaning they are only found in the Cerrado region and may be extinct if their habitats are destroyed.

4. Conceptual stretching occurs when researchers inappropriately apply established theories in new contexts. In doing so, the explanatory scope of certain concepts is stretched, however, at the risk of compromising their analytical capacity and, consequently, leading to pseudo-equivalences.

REFERENCES

Becker, Bertha. Geopolítica da Amazônia [Amazon Geopolitics]. Estudos Avançados, 19 (53), 2005.

Cook, James. *Journal of Captain James Cook kept on HMS Resolution on his second voyage to the Pacific*. Volume 2 1772–1775 Series. The National Library of Australia, Online Historic Collection Section, (as filmed by the AJCP) [microform]: [M722]. Consulted November 25, 2022. https://nla.gov.au/nla.obj -1402274252/view.

Haass, R. World order 2.0: the case for sovereign obligation. Foreign Affairs, v. 96, n. 1, p. 1–9, 2017.

Kron, W. Coasts: the high-risk areas of the world. *Nat Hazards* 66, 1363–1382, 2013.

Lenton, T.; Held, H.; Kriegler, E.; Hall, J.; Lucht, W.; Rahmstorf, S; Schellnhuber. Tipping elements in the Earth's climate system. PNAS, 2007. Available at: https://www.pnas.org/doi/epdf/10.1073/pnas.0705414105.

Smith, S. Percy. Hawaiki: the whence of the Maori, being an introduction to Rarotongan history. The Journal of the Polynesian Society. Volume 8, No. 1, March 1899. pp. 01–48. Available at: https://www.jps.auckland.ac.nz/document/Volume _8_1899/Volume_8%2C_No._1%2C_March_1899/Hawaiki%3A_the_whence _of_the_Maori%2C_being_an_introduction_to_Rarotongan_history%3A_Part_III %2C_by_S._Percy_Smith%2C_p_1-48/p1.

PART I

Brazilian Geopolitical Perceptions for Amazonia

Chapter 1

Amazonian Geopolitics of Climate Change

José Antonio Marengo Orsini and
Gilberto Fernando Fisch

The Amazon region has undergone notable structural changes in which new actors, from academia, organized civil society, regional and federal governments, and international organizations, have played a decisive role. The region extends into several countries like Brazil, Venezuela, Peru, Bolivia, Colombia, Ecuador, Guyana, French Guiana (France), and Suriname. It hosts the world's largest tropical rainforest with the most expressive percentage of biodiversity. However, perceptions of its challenges differ among Amazon countries, which reflect different global, national, and regional interests resulting in conflicts that make it difficult to implement appropriate and adequate public policies. Therefore, the Amazon requires an approach to consolidate its development as a region. Strengthening institutions, new science, technology, innovation advances, and regionalization are suggested strategies (Becker, 2016).

The Amazon region is experiencing illegal mining, fishing, and deforestation. In addition, Indigenous people face menaces from economic groups that try to take their lands for timber. These are examples of how climate change may impact sociopolitical environmental crises. This implication means that Amazonia will struggle to control geographical entities with an international and global dimension and use them for political advantage.

Geopolitics is a relevant tool for understanding the complex world around us. It represents the study of the influence of factors such as geography, anthropic aspects, economics, environment, and demography on politics, especially a state's foreign policy. In general, geopolitical examples of these interactions may include activities or initiatives such as trade agreements, war treaties, border or territorial acknowledgments, and climate agreements.

Dagicour (2020) and the recent results of the Science Panel for Amazonia (Science Panel for the Amazon, 2021; SPA) suggest that the Amazon basin represents an irreplaceable reservoir of biodiversity and freshwater, and the region has become extremely important in this age of climate disruption. The "once-in-a-century" droughts and floods that have affected Amazonia since the beginning of the twenty-first century and their impacts on natural and human systems are examples of how climate change may already affect the Amazon region. It functions as an entity where climate change may affect the region and the entire planet (Marengo et al., 2021b). The fires that struck the Amazon rainforest in 2019 revealed the fragility of this area and shed light on the profound divergences between the Brazilian government, the scientific sector, and the international community.

Deforestation in the Brazilian Amazon has almost doubled since 2018, with industrial, agricultural monoculture, and mineral extraction making ever-greater inroads into the tropical belt. There is a dilemma in which some federal government sectors believe that economic development is more important than protecting the environment. In the face of the global ecological and climate crisis, tension has emerged between the sovereignty of Amazon states and the argument that, in this case, a set of international rules should be applied.

Facing Brazil's commitments at the Paris Agreement in 2015 and renewed in the COP-26 in Glasgow in 2021, the Brazilian government's recent geopolitical positioning has cast a veil of uncertainty over the conservation of the Amazon rainforest, potentially negating recent progress in multilateral governance on climate change. In any case, one may ask if Brazil will fail to fulfill its promises to reduce deforestation and greenhouse gas emissions, committed in Paris and Glasgow.

This increasingly diverse web of local, national, and international stakeholders proves the need for awareness of the Amazon's critical role in regulating the earth's climate. Moreover, it raises questions about the wisdom of the development model being pursued.

The Pact of Leticia, a commitment signed by Amazonian nations in 2019 to intensify their collaboration in satellite monitoring and combating deforestation, contains very few concrete measures. Nevertheless, the Leticia summit brought new focus to the perennial difficulty of bringing about genuine regional cooperation in the face of powerful national interests.

With the new scientific knowledge provided by SPA (2021) and the IPCC Assessment Report (AR6) documents (IPCC 2021, 2022), we offer some scientific issues: What challenges and threats hang over the Amazon today, placing its ecosystems and populations at risk? How considerable and accurate is the risk of climate change making the Amazon rainforest reach a tipping point? Is it a case of suffering the dieback of its tropical forest becoming a savanna biome, thus affecting the local, regional, and global water, energy, and carbon cycles? How should the Amazon rainforest and its resources be governed in an environmental emergency? In this chapter we try to answer these questions from a scientific point of view. In addition, we provide some insights that could be useful in the geopolitical discussions on the Amazon region and its strategic role in the socioenvironmental development of the region.

1. THE AMAZON'S ROLE IN WORLDWIDE REGIONAL AND GLOBAL CLIMATE STABILITY

Macedo (2021) points out the importance of the Amazon for keeping global climate balance, the drastic change to the environmental agenda of Brazilian diplomacy, and the growing call in international public opinion for a globally coordinated action to reverse deforestation in the region. The Amazon plays a crucial role as a sink of carbon dioxide (the forest absorbs about two billion tons of carbon dioxide per year, which is approximately 5 percent of the planet's annual emissions), and it is at the center of the debate about reversing climate change (Brando, 2020).

However, it is clear today that, in addition to decreasing the gas absorption capacity, deforestation is releasing a significant additional amount of carbon dioxide into the atmosphere and, as a result, accelerating the process of global warming. The situation is more evident along the deforestation arc in southeastern Amazonia, where observations show that, in recent decades, this section of Amazonia has been experiencing warming and drying, becoming a source of carbon (Gatti et al., 2021; Boulton et al., 2022). This scenario is consistent with previous works by Lovejoy and Nobre (2018) and Covey et al. (2021). They suggest that the dynamics of gaseous exchanges between the Amazon rainforest and the atmosphere is already hostile. We may have already passed the tipping point, so the emission of gasses from the forest might have accelerated climatic change.

Recent climate-modeling studies consider the Amazon basin deforestation (SPA, 2021). However, because climate, hydrology, and deforestation data are available for Brazil, most scientific studies have been conducted for the Brazilian Amazon (Amazônia Legal). Given the importance of the entire Amazon basin, encompassing its broad Pan-Amazonia perspective, we should consider that the atmosphere and rivers do not care about political boundaries. Therefore, future observations, mapping studies, and analyses must break through national boundaries, following the example of projects such as Rede Amazônica de Informação Socioambiental Georreferenciada (RAISG), with its extensive, integrated surveys on human pressure on the Amazon (RAISG, 2012).

The Amazon Forest comprises nine countries, and 60 percent of its land is inside Brazil's territory. This composition reaffirms the importance of Brazil's active engagement in preservation initiatives and global climate security in general. In 2021, Brazil reported approximately 184,000 wildfire outbreaks, the highest occurrences in South America. Most of these fires occurred due to deforestation: almost 41 percent in the Amazon region, followed by the Cerrado (34%). Dry conditions in southern and eastern Amazonia favored these circumstances.

According to the National Institute of Space Research, deforestation increased 34 percent in 2019 compared to the previous year, despite the economic crisis. Also, it increased again in 2020, despite the COVID-19 pandemic. In 2021 alone, deforestation in the Brazilian Amazon rainforest reached its highest level in more than fifteen years (see Figure 1), increasing by 22 percent.

1.1 Amazonian and South American Water, Food, and Energy Security

The Amazon is home to about three million species of plants and animals and one million Indigenous people. The Amazon biome plays a critical role

Amazon deforestation highest since 2006
Annual rate in square kilometres

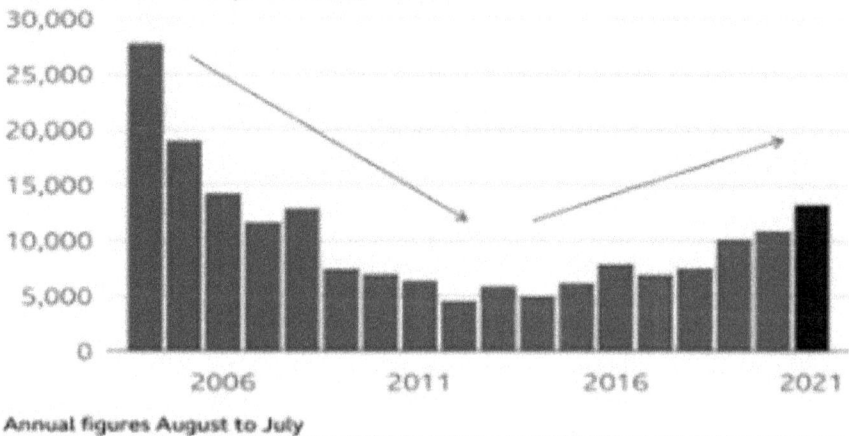

Annual figures August to July

Figure 1.1.   Deforestation Rate in the Brazilian Amazon to 2021. PRODES-INPE-National Institute for Space Research

in the regional and global water cycle and in regulating climate variability. It is a crucial carbon storage and sink, storing approximately 150–200 billion tons of carbon in soils and vegetation (SPA, 2021 and references quoted in). Rainfall in the Amazon region is partially due to a significant amount of atmospheric moisture from the tropical Atlantic Ocean. The humid air masses from the tropical Atlantic gain extra moisture due to water recycling of the forest when crossing the Amazon. Later, this moisture flows to southeastern South America via the so-called aerial rivers (Marengo et al., 2021b), suggesting that the Amazon region is an essential water source for ecosystems beyond the basin, like south and southeastern South America.

The term "aerial river" suggests, and stresses, the understanding that the volume of moisture transported by these atmospheric regions is somewhat equivalent to the discharge of the Amazon River into the Atlantic Ocean (Arraut et al., 2012). The aerial river to the east of the Andes contributes to precipitation over southern Brazil and the La Plata River basin via the South American low-level jet east of the Andes (SALLJ; Marengo et al., 2008). This moisture feeds intense mesoscale convective systems and heavy precipitation, frequently developing near its exit (Zipser et al., 2006). The SALLJ transports large amounts of moisture from the Amazon basin toward the subtropics of South America, and evapotranspiration from the Amazon basin contributes substantially to regional precipitation patterns (Zemp et al., 2014; Gimeno et al., 2016; Staal et al., 2018).

Montini et al. (2019) showed significant increases in the SALLJ. It demonstrates that, in recent decades, the northwesterly moisture flux, especially in austral spring, summer, and fall, has possibly enhanced precipitation and extremes over southeastern South America. Jones (2019) shows substantial growth in the activity of the SALLJ northern branch in the last thirty-nine years and explains the dynamic reasons for that. The frequency and intensity of the SALLJ in the Northern Andes emphasize this expansion in activity.

During the significant drought in the southern Amazon in the summer of 2005, the number of SALLJ events during January 2005, at the height of the rainy season, was meager, suggesting a disruption of moisture transport from the tropical North Atlantic. Furthermore, throughout the drought in southeastern Brazil in 2013–2015 (Nobre et al., 2016a) and over Pantanal in 2020 (Marengo et al., 2021a), we verified that the moisture coming from Amazonia did not reach the region due to an atmospheric synoptic blocking system during summer.

The drought in 2013–2015 affected water and energy security in Sao Paulo, and in 2005 it increased the risk of fire over southern Amazonia, while in 2020 it triggered the worse drought in Pantanal. In all those years, the SALLJ was almost absent during the summertime. In Pantanal, the number of fire events was extremely high in 2020, increasing by more than 200 percent compared to previous years. In 2019–2020, the drought-heat stress compound event in Pantanal affected river transportation during those years and a large-scale fire with a vast loss of biodiversity. In 2022, this situation persists.

Other effects of extremes of climate variability in the form of drought, floods, and climate change may increase through the destruction of the Amazon forests and related land use changes. The loss of habitable and arable land due to droughts, floods, and forced migrations of people are potential consequences (Macedo, 2021). Moreover, there are risks to food supply chains and food security in developed and developing countries, as well as to energy supply in case of a dam collapse, and droughts, besides political and economic instability.

Gloor et al. (2013) and Barichivich et al. (2018) verified the modification of the hydrological cycle in the Amazon in the last decades. It is partly explained by changes in moisture transport coming from the tropical Atlantic, presumably caused by sea surface temperature (SST) induced northward displacement of the Inter Tropical Convergence Zone (ITCZ) (Marengo et al., 2013, 2018; Gimeno et al., 2020). Furthermore, at the beginning of the twenty-first century, there has been an unprecedented number of extreme drought and flood events. The changes in SST gradients and atmospheric circulation may also be related to the large-scale conversion of forests to pasture and cropland over the last decades across the region.

This panorama alters the land-atmosphere interface and contributes to changes in the regional and local hydrological cycle (Zemp et al., 2017a, b; Garcia et al., 2018). Therefore, the observed extreme climatic events in the region, such as droughts and floods, or changes in the rainy and dry seasons, augmented fire risk with associated impacts on climate, health, and biodiversity; these suggest an increase in climate variability in the region (Aragão et al., 2018).

In summary, around 50 percent of the Amazon's annual rainfall originates from the evapotranspiration of Amazonian trees. Land-use change in these regions may weaken moisture recycling processes and have more decisive consequences for rainfed agriculture and natural ecosystems regionally and downwind than previously thought (Zemp et al., 2014). Removal of forests increases temperature, reduces evapotranspiration, and diminishes precipitation downwind of deforested areas (Nobre et al., 2016a; Staal et al., 2018; Sierra et al., 2021). Besides current consequences, deforestation and the degradation of terrestrial and aquatic systems put human health, food, and water security at risk, decreasing the Amazon's people and wildlife capacity to adapt to further and future anthropogenic changes. Consequently, the resilience of the biome will decrease.

1.2 Climate Extremes and Impacts on Population and Biomes

The positive feedback between changes in climate and land use, mainly deforestation, is a threat to the Amazon rainforest, increasing fire occurrence, forest degradation, and long-term loss of forest functional structure. The combined effect of both impacts will lead to a long-term decrease in carbon stocks in forest biomass, compromising Amazonia's role as a carbon sink, largely conditional on the forest's responses to elevated atmospheric CO_2 (Gatti et al., 2021).

Amazonia hosts the earth's most extensive tropical forests and has been a vital carbon sink over recent decades. However, this carbon sink seems to decline with time due to deforestation and climate change. Even when deforestation rates declined significantly from 2005 to 2014 (75%) in the Brazilian Amazon, the number of vegetation fires did not decline at the same rate. Due to the increased frequency of extreme droughts, higher temperatures, and increased forest degradation, the rainforest becomes more vulnerable to fires as time passes (Aragão et al., 2018).

The rainforest's transformation into a savanna brings biodiversity loss and alterations in ecosystem functions and services (Sampaio et al., 2019). In the Amazon basin, the synergic effects of deforestation, fire, agricultural frontier expansion, infrastructure development, extractive activities, climate change, and extreme events may exacerbate the risk of savannization, leading to more frequent, stronger, and persistent drought periods (Nobre et al., 2016b). This direction will result in temperature increases and a decline in annual rainfall. Consequently, there will be reduced availability of the ecosystem services the forest offers for local people.

2. CLIMATE CHANGE: CLIMATE SECURITY RISKS IN AMAZONIA

Climate change became a security issue, and public opinion turned it into a topic of public debate alongside complementary agendas such as identity, human, and food security. As a result, the concept of climate or environmental security encompasses a prospective debate on climate change and its effects on land, biodiversity, atmosphere, water, and forests. Moreover, consolidating the concept of climate security brings implications for framing the current situation in the Amazon as a matter of security, not only on a local scale but also from regional and global perspectives.

A complex chain of interrelated events exists between the Amazon and all dimensions of human activity and the ecosystem. Therefore, any threat to the survival of the Amazon represents an existential resilience to an unlimited variety of services that require protection. It is precisely for its multifaceted nature that the Amazon is valuable, and the forest's delicate balance must not be broken (Macedo, 2021).

This level of consciousness stems from accumulating and overlapping scientific research findings and political agendas. Environmental threats are now beginning to emerge on a global scale and perspective. The most worrisome of these are the possible consequences of global warming caused by the atmospheric buildup of greenhouse gasses. Slowing or adapting to climate change is essential for reducing population risks. Conflicts between scientific and political agendas must be solved to help societies reach adaptation and resilience (IPCC, 2021, 2022; UNDP, 2021).

2.1 Drought and Risk of Fire and Floods in the Region: Past, Present, and Future

The Amazon rainforest is particularly vulnerable to climate change. Consequently, there are interconnected risks of deforestation, forest degradation, and climate change, increasing forest fires' risk and prevalence, reducing forest resilience, soaring tree mortality, drought stress, and loss of biodiversity.

Dry seasons in the Amazon have become more intense, longer, and drier in recent decades, leading to more significant forest biodiversity loss and increasing fire risk. Studies have shown evidence of the lengthening of the region's dry season, primarily over the southern Amazon, since the 1970s (Marengo et al., 2011, 2018, 2021b; Fu et al., 2013). This tendency can be related to the large-scale influence of meridional SST gradients across the North and South Atlantic. However, alternative explanations indicate the strong influence of dry season evapotranspiration in response to a seasonal increment of solar radiation (Dubreuil et al., 2012; Fu et al., 2013; Marengo et al., 2018).

In addition, we must consider other consequences. On the one hand, a poleward shift influences the southern hemispheric subtropical jets (Fu et al., 2013), on the other hand there is an equatorward contraction of the ITCZ (Arias et al., 2015). In addition, Wang et al. (2011), Alves et al. (2017), and Leite-Filho et al. (2019) suggest that land-use change influences the dry season's length in the Amazon. Therefore, a consequently longer dry season induces a late onset of the rainy season, which impacts the hydrology and the risk of fire in the region.

According to Tomasella et al. (2011) and Marengo et al. (2018), the substantial interannual rainfall variability over the Amazon basin directly impacts the Amazon River's water balance. Because of this variability, the

Amazon basin is affected by recurrent droughts and floods of variable intensity. Drought not only implies a shortage of precipitation but is also generally associated with increased surface air temperature. Usually, most of the severe droughts in the Amazon region are El Nino-related events (Cai et al., 2020). However, in 1963 and 2005, the Amazon was affected by a severe drought that was not El Niño-related: most rainfall anomalies in the southwestern Amazon resulted from SST irregularities in the tropical North Atlantic (TNA). In fact, during the last twenty years, the three "megadroughts" (2005, 2010, and 2015/16) (Jiménez-Muñoz et al., 2016; Marengo and Espinoza, 2016) were events classified at the time as "one-in-a-one hundred-year events." Past megadroughts identified in 1925–1926, 1982–1983, and 1997–1998 had El Niño as a consequence (Marengo et al., 2018). In contrast, "megafloods" were detected in 2009, 2012, 2014, and 2021 (Marengo and Espinoza, 2016; Espinoza et al., 2022).

Historical drought and flood maintain connections with tropical Pacific and Atlantic influences. For instance, the historic drought in 2010 involved El Niño during the austral summer and a combined warmer-than-usual tropical Atlantic SST during the austral winter and spring (Marengo and Espinoza, 2016). In 2021, in a similar context, the flood caused the intensification of the atmospheric upward motion in northern Amazonia: as a result, the Walker cell circulation[1] (Espinoza et al., 2022). In addition, as documented in the previous significant floods of the twenty-first century (2009 and 2012), the 2021 flood also occurred under La Niña conditions in the central equatorial Pacific. Therefore, during the 2021 flood, an intensification of the continental Hadley cell circulation[2] was also reported, producing in June 2021 the highest water levels of the Rio Negro at Manaus in 120 years of record. This flood surpassed the "once-in-a-century" Amazon flood of 2012 (Espinoza et al., 2022).

An international initiative is to study the performance of the coupled atmosphere-ocean general circulation models led by the IPCC. The Climate Model Intercomparison Project,[3] named CMIP6, facilitates the assessment of the strengths and weaknesses of climate models. For example, phase 6 (CMIP6) shows that future climate projections agree on the sign of decreasing future rainfall trends in the Amazon, with droughts projected to increase in duration and intensity under global warming (Ukkola et al., 2020). Especially, CMIP6 models show drying across the eastern and southern Amazon in the twenty-first century (Parsons et al., 2020). In addition, most CMIP6 models agree on future decreases in soil moisture and runoff across most of the Amazon in all emissions scenarios (Cook et al., 2020).

Under different global warming scenarios, the Amazon is central. Projections indicate an increase of 75 percent in the number of hot days (global warming above 4°C compared to the long-term climatology) and a decrease in the highest five-day precipitation amount (Rx5day).[4] In addition, this region increased meteorological droughts (Santos et al., 2020). Lastly, Oliveira et al. (2021) show that the combined effects of large-scale Amazon deforestation and global warming can subject millions of people in the Amazon region to a heat stress index beyond the level of survivability by the end of the twenty-first century. Furthermore, it is also an indication that the effects of deforestation alone are comparable to those of the worst-case global warming scenarios under RCP8.5.[5]

2.2 The Risk of a Future Amazon Rainforest Dieback

For Amazonia, the current generation of climate models from CMIP6 projects the possibility of two equilibrium points: one that favors the forest (humid, the current and historical state of the Amazon basin) and another that favors the savanna (drier, the current conditions in the Cerrado, a potentially bleak future for the Amazon basin (Nobre, 2014).

In the face of warming climate, increased deforestation and ecosystem degradation, and wildfires, the Amazon could soon reach a tipping point beyond which recovery may be impossible. Moreover, the climate of the Amazon could soon reach a tipping point of global consequence, beyond which most of the remaining rainforest would irreversibly change to a different and highly degraded ecosystem, which is named Amazon forest dieback.

Lovejoy and Nobre (2018) and Marengo et al. (2021) warn that the Amazon rainforest could soon cross this tipping point, resulting in a rapid shift from rainforest to degraded dry ecosystems with reduced tree cover. Crossing the Amazon's biophysical tipping point would have devastating local and global effects: a sudden crash in biodiversity and rapid rainforest dieback, the release of vast amounts of carbon into the atmosphere due to tree death, and drastic changes to the regional water cycle, with heavy impacts projected on Brazilian aquifers, agribusiness, and urban water supplies.

A recent study by Gatti et al. (2021), using CO_2 observations from 2010 to 2018, investigated Amazonia's carbon budget and the main drivers responsible for its change into a carbon source and found that total carbon emissions are more significant in eastern Amazonia than in the western part. Southeastern Amazonia acts as a net carbon source (total carbon flux minus fire emissions) to the atmosphere, along with higher temperature increases and rainfall decreases in deforested areas of eastern Amazonia (Gatti et al., 2021). Researchers explore the effect of climate change and deforestation trends on carbon emissions at the study sites and find that the intensification of the dry season and an increase in deforestation seem to promote ecosystem stress, increase in fire occurrence, and higher carbon emissions in the eastern Amazon.

Previously, Hubau et al. (2020) found evidence that African and Amazonian tropical forests are losing their carbon sinking capacities. This trend presents different time frames in the biomes since the carbon sinking capacity is shrinking more rapidly in the Amazon. As a result, in some regions of the Amazon there is an increase of carbon released into the atmosphere, further contributing to increasing temperatures and having future effects on mean global temperatures. In fact, over the past forty years, eastern Amazonia has dealt with more deforestation, warming, and moisture stress than the western part, especially during the dry season, with the southeast experiencing the most notable trends (Spracklen et al., 2015; Leite-Filho et al., 2019; Marengo et al., 2021b).

A recent study by Boulton et al. (2022) suggests that the world's largest rainforest is losing its ability to bounce back from damage caused by droughts, fires, and deforestation. Large swathes could become sparsely forested savannahs, much less efficient than tropical forests at sucking carbon dioxide from the air. Resilience is being lost faster in regions with less rainfall and parts of the rainforest closer to human activity. Researchers provide direct empirical evidence that the Amazon rainforest is losing resilience, risking dieback with profound implications for biodiversity, carbon storage, and climate change on a global scale.

There are signs of loss of resilience in more than 75 percent of the forest, with trees taking longer to recover from droughts primarily driven by climate change and human impacts such as deforestation and fires. This vicious cycle of damage could trigger dieback. According to Lovejoy and Nobre (2018), there is a potential tipping point if deforestation exceeds 20 percent–25percent of its total forest area. As of this writing, this rate is about 17 percent.

Potential losses of biodiversity and ecosystem services show strong dependence on nonclimatic drivers, particularly land-use change, deforestation, and forest fire practices. Currently, there is low capacity to monitor and control deforestation. Since 2014, however, policies and institutions have weakened, and Amazon deforestation rates have risen, sharpening in recent years (Silva Junior et al., 2021). As a result, conservation incentives and a new complementary and allegedly cost-effective approach expanded. They include payment for ecosystem services, REDD+, environmental certification, and conservation easements, but they remain controversial. So, effectiveness depends on more research, with potential implications for possible adverse side effects, participatory management systems, and collective decision-making processes.

In summary, climate and land-use changes push the Amazon closer to the projected "bio-climatic tipping point" faster than any other tropical forest, especially in the eastern and southern Amazon basin. Hence, this condition is happening despite significant uncertainties in defining thresholds for tipping points.

3. INTERNATIONAL COOPERATION IN THE AMAZON'S ENVIRONMENT STUDIES: FROM THE AMAZON COOPERATION TREATY ORGANIZATION TO THE AMAZON SCIENCE PANEL

The Amazon region comprises a territory where ecosystems are exposed to continuous and recent degradation, putting their continuity at risk, which implies severe impacts on the natural environment and human populations at global, regional, and local levels. The Amazon region, with an area of nearly 741 million hectares, covers about 44 percent of the surface of South America (ACTO, 2018). In the following sections, we explore two initiatives involving Geopolitics in Amazonia: the Amazon Cooperation Treaty Organization (ACTO) as a political integration activity and the Amazon Science Panel (SPA) for scientific collaboration. The description of both follows below.

3.1 The Amazon Cooperation Treaty Organization

Amazonian countries have made exciting progress since the signing of the Amazon Cooperation Treaty, or ACTO. In the context of the cooperation process, Amazon countries promoted and reaffirmed their renewed role through ACTO: a forum for cooperation, exchange, and knowledge. Jointly, they plan to strengthen, deepen, and broaden the dialogue, continue to preserve and protect the Amazonian territories, facilitate rapprochement among their peoples, and promote harmonious, participatory, and sustainable development. ACTO's agenda incorporates a cross-cutting and multisectoral approach in all the programs, projects, and activities identified to respond to the member countries' concerns and requirements and ACTO's mandates.

ACTO's mission is to be a permanent forum for cooperation, exchange, and information.[6] Guided by the principle of reducing regional asymmetries, members agree to coordinate actions, cooperate in national processes for socioeconomic progress, and enable the gradual incorporation of these vast territories into the national economies. As a consequence, they promote regional cooperation actions to improve the quality of life of Amazonian inhabitants, working under the principle of sustainable development and sustainable livelihoods in harmony with nature and the environment, and considering the internal laws of the member countries (ACTO, 2018).

ACTO is oriented to promote the harmonious development of the Amazonian territories. Through joint actions, Amazonian countries produce equitable and mutually beneficial results in achieving the sustainable development of the Amazon region. According to the thematic approach, the issue of conservation, protection, and sustainable use of renewable natural resources has as its objective the contribution to sustainable development and sustainable life and the maintenance of a clean and healthy environment, establishing the following subthemes: forests, water resources, management, monitoring and control of wild flora and fauna species endangered by trade, protected areas, sustainable use of biodiversity and promotion of bio trade and research, technology, and innovation in Amazon biodiversity. Other themes include Indigenous people, health, tourism, infrastructure, and transport, to mention a few.

3.2 Scientific Panel of Amazonia

Concerned by the growing urgency of catastrophic threats to the Amazon and inspired by the Leticia Pact, a group of over two hundred prominent scientists from the region and global partners have united to form the unprecedented Science Panel for the Amazon, or SPA.[7] The Panel completed a first-of-its-kind scientific assessment of the state of the art in the Amazon basin, current trends, and policy-relevant considerations for the long-term sustainability of the ecosystem and its peoples. The Panel's recommendations aim to promote conservation and advance sustainable development pathways for the region, with a vision of a healthy, standing forest, flowing rivers, bio-economy based on exchange and collaboration between local and Indigenous knowledge, science, technology, and innovation (SPA, 2021).

The SPA Report released in 2021 at COP 26 in Glasgow (SPA, 2021) identifies sustainable development pathways. It thoroughly analyzes the Amazon basin as a one-of-a-kind scientific assessment. The report underscores the significance of offering science-based, data-driven recommendations, encouraging technological innovation, and nature-based solutions combined with Indigenous peoples' and local communities' knowledge to guide decision-making and policy making.

4. BRAZILIAN POSITION ON THE AMAZON'S PROTECTION AND CLIMATE MITIGATION

Ensuring the integrity of hydrological systems, biodiversity, and the fundamental role of the Amazon as a global climate regulator requires about 80 percent of forests to remain preserved. In order to sustain this condition, an urgent priority is to achieve zero deforestation and ecosystem degradation and combat wildfires in the Amazon before 2030. In addition, a complete and immediate deforestation, wildfire, and ecosystem degradation moratorium in areas nearing a tipping point are also needed (SPA, 2021).

Protecting Indigenous peoples' and local communities' land and water rights in Amazonian countries is critical for social justice and conservation outcomes. Providing secure land tenure rights and the institutional environment for enforcing these rights is an important and cost-effective way for countries to protect their forests and culture. People from the Amazon could benefit from payment from ecosystem services, securing some rent while protecting the forest and thus reducing deforestation. The great majority of indigenous Brazilians choose environmental conservation and reject such illegal models of economic development based on soybean expansion.

5. GEOPOLITICS OF AMAZON PRESERVATION

The conservation and preservation of the Amazon biome is an urgent need, not only due to its impact in Brazil, but also from the global perspective. As has been described before, the Amazon region may influence several indicators: the CO_2 budget (that drives global warming),[8] the nexus of food-water-energy on local, regional, and global scales, and the moisture export to southern Brazil, which influences the water cycle and level of reservoirs, including the La Plata River Basin. Also, the forecast increase in air temperature, the number of hot days, and the extension of the dry season are connected. Therefore, they are associated with global warming, added by deforestation, which will impact the population of Amazonia, estimated at twenty million inhabitants, most of whom (around 70%) live in urban areas/cities.

Surpassing a tipping point in terms of deforestation and subsequent forest dieback will lead to abrupt and irreversible shifts between alternative ecosystem states, potentially incurring high societal costs and significant impacts on local and regional economies. Tipping points will lead to abrupt and possibly irreversible changes between alternative ecosystem states, potentially incurring high societal costs and significant impacts on local and regional economies.

According to Cardozo et al. (2023), the water resources within the Amazon basin can be considered a global public good. The authors highlight that its spatial influence affects the people living on river shores. It includes the regional effects of the aerial rivers and the Amazon plume (sediments and organic matter spread out to other countries like French Guiana and Suriname). Also, Ramos et al. (2019) describe that the moisture transported by the aerial rivers could affect the moisture/rainfall in Africa, so any change in the Amazon biome will affect this continent. Another vital issue is how to estimate the value of preservation of the Amazon rainforest in order to regulate water, energy, and carbon sources/sink. According to Strand et al. (2018), although the Amazon rainforest is recognized for its ecosystem services locally and regionally, its attributing economically measurable values are still scarce and difficult to make. The authors estimate that the Amazon could contribute US$ 8–10 billion to Brazil's economy annually.

So, climate adaptation policies are needed more than ever to keep the region resilient. Tackling this issue demands an approach considering and implementing the Sustainable Development Goals indexes for the 2030 agenda. We can suggest that index numbers 1, 2, 3, 5, 6, 10, 11, 12, 15, and 16 all apply to the Amazon region and, of course, are associated with and connected to number 13, which represents climate change issues.

CONCLUSION AND RECOMMENDATIONS

As shown by model projections, large-scale deforestation, and the prospects of global climate changes can intensify the risk of a drier and warmer Amazon. Still, changes in seasonal rainfall distribution and the duration of the dry season may have significant impacts on Amazon hydrology and other sectors since rainfall reductions may occur predominantly in the dry-to-wet transition season. While land use change posed by the rate of deforestation is the most visible threat to the Amazon ecosystem, climate change is emerging as the most insidious threat to the region's future, creating feedback loops and synergies with land use changes.

There is a strong need for better education of local people and policy and decision makers on climate, hydrology, and the atmospheric sciences, especially the impacts of land use and climate change on their livelihoods. Traditional and cultural knowledge are also invaluable sources of climate-proxy information. We must improve ground monitoring, data accessibility and quality, research infrastructure, and climate model development. Furthermore, to investigate possible future climate scenarios that include greenhouse gas increases and land use changes, key research centers and universities must do research on model development and calibration.

This interaction between climate scientists and modelers in the region can help promote collaboration among scientists from Amazon countries and the rest of the world, following the strategy of previous and current collaborations, such as LBA[9] and ATTO.[10] The best option is coproduction between the scientific and the decision-making stakeholder communities. In doing so, governments can better understand and assimilate research findings to develop and improve environmental policies for Amazonia.

NOTES

1. The Walker cell circulation is a conceptual model of the airflow in the tropics in the lower atmosphere caused by differences in heat distribution between ocean and land.

2. Hadley cell circulation is a global-scale tropical atmospheric circulation consisting of a single wind system in each hemisphere, with westward and equatorward flow near the surface and eastward and poleward flow at higher altitudes.

3. Climate Data Guide, "Pairing climate data with climate data experts."

4. The highest five-day precipitation amount (RX5day) is a measure of heavy precipitation, meaning a maximum of five-day precipitation amount in a given period. With time, an increase in this index means the chance of flood conditions will increase.

5. The scenario known as RCP 8.5 (Representative Concentration Pathway) predicts an average concentration of carbon dioxide corresponding to a radiative forcing of 8.5 watts per square meter across the planet, which would lead to an increase in the global average temperature of about 5°C by 2100.

6. ACTO is an intergovernmental organization created to strengthen and implement the objectives of the Amazon Cooperation Treaty, with a broad vision of the South-South cooperation process from three different dimensions—political-diplomatic, strategic, and technical—building synergies among governments, multilateral organizations, cooperation agencies, organized civil society, social movements, the scientific community, productive sectors, and society (see chapter 4).

7. Science Panel for the Amazon, "The Amazon we want."

8. The term "CO_2 budget" illustrates how much CO_2 we can create individually through our lifestyles if global warming is to be limited to 1.5°C.

9. The Large-Scale Biosphere-Atmosphere Experiment in Amazonia (LBA) was an intensive scientific investigation of the tropical rainforest of Brazil and portions of adjacent countries. For additional information, see:https://daac.ornl.gov/cgi-bin/dataset_lister.pl?p=11.

10. Amazonian Tall Tower Observatory. This research site is located in the middle of the Amazon rainforest in northern Brazil. Scientists from Germany and Brazil jointly manage it. ATTO's objective is to continuously gather meteorological, chemical, and biological data, such as the concentration of greenhouse gases.

REFERENCES

Amazon Cooperation Treaty Organization. "Regional report on the status of forests in the Amazon Region." (2018) Accessed July 12, 2022. http://otca.org/en/project/regional-report-on-the-status-of-forests-in-the-amazonregion/.

Alves, Lincoln Muniz, José A. Marengo, Rong Fu, and Rodrigo J. Bombardi. "Sensitivity of Amazon Regional Climate to Deforestation." *American Journal of Climate Change* 6, no.1 (2017):75–98.

Aragão, L. E. O. C., Liana O. Anderson, Marisa G. Fonseca, Thais M. Rosan, Laura B. Vedovato, Fabien H. Wagner, Camila V. J. Silva, Celso H. L. Silva Junior, Egidio Arai, Ana P. Aguiar, Jos Barlow, Erika Berenguer, Merritt N. Deeter, Lucas G. Domingues, Luciana Gatti, Manuel Gloor, Yadvinder Malhi, Jose A. Marengo, John B. Miller, Oliver L. Phillips, and Sassan Saatchi. "21st Century drought-related fires counteract the decline of Amazon deforestation carbon emissions." *Nature Communications* 9, no.536 (2018):1–12.

Arraut, Josefina Moraes, Carlos Nobre, Henrique M. J. Barbosa, Guillermo Obregon, and José Marengo. "Aerial Rivers and Lakes: Looking at Large-Scale Moisture Transport and Its Relation to Amazonia and to Subtropical Rainfall in South America." *Journal of Climate* 25, no.2 (2012): 543–556.

Arias, Paola. A., J. Alejandro Martínez, and Sara C. Vieira. "Moisture sources to the 2010–2012 anomalous wet season in northern South America." *Climate dynamics* 45, no.9 (2015): 2861–2884.

Barichivich, J, Emanuel Gloor, Philippe Peylin, Roel J. H. Brienen, Jochen Schöngart, Jhan Carlo Espinoza, and Kanhu C. Pattanayak. "Recent intensification of Amazon flooding extremes driven by strengthened Walker circulation." *Science advances* 4, no. eaat8785 (2018):1–7

Becker, Bertha. *Amazônia, Geopolítica na Virada do III Milênio*, Rio de janeiro: Garamond, 2006.

Boulton, Chris.A., Timothy M. Lenton, and Niklas Boers. "Pronounced loss of Amazon rainforest resilience since the early 2000s." *Nature Climate Change* 12 (2022): 271–278.

Brando, P. M., B. Soares-Filho, and L. Rodrigues, A. Assunção, D. Morton, D.Tuchschneider, E.C.M. Fernandes, M.N. Macedo, U. Oliveira, M.T. Coe. "The gathering firestorm in southern Amazonia." *Science advances* 6, no.02, eaay1632, (2020):1–09.

Cai, Wenju, McPhaden Michael J., Alice M. Grimm, Regina R. Rodrigues, Andréa S. Taschetto, René D. Garreaud, Boris Dewitte, Germán Poveda, Yoo-Geun Ham, Agus Santoso, Benjamin Ng, Weston Anderson, Guojian Wang, Tao Geng, Hyun-Su Jo, José A. Marengo, Lincoln M. Alves, Marisol Osman, Shujun Li, Lixin Wu, Christina Karamperidou, Ken Taakahashi, and Carolina Vera. "Climate impacts of the El Niño–Southern Oscillation on South America." *Nat Rev Earth Environ* 1 (2020):215–231.

Cardozo, Mónica Lizeth, Marcelo Bentes Diniz, and Claudio Fabian Szlafsztein. "Amazon Basin water resources ecosystem services on the approach of Global Public Goods." *Agua Y Territorio* 21, (2023): 103–119

Climate Data Guide. "Pairing climate data with climate data experts." Accessed November 20, 2022. https://climatedataguide.ucar.edu.

Cook, B. I., J. S. Mankin, K. Marvel, A. P. Williams, J. E. Smerdon, and K. J. Anchukaitis. "Twenty-First Century Drought Projections in the CMIP6 Forcing Scenarios." *Earth's Futur* 8, no. e2019EF001461 (2020): 1–20.

Convey, Kristofer, Fiona Soper, Sunitha Pangala, Angelo Bernardino, Zoe Pagliaro, Luana Basso, Henrique Casso, Philip Fearnside, Diego Navarrete, Sidney Novoa, Henrique Sawakuchi, Thomas Lovejoy, Jose Marengo, Carlos A. Peres, Jonathan

Baillie, Paula Bernasconi, Jose Camargo, Carolina Freitas, Bruce Hoffman, Gabriela B. Nardoto, Ismael Nobre, Juan Mayorga, Rita Mesquita, Silvia Pavan, Flavia Pinto, Flavia Rocha, Ricardo de Assis Mello, Alice Thuault, Alexis Anne Bahl, and Aurora Elmore. "Carbon and beyond: the biogeochemistry of climate in a rapidly changing Amazon." *Frontiers in Forest and Global Change* 4, no. 618401, (2021): 01–20.

Dagicour, Ombelyne. "The geopolitics of the Amazon." *Politique étrangère* 1, (2020):135–146.

Dubreuil, Vincent, Nathan S. Debortoli, Beatriz Funatsu, Vincent Nédélec, and Laurent Durieux. "Impact of land-cover change in the Southern Amazonia climate: a case study for the region of Alta Floresta, Mato Grosso, Brazil." *Environ Monit Assess* 184 (2012): 877–91.

Espinoza, Jhan Carlo, José Antonio Marengo, Jochen Schongart, and Juan Carlos Jimenez. "The new historical flood of 2021 in the Amazon River compared to major floods of the 21st century: Atmospheric features in the context of the intensification of floods." *Weather and Climate Extremes* 35, no.100406, (2022):1–12.

Fu, Rong, Lei Yina, Wenhong Lib, Paola A. Ariasc, Robert E. Dickinsona, Lei Huanga, Sudip Chakrabortya, Katia Fernandesd, Brant Liebmanne, Rosie Fisher, and Ranga B. Myneni. "Increased dry-season length over southern Amazonia in recent decades and its implication for future climate projection." *Proc. Natl. Acad. Sci.* 110, no.45 (2013): 18110–18115.

Garcia, Beatriz Nunes, Renata Libonati, and Ana M.B. Nunes. "Extreme Drought Events over the Amazon Basin: The Perspective from the Reconstruction of South American Hydroclimate." *Water* 10, no.1594 (2018):1–16.

Gatti, Luciana Vanni, L. S. Basso, John B. Miller, Manuel Gloor, Lucas Domingues, H. L. G Cassol, Graciela Tejada, L. E. O. C. Aragão, Carlos A Nobre, W. Peters, Luciano Marani, E. Arai, Alber Ipia, S. M. Corrêa, Liana O. Anderson, C. Von Randon, S. C. S Correia, S. P. Crispim, and R. A. L. Neves. "Decrease in Amazonia carbon uptake linked to trends in deforestation and climate." *Nature*, 595 (2021):388–393.

Gimeno, Luis, Francina Dominguez, Raquel Nieto, Ricardo Trigo, Anita Drumond, Chris J. C. Reason, Andréa S. Taschetto, Alexandre M. Ramos, Ramesh Kumar, and José Marengo. "Major mechanisms of atmospheric moisture transport and their role in extreme precipitation events." *Annu. Rev. Environ. Resour.* 41, (2016):117–141.

Gimeno, Luis, MartaVázquez, Jorge Eiras-Barca, RogertSorí, Milica Stojanovic, Iago Algarra, RaquelNieto, Alexandre M.Ramos, Ana María Durán-Quesada, and Francina Dominguez. "Recent progress on the sources of continental precipitation as revealed by moisture transport analysis." *Earth-Science Rev.* 201, (2020):103070.

Gloor, M., R. J. Brienen, D. Galbraith, T. R.Feldpausch, J. Schöngart, J. L. Guyot, J. C. Espinoza, J. Lloyd, O. L. Philips. "Intensification of the Amazon hydrological cycle over the last two decades." *Geophys. Res. Lett.* 40, no.9 (2013): 1729–1733.

Hubau, W., S. L. Lewis, O. L. Phillips, K. Affum-Baffoe, H. Beeckman, A. Cuní-Sanchez, A. K. Daniels, C. E. N. Ewango, S. Fauset, J. M. Mukinzi, D. Sheil,

B. Sonké, M. J. P. Sullivan, T. C. H. Sunderland, H. Taedoumg, S.C. Thomas, L. J. T. White, K. A. Abernethy, S. Adu-Bredu, C. A. Amani, T. R. Baker, L.F. Banin, F. Baya, S. K. Begne, A. C. Bennett, F. Benedet, R. Bitariho, Y. E. Bocko, P. Boeckx, P. Boundja, R. J. W. Brienen, T. Brncic, E. Chezeaux, G. B. Chuyong, C. J. Clark, M. Collins, J. A. Comiskey, D. A. Coomes, G. C. Dargie, T. de Haulleville, M. N. D. Kamdem, J. L. Doucet, A. Esquivel-Muelbert, T. R. Feldpausch, A. Fofanah, E. G., Foli, M. Gilpin, E. Gloor, C. Gonmadje, S. Gourlet-Fleury, J. S. Hall, A.C. Hamilton, D. J. Harris, T. B. Hart, M. B. N. Hockemba, A. Hladik, S. A.Ifo, K. J. Jeffery, T. Jucker, E. K. Yakusu, E. Kearsley, D. Kenfack, A. Koch, M. E. Leal, A. Levesley, J. A. Lindsell, J. Lisingo, G. Lopez-Gonzalez, J. C. Lovett, J. R. Makana, Y. Malhi, A. R. Marshall, J. Martin, E. H. Martin, F. M. Mbayu, V. P. Medjibe, V. Mihindou, E. T. A. Mitchard, S. Moore, P. K. T. Munishi, N. N. Bengone, L. Ojo, F. E. Ondo, K. S. Peh, G. C. Pickavance, A. D. Poulsen, J. R. Poulsen, L. Qie, J. Reitsma, F. Rovero, M. D. Swaine, J. Talbot, J. Taplin, D. M. Taylor, D.W. Thomas, B. Toirambe, J. T. Mukendi, D. Tuagben, P. M. Umunay, G. M. F. van der Heijden, H. Verbeeck, J. Vleminckx, S. Willcock, H. Wöll, J. T. Woods, L. Zemagho. (2020). "Asynchronous carbon sink saturation in African and Amazonian tropical forests.: *Nature* 579 (2020)**:** 80–87.

IPCC. "Summary for Policymakers." In *Climate Change*, The Physical Science Basis. Contribution of Working Group I to the Sixth Assessment Report of the Intergovernmental Panel on Climate Change, edited by Masson-Delmotte, V., P. Zhai, A. Pirani, S. L. Connors, C. Péan, S. Berger, N. Caud, Y. Chen, L. Goldfarb, M. I. Gomis, M. Huang, K. Leitzell, E. Lonnoy, J. B. R. Matthews, T. K. Maycock, T. Waterfield, O. Yelekçi, R. Yu and B. Zhou. New York: Cambridge University Press, 2021.

IPCC. *Climate Change 2022: Impacts, Adaptation, and Vulnerability.* Contribution of Working Group II to the Sixth Assessment Report of the Intergovernmental Panel on Climate Change, edited by H.-O. Pörtner, D.C. Roberts, M. Tignor, E.S. Poloczanska, K. Mintenbeck, A. Alegría, M. Craig, S. Langsdorf, S. Löschke, V. Möller, A. Okem, B. Rama. New York: Cambridge University Press, 2022.

Jiménez-Muñoz, Juan C., Cristian Mattar, Jonathan Barichivich, Andrés Santamaría-Artigas, Ken Takahashi, Yadvinder Malhi, José A. Sobrino, and Gerard van der Schrier. "Record-breaking warming and extreme drought in the Amazon rainforest during the course of El Niño 2015–2016." *Sci. Rep.* 6 (2016): 33130.

Jimenez, Juan C., Jose A. Marengo, Lincoln M. Alves, Juan C. Sulca, Ken Takahashi, Samantha Ferrett, Matthew Collins. "The role of ENSO flavours and TNA on recent droughts over Amazon forests and the Northeast Brazil region." *Int. J. Climatol.* 41, no 7 (2019): 3761–3780.

Jones, Charles. "Recent changes in the South America low-level jet." npj *Clim Atmos Sci* 2, no 20 (2019): 1–8.

Leite-Filho, A. T., V. Y. Sousa Pontes, M. H. Costa. "Effects of Deforestation on the Onset of the Rainy Season and the Duration of Dry Spells in Southern Amazonia." *J. Geophys. Res. Atmos* 124 (2019): 5268–5281.

Lovejoy, T. E., and C.A. Nobre. "Amazon Tipping Point." *Science Advances*, vol. 4, n. 2 (2018): 1–2.

Macedo, Gustavo. "Climate Security, the Amazon, and the Responsibility to Protect." *Brazilian Political Science Review Forum* 15, no.3 (2021):1–27.

Marengo, J. A., L. M. Alves, W. R. Soares, D. Rodriguez, H. Camargo, M.P. Riveros, A. D. Pabló. "Two contrasting severe seasonal extremes in tropical South America in 2012: flood in Amazonia and drought in northeast Brazil." *J Clim.* 26 (2013): 9137–9154.

Marengo, J. A., J. C. Espinoza. "Extreme seasonal droughts and floods in Amazonia: causes, trends and impacts." *Int J Climatol* 36 (2016): 1033–1050.

Marengo, J. A., Wagner Rodrigues Soares, A. Celeste Saulo, Matilde Nicolini. "Climatology of the low-level jet east of the Andes as derived from the NCEP—NCAR reanalyses: Characteristics and temporal variability." *J Clim* 17, no.2 (2008): 2261–2280.

Marengo, J. A., Carlos M. Souza Jr., Kirsten Thonicke, Chantelle Burton, Kate Halladay, Richard A. Betts, Lincoln M. Alves, and Wagner R. Soares. "Changes in climate and land use over the Amazon region: current and future variability and trends." *Front Earth Sci* 6, no.228 (2018): 1–21.

Marengo, J. A., Ana P. Cunha, Luz Adriana Cuartas, Karinne R. Deusdará Leal, Elisangela Broedel, Marcelo E. Seluchi, Camila Miranda Michelin, Cheila Flávia De Praga Baião, Eleazar Chuchón Angulo, Elton K. Almeida, Marcos L. Kazmierczak, Nelson Pedro António Mateus, Rodrigo C. Silva, and Fabiani Bender. (2021a). "Extreme Drought in the Brazilian Pantanal in 2019–2020: Characterization, Causes, and Impacts." *Front Water* 3, no 3 (639204) (2021a):1–20.

Marengo, J. A., J. C. Espinoza, R. Fu, J. C. J. Muñoz, L. M. Alves, H. R. Rocha, J. Schöngart. "Long-term variability, extremes and changes in temperature and hydrometeorology in the Amazon region." In *Amazon Assessment Report 2021*, edited by Nobre C, Encalada A, Anderson E, Roca Alcazar FH, Bustamante M, Mena C, Peña-Claros M, Poveda G, Rodriguez JP, Saleska S, Trumbore S, Val AL, Villa Nova L, Abramovay R, Alencar A, Rodríguez Alzza C, Armenteras D, Artaxo P, Athayde S, Barretto Filho HT, Barlow J, Berenguer E., Bortolotto F., Costa FA, Costa MH, Cuvi N, Fearnside PM, Ferreira J, Flores BM, Frieri S, Gatti LV, Guayasamin JM, Hecht S, Hirota M, Hoorn C, Josse C, Lapola DM, Larrea C, Larrea-Alcazar DM, Lehm Ardaya Z, Malhi Y, Marengo JA, Melack J, Moraes R M, Moutinho P, Murmis MR, Neves EG, Paez B, Painter L, Ramos A, Rosero-Peña MC, Schmink M, Sist P, ter Steege H, Val P, van der Voort H, Varese M, Zapata-Ríos G. New York: United Nations Sustainable Development Solutions Network, 2021b.

Marengo, J. A. Carlos M. Souza Jr., Kirsten Thonicke, Chantelle Burton, Kate Halladay, Richard A. Betts, Lincoln M. Alves, and Wagner R. Soares. "Changes in climate and land use over the Amazon region: current and future variability and trends." *Front. Earth Sci.* 6, no.228 (2018):1–21.

Marengo, J. A., Javier Tomasella, Lincoln M. Alves, Wagner R. Soares, Daniel A. Rodriguez. "The drought of 2010 in the context of historical droughts in the Amazon region." *Geophys. Res. Lett.* 38, no.12 (2010): 1–5.

Montini, T. L., C. Jones, and L. M. V. Carvalho. "The South American low-level jet: A new climatology, variability, and changes." *J Geophys Res Atmos* 124 (2019):1200–18.

Nobre, Antonio Donato. *The Future Climate of Amazonia, Scientific Assessment Report*. São José dos Campos: CCST-INPE, INPA and ARA, 2014.

Nobre, C. A., Gilvan Sampaio, Laura S. Borma, Juan Carlos Castilla-Rubio, José S. Silva, and Manoel Cardoso. "Land-use and climate change risks in the Amazon and the need of a novel sustainable development paradigm." *Proc. Natl. Acad. Sci.* 113, (2016a): 10759–10768.

Nobre C. A., J. A. Marengo, M. E. Seluchi, L. A. Cuartas, L. Alves. "Some Characteristics and Impacts of the Drought and Water Crisis in Southeastern Brazil during 2014 and 2015." *Journal of Water Resource and Protection* 8 (2016b): 252–262.

Oliveira, Beatriz Fátima Alves de, Marcus J. Bottino, Paulo Nobre, and Carlos A. Nobre. "Deforestation and climate change are projected to increase heat stress risk in the Brazilian Amazon." *Commun Earth Environ* 2, no. 207 (2021): 1–8.

Parsons, L.A. "Implications of CMIP6 projected drying trends for 21st century Amazonian drought risk." *Earth's Futur* 8 (2020): e2020EF001608.

RAISG (2012) Red Amazónica de Información Socioambietal Georreferenciada. Accessed November 20, 2022. https://www.raisg.org/en/publication/amazonia-under-pressure/.

Ramos, A. M., R. C. Blamey, I. Algarra, R. Nieto, L. Gimeno, R. Tomé, C. J. Reason, and R. M. Trigo. "From Amazonia to Southern Africa: Atmospheric moisture transport through low level jets and atmospheric rivers." *Annals of the New York Academy of Sciences* 1436, no 1 (2019): 217–230.

Sampaio, G., L. S. Borma, M. Cardoso, L. M. Alves, C. von Randow, D. A. Rodriguez, C. A. Nobre, F.F. Alexandre. "Assessing the Possible Impacts of a 4 °C or Higher Warming in Amazonia." In *Climate Change Risks in Brazil*, edited by C. A. Nobre, José A. Marengo, and Wagner R. Soares, 201–218, Cham: Springer international Publishing, 2019.

Santos, Diego Jatobá dos, George Ulguim Pedra, Marcelo Guatura Barbosa da Silva, Carlos Augusto Guimarães Júnior, Lincoln Muniz Alves, Gilvan Sampaio, José Antônio Marengo. "Future rainfall and temperature changes in Brazil under global warming levels of 1.5°C, 2°C and 4°C." *Sustentabilidade Em Debate* 11, no. 3 (2020): 57–90.

Sierra, Juan Pablo Sierra, Clementine Junquas, Jhan Carlo Espinoza, Hans Segura, Thomas Condom, Marcos Andrade, Jorge Molina-Carpio, Laura Ticona, Valeria Mardoñez, Luis Blacutt, Jan Polcher, Antoine Rabatel, and Jean Emmanuel Sicart. "Deforestation Impacts on Amazon-Andes Hydroclimatic Connectivity." *Climate Dynamics* 58 (2021): 2609–2636.

Silva Junior, Celso H. L. Silva Junior, Nathália S. Carvalho, Ana C. M. Pessôa, João B. C. Reis, Aline Pontes-Lopes, Juan Doblas, Viola Heinrich, Wesley Campanharo, Ane Alencar, Camila Silva, David M. Lapola, Dolors Armenteras, Eraldo A. T. Matricardi, Erika Berenguer, Henrique Cassol, Izaya Numata, Joanna House, Joice Ferreira, Jos Barlow, Luciana Gatti, Paulo Brando, Philip M. Fearnside, Sassan

Saatchi, Sonaira Silva, Stephen Sitch, Ana P. Aguiar, Carlos A. Silva, Christelle Vancutsem, Frédéric Achard, René Beuchle, Yosio E. Shimabukuro, Liana O. Anderson, and Luiz E. O. C. Aragão. "Amazonian forest degradation must be incorporated into the COP26 agenda." *Nature Geoscience* 14 (2021): 634–635.

Spracklen, D. V., and L. Garcia-Carreras. "The impact of Amazonian deforestation on Amazon basin rainfall." *Geophys. Res. Lett.* 42, (2015): 9546–9552.

Science Panel for the Amazon. *Executive Summary of the Amazon Assessment Report 2021*, edited by C. Nobre, A. Encalada, E. Anderson, F.H. Roca Alcazar, M. Bu mante, C. Mena, M. Pe a-Claros, G. Poveda, J.P. Rodriguez, S. Saleska, S. Trumbore, A.L. Val, L. Villa Nova, R. Abramovay, A. Alencar, A.C.R. Alzza, D. Armenteras, P. Artaxo, S. Athayde, H.T. Barretto Filho, J. Barlow, E. Berenguer, F. Bortolotto, F.A. Costa, M.H. Costa, N. Cuvi, P.M. Fearnside, J. Ferreira, B.M. Flores, S. Frieri, L.V. Gatti, J.M. Guayasamin, S. Hecht, M. Hirota, C. Hoorn, C. Josse, D.M. Lapola, C. Larrea, D.M. Larrea-Alcazar, Z. Lehm Ardaya, Y. Malhi, J.A. Marengo, M.R. Moraes, P. Moutinho, M.R. Murmis, E.G., Neves, B. Paez, L. Painter, A. Ramos, M.C. Rosero-Pe a, M. Schmink, P. Sist, H. ter Steege, P. Val, H. van der Voort, M. Varese, G. Zapata. New York: United Nations Sustainable Development Solutions Network, 2021.

Science Panel for the Amazon, "The Amazon we want." Accessed November 20, 2022. https://www.theamazonwewant.org.

Staal, A. Arie Staal, Obbe A. Tuinenburg, Joyce H. C. Bosmans, Milena Holmgren, Egbert H. van Nes, Marten Scheffer, Delphine Clara Zemp & Stefan C. Dekker. "Forest-rainfall cascades buffer against drought across the Amazon." *Nat. Clim. Chang.* 8 (2018): 539–543.

Strand, Jon, Britaldo Soares-Filho, Marcos Heil Costa, Ubirajara Oliveira, Sonia Carvalho Ribeiro, Gabrielle Ferreira Pires, Aline Oliveira, Raoni Rajão, Peter May, Richard van der Hoff, Juha Siikamäki, Ronaldo Seroa da Motta & Michael Toman. "Spatially explicit valuation of the Brazilian Amazon Forest's Ecosystem Services." *Nat Sustain* 1 (2018): 657–664.

Tomasella, J., L. S. Borma, J. A. Marengo, Javier Tomasella, Laura S. Borma, José A. Marengo, Daniel A. Rodriguez, Luz A. Cuartas, Carlos A. Nobre, Maria C.R. Prado. "The droughts of 1996—1997 and 2004—2005 in Amazonia: hydrological response in the river main-stem." *Hydrol Process* 25 (2011): 1228–1242.

Ukkola, A. M., M. G. De Kauwe, M. L. Roderick, G. Abramowitz, A. J. Pitman. "Robust future changes in meteorological drought in CMIP6 projections despite uncertainty in precipitation." *Geophysical Research Letters* 46, (2020): e2020GL087820.

United Nations Development Programme, *Supporting climate Security*, 2021. Accessed April, 30, 2021. https://www-dev.undp.org/2030-agenda-for-sustainable -development/peace/conflict-prevention/climate-security.

Wang, G., S. Sun, and R. Mei. "Vegetation dynamics contributes to the multi-decadal variability of precipitation in the Amazon region." *Geophys Res Lett* 38, no.19 (2011): 1–5.

Zemp, Delphine Clara, C.-F. Schleussner, H. M. J. Barbosa, R. J. van der Ent, J. F. Donges, J. Heinke, G. Sampaio, and A. Rammig. "On the importance of cascading moisture recycling in South America." *Atmos Chem Phys* 14: (2014): 13337–13359.

Zemp, Delphine Clara, C.-F. Schleussner, H. M. J. Barbosa, A. Rammig. "Deforestation effects on Amazon forest resilience." *Geophys. Res. Lett.* 44 (2017a): 6182–6190.

Zemp, Delphine Clara, Carl-Friedrich Schleussner, Henrique M. J. Barbosa, Marina Hirota, Vincent Montade, Gilvan Sampaio, Arie Staal, Lan Wang-Erlandsson, and Anja Rammig. "Self-amplified Amazon forest loss due to vegetation-atmosphere feedbacks." *Nat. Commun.* 8, (2017b):1–10.

Zipser, Edward J. Zipser, Daniel J. Cecil, Chuntao Liu, Stephen Nesbitt, David P. Yorty. "Where are the most intense thunderstorms on Earth?" *Bull Am Meteorol Soc* 87 (2006): 1057–72.

Chapter 2

Environmental Geopolitics and the Amazon in the Context of Hybrid Warfare

Public Opinion and National Security in Brazil

Rodrigo Augusto Lima de Medeiros

This chapter seeks to analyze narratives that form the basis of conceptions about the Brazilian Amazon. The goal is to understand its geopolitical and environmental implications in disputes to take over concepts, resources, hearts, and minds. The Amazon's environmental geopolitics implicates vocabulary standardization, knowledge creation, and rules operationalization, thus promoting institutionalization. These processes occur in specialized bureaucracies, either state (military and civil) and nonstate (media, business, NGOs, and social movements). They nominate and establish practices for the Amazonian territory. On the other hand, the political-institutional elaborations involved in the spectrum of national security (geopolitics) and environmental issues (political ecology) constitute narratives of a governing nature, thus providing a reflexive basis for the alleged environmental geopolitics of the Amazon.

We use narrative and inquiry to reflect on what intellectuals say about the Amazon and its geopolitics. The notion of narrative is present in philosophy and literary criticism by authors such as Walter Benjamin (1985), Roland Barthes (1984), and Edward Said ([1978]1990), to interpret how social tensions, political dramas, and webs of meaning build experiences of institutional legitimation. Narrative, as discourse, is defined as a way of structuring and legitimating meanings of actions, mainly in political and institutional contexts (Geertz, 1989). The narratives' focus of analysis closely relates to political struggles over the institutionalization of meanings in Amazonian space. In these terms, a more substantive (less adjectival) analysis of the Amazonian subject and its geopolitics would only succeed if it acquired cross-cutting descriptions that combine aspects of specific statements, elaborated both in and out of Amazonian countries.

The perspective proposed in this chapter brings forth an approach for different sectors, such as the military (sovereignty, geopolitics, defense, intelligence), environmentalists (environmental conservation, forest, protected areas, climate change), organic intellectuals (think tanks), and the media (public opinion). Thus, narrative content on the Amazon, and its geopolitics, in political-administrative inquiries is found. Three argumentative axes demonstrate this scope: 1) intellectual propositions that build institutional territorialities designed to govern the Amazonian territory; 2) media coverage that produces political imaginaries of the Amazon and; 3) institutional practices that mobilize political resources in the formulation of state and nonstate territorialities. These axes converge toward practical meanings of the Amazonian territory, seeking to give it valuable contours. Data formulations regarding the territory guide the agents' decisions, transforming the vocabulary used to deal with the Amazon.

The dissemination of public opinion seeks to establish truths about intentions, preferences, and choices that are sometimes sold as the very manifestation of the people's will. However, at a certain level of analysis, disclosure and public opinion are parts of battles fought in the shadows to win ideological convictions in the context of a hybrid war[1] (Wither, 2016; Leiner, 2020). This seemingly "neutral" situation hides intense political strategizing that uses specialized knowledge and media repercussions to push governmental and private actions in specific directions.

Public opinion spreads in both digital and conventional media simultaneously with public policies in environmental and defense issues. As a result, they disseminate the narratives of specific groups, capitalized or instrumentalized in both the state and the private sector, through which they elaborate hegemonic territorial practices on the Amazon. Pragmatically, these practices influence specific territorial routines. Specialists from distinct academic backgrounds, whether or not they occupy positions in public administration (public agents) and private administration (private agents), compete inside niches of power-knowledge (Foucault, [1973] 2003; [1981] 2007). Knowledge from different areas, such as law, military sciences, geology, geography, ecology, economics, sociology, anthropology, biology, agronomy, and engineering, seeks to establish truths that make up fractions of the Amazonian reality. In all areas, there is an endeavor to demonstrate their correctness through evidence anchored either in scientific methods (experiments) or the art of rallying forces supporting their convictions (Latour 2000, 2014).

Thus, processes aim to indicate solutions for the Amazonian equation, enunciated in proposals capable of remodeling local and national realities. However, the restriction of Amazon territorialities diminishes the plurality of groups that inhabit the region, impacting their existences and experiences. This delimitation is formed through treaties, occupations, possessions, fortifications, integration programs, and settlements. Complementarily, anthropic intervention operates in terms of narratives: infrastructure (hydroelectric dams and roads), free trade, migratory flows, alliances for progress, economic cycles, biopiracy, climate change, human rights, demarcations of indigenous lands, ecological parks, regulatory frameworks, global governance, among others (Medeiros, 2018). Ultimately, such delimitations constitute part of the same process of territorialization of administrative practices.

This chapter intends to focus on the so-called news (or speech, in Barthes's perspective), that is, on what is informed. The task is to analyze how information influences narratives that constitute territorial practices. From a critical perspective, decoding this fact is proposed in order to go beyond conventional or digital media vehicles spread in terms of a pragmatic narrative. It should be pointed out that there is no concern with the integrity or verifiability of reported data. There will be no fact finding. Instead, this chapter will show the articulations of statements that justify opinion forming discursive practices besides concrete proposals that mobilize networks, resources, policies, and knowledge, which will articulate the national interest and national sovereignty, on the one hand, and legitimize conceptions of human rights, minority rights, and environmental rights, in the inscription of new territorial practices, on the other.

Within a vast web of disputes, conventional and digital media give evidence of the dynamics that form Amazonian territorialities. Debate forums clarify it, demonstrating that it transcends people's local territorialities and the Amazon's inhabitant groups. Despite running the contributing risk, it denies the heterogeneity of cognitive maps and ways of acting in the Amazonian territory. It forms groups on the practices under state territoriality. Furthermore, it allows us to see the reflections, experiences, and knowledge that forge hegemonic territoriality. The limited number of social actors who have a voice in the formulation of public policies and the media leads to a more hegemonic (dominant) bias of the themes addressed, to the extent that marginalized groups in national and transnational social disputes remain without a voice or representation. The disruptive technology of social networks presents the illusion of the democratization of informing. However, this proves to be as illusory as ideological (Wu, 2011).

In this sense, we access discursive repertoires that propose to institute Amazonian territorialities. It becomes clear when discussing Amazonian issues: mainly when subjects are about national security, territorial possession, environmentalism, developmentalism, indigenous issues, infrastructure, global governance, climate change, international trade, environmental responsibility, and technological progress, among other topics. Pressure groups, political parties, congress members, governors, professional associations, NGOs, foundations, intellectuals (researchers), activists, and social movement leaders, find some space within the conveniences of the media to inform (form) public opinion. However, there is little room for otherness, for disadvantaged minorities, and for proposals that go against hegemonic powers. Because of the bias existing in the written media, our interest is in inquiring about the themes dealt with in this chapter, focusing more on the taxological artifacts that structure enunciates that form territorial practices.

Combining environmental actions with national security measures in digital and conventional media should conceptually enhance the theme of environmental geopolitics. In summary, this chapter offers three sections. The first section seeks to lay out elements of green narratives in a geopolitical context, seeking to collate new scenarios in formulating new territorialities. The second section examines the insertion of ecological subject matter in the context of the primary official documents that guide national security policies. Finally, the third section systematizes notes for a concept of environmental geopolitics in the context of Brazil's challenges in the environmental and national security areas. The conclusion establishes that the link between public opinion and green and national security agendas can be promising, as Brazil wants to assume a leading role in environmental geopolitics. Moreover, the environmental program is the gateway for Brazil to expand its international projection, favoring it's insertion into the global market and consolidating its leadership in multilateral forums.

It is necessary to undo the belief that the environmental agenda threatens sovereignty, development, and national interests. This misguided understanding of environmental policy no longer fits an interdependence and interconnectivity system. However, it may favor Brazil's intention to expand its interests in the international market. The hypothesis in this research proposes that Brazilian geopolitical projection depends on whether it can assume an environmental leadership role in the context of hybrid warfare in the concert of nations. Hence, this chapter proposes to examine both national security in the environmental agenda and the environment in the national security agenda.

1. ENVIRONMENTAL NARRATIVES IN A GEOPOLITICAL CONTEXT: OTHER VALUES COUNTERBALANCING PROPOSALS FOR THE AMAZON

In order to achieve national objectives, the tools available to nation-states must bring forth conceptual calibration about how they operate in increasingly complex international contexts. South American countries in general, and Brazil in particular, face the challenge of promoting national development in a world order with a preestablished international division of labor (Wallerstein, 1992). However, it is possible to glimpse the horizon and alternatives to the hegemonic models of developed countries, and it is up to developing countries to find their paths (Escobar, 1995; Chang, 2004).

With a territorial area of 8,515,767 km² (851,576,700 ha), an estimated population of 210.3 million (IBGE, 2019), a gross domestic product of R\$ 6.8 trillion (Central Bank, 2018), and 5.7 million km² of ocean area along the coast, Brazil has multiple challenges at both the security and national defense agenda (Queiroz, 2012) and the environmental agenda fronts (Medeiros, 2018). There is a general feeling of frustration when considering that the immense potential of human, mineral, forest, fishing, soil, biodiversity, ecosystem services, and timber resources does not have substitutes for sustainable economic growth, international projection, comparative advantages, or social justice. The end of the twentieth century and the dawn of the twenty-first century brought, with greater intensity, two orders of phenomena to state public policies: environmental interdependencies (nonrenewable resources, climate vulnerabilities) and socioeconomic interconnections (global flows of capital, goods, information, people). It is by reflecting on this context of interdependencies and interconnections that this chapter will analyze the challenges of the Brazilian national state in the defense of sovereignty (Heller, 1947; Tokatlian, 1990; Castro, 2004; Queiroz, 2012), in the rational use of territory (Sachs, 2005) and the promotion of citizenship with social justice (Marshall, 1967; Rawls, 1997).

To scale dependent variables as a function of policy choices, we problematize the strategic boundaries between the environmental national security and defense agendas, examining the space-actors-power triad. According to the specialized literature of Policy Analysis (Beyme, 1985), a plan is a diverse set of problems, issues, and solutions on which politicians, citizens, interest groups, media, civil servants, business people, and experts, among others, focus their attention at a given time (Birkland, 2007; Souza, 2007).

The interaction between different social actors in a given field of knowledge generates formulations that will inform the decision-making of political agents (Cobb and Ross, 1976). This chapter proposes to problematize analytical parameters for the adequacy of environmental and security issues, and defense actions within the scope of the Brazilian state (actor) in the execution of actions (power/government) for the Brazilian territory (space). Thus, it will seek to tie the argument conceptually to the notion of Geopolitics (Castro, 1999; Miyamoto, 1991; Fernandes, 2002; Costa, 1992 and 2019; Medeiros, 2018) applied to environmental vulnerabilities (Queiroz, 2012). In other words, the chapter frames the arguments in the conception of environmental geopolitics.

For Bertha Becker, geopolitics is the "field of knowledge that analyzes relationships between power and space" (2005, 71). The state is the leading geopolitical actor insofar as it has the legitimate monopoly of physical violence (Weber, [1921] 2004). Moreover, the state imposes the sovereignty of its legal-institutional order within its territory and can, pretentiously, impose its territorial conceptions on other states under asymmetric negotiation conditions. However, the state is not the only actor in the geopolitical game.[2]

At the national level, equating the use (occupation) of the soil between demands for increased productivity and conservation of ecosystem services is imperative to unlock the issue of development (Escobar, 1995; Furtado, 1987). In international relations, Brazil's economic insertion into the international market should not reproduce the cycle of technological dependence (Becker, 1993; Baer, 2002). This chapter finds enough evidence to recognize that the path of conjugation between the environmental and national security agendas may become the gateway to the more significant insertion of Brazil in the international market, consequently, to the much-desired national development.

2. Brazil's Environmental Policy for the Amazon: International Pressure, National Motivation, and Defense of Sovereignty

Brazil is a country with environmental superlatives. It has the largest continuous area of tropical forests (FAO, 2006), approximately 16 percent of the planet's freshwater in the liquid state (Tundisi, 2005) and approximately 20 percent of the planet's biodiversity (Lewinsohn, 2006), assets that accredit Brazil to global environmental leadership. However, besides a global context of maturing the environmental agenda, Brazil's adherence follows its path. According to Souza (2000), Brazil is an intermediate country when it comes to the application of environmental policy instruments. In other words, according to the Souza (2000, 274–313), even though Brazil does not have an environmental protection system as old and organized as that of some developed countries, it is one of the most prominent pioneers among developing countries, with a system that is superior to most.

It is not easy to equate the external influence to the internal political arrangements concerning the construction of the environmental agenda in Brazil; it is, however, important to emphasize that there are enough national motivations to trigger an autochthonous environmental policy. It has always been an issue of the modern national state to control and use natural resources (Queiroz, 2012; Scott, 1998) without proselytizing nature conservation. However, the European industrial revolution during the nineteenth century allowed humankind to consume natural resources voraciously (Hobsbawm, 1997). As a result, throughout the twentieth century, the environment gained protagonism. It alters industrialization, demography, natural resources use, mass-production consumption, urbanization, agriculture, and cattle ranching (Santos, 1993).

The status of the green issue has increased with the creation of the United Nations' program Environment Programme (UNEP, 1972) to coordinate environmental activities and promote cooperation. The slogan "Think globally, act locally" became a catchphrase for the organization (Giddens 1991, 2010). Considering that the environmental issue concerns all humankind, since the limits set by the physical boundaries of national states are not barriers to climate effects, it is questionable to what extent the structure created under the aegis of the UN enables the democratic expression of the different interests involved. The UN's liberal conception does not undo the realistic observation that power relations between the world and the UN are asymmetrical. Power, cooperation, market, defense, and geopolitics guide the relations between national states (Nogueira and Messari, 2005). The environmental issue is close to these variables. Global environmental governance has its limits. The self-determination and sovereignty of national states should not be the object of environmental disputes.

The environmental agenda's expansion occurred during the last decade of the twentieth century and throughout the first two decades of the twenty-first century. Therefore, a change in perspective will affect environmental management from 2019 to 2022. Nevertheless, over the 130 years of the republic, despite its normative evolution, the Brazilian environmental agenda has never been at the center of the government's concerns (Medeiros, 2018; Souza, 2000; Santos, 1993).

These political-administrative inquiries serve the purpose of governing territories. To govern (or create) territories means establishing sets of institutional inquiries, that is, to establish procedures, analyses, reflections, calculations, and tactics that allow the exercise of singular and complex forms of power that target population and space. It also means constituting specific forms of knowledge, such as political economy, political ecology, diplomacy, military strategy, and public opinion. It relentlessly leads to the preeminence of a kind of power that is referred to as the government of a territory, as it addresses relational geographic space (Massey, [2005] 2008). All this leads to institutionalizing a series of specific government apparatuses and a set of knowledge (Foucault, [1978] 1996, 289). Michel Foucault synthesizes the concepts of power and discipline in the concept of government. The goal is to mark the genealogy of the technology of governing.

The analysis involves, as a first necessary step, recognizing the expression "internationalization of the Amazon," a narrative reference that names practices and guides actions for the governing (or creation of an economy) of the Amazonian territory. That is a symbolic economy of the Amazonian territory (Bourdieu, 2004). Amazonian geopolitics hides the pretension of defining territorial practices. Instead, these practices are social actions capable of configuring a specific way of projecting the Amazon (Weber, [1921] 2004). Thus, in analyzing the content that characterizes the environmental geopolitics of the Amazon, this chapter examines practical narratives that engender domains of knowledge for the territory and founding power relations.

3. "ETERNAL RECURRENCE": STRUCTURED NARRATIVES

In Brazil, the environmental issue is within the scope of national public management, with national environmental law being the first line of environmental protection. However, as could not be otherwise, the green issue, by definition, goes beyond the border limits between national states: it demands an international consensus set up around political, scientific, and multilateral debates on climate change, species survival, biodiversity maintenance, and human vulnerabilities, contributing to form international ecopolitics (Le Prestre, 2000). Some countries are more relevant than others when concerning the environmental. Within this international game, authors such as Anthony Giddens (2010) see Brazil as an insurance state, a kind of guarantor of humankind's decisions to combat climate change. Is there a geopolitical gain to this?

The turning point of the environmental agenda concerning national security is part of the so-called global environmental governance. According to the UN Commission on Global Governance, governance is how individuals and institutions manage their everyday problems. In other words, governance is a

> continuous process by which conflicting interests can be accommodated and cooperative actions can be achieved (. . .) concerns not only formal institutions and regimes authorized to enforce obedience, but informal arrangements

that serve the interests of individuals and institutions. (Commission on Global Governance 1996, 2)

In some environmental disputes, global governance processes threaten national sovereignty. The fact is that global governance presents the classical trade-offs of international relations: power/sovereignty versus cooperation/ interdependence (Nogueira and Messari, 2005), which subsist in the classical division proposed by Edward H. Carr (1939) and Morgenthau (1948) between realists and idealists/utopians. These radical dichotomies find new meanings in complex, contemporary international relations. Since the United Nations Conference on the Human Environment (Stockholm 1972) and the United Nations Conference on Environment and Development (Rio 1992), there has been increasing evidence of the engagement of multilateral international organizations and nongovernmental civil society organizations (NGOs) in environmental protection.

Invariably, during almost all periods in Brazil's history, with greater intensity in some specific moments over others, some groups that were more sensitive to issues of national sovereignty do the internal reading that environmental actions (including struggles of social movements claiming land) represent "threats to Brazilian territorial integrity" (Medeiros, 2018). Unsurprisingly, this issue is sensitive for national security policymakers. For example, people fear that US and European NGOs operating in Brazil are primarily responsible for the propagation of false environmentalist theses that preach "shared sovereignty of the Amazon" or "international statutory regimes to deal with the Amazon" (Medeiros, 2018).

In the area of international security, the theoretical-methodological per-spective of the Copenhagen School holds that security concerns should encompass not only military threats but also those arising from political, eco-nomic, environmental, and social areas (Buzan, 1998). Thus, there are threats in these areas where the state expands its activities and consequently, should compose the scope of defense policies of national states. Still, uncertainties about the environmental agenda imply consequences for national security objectives. For example, we can mention future political structures that gov-ern environmental issues and the advancement of the environmental agenda in the political party composition of the world's military and economic pow-ers (Buzan, 1998). These realms potentially affect countries' environmental policies toward the rest of the world (especially Brazil).

According to Grace Tanno's (2002) diagnosis, the European environmental structure is still heterogeneous, without unity in social movements, epistemic communities, international organizations, and nongovernmental organiza-tions. However, there is pressure from European NGOs (e.g., Greenpeace and WorldWatch Institute) to securitize issues in the environmental sector.

In Tanno's (2002) analysis of the environmental issue, the Copenhagen School warns that two types of agendas coexist—governmental agendas and scientific agendas: "The problem lies in the authority of the scientific community to support the 'securitization move'" (2002, 68). Experts (scientists and environmentalists) can define which direction to take, including suggesting securitizing environmental demands. However, there is still a general understanding that "environmental threats should be dealt with at the local level, even if they affect the whole world" (Tanno 2002, 67). Therefore, the dispute would be more on the subject of regionalization of the issue with local referrals.

Constructivism, as a theoretical strand in international relations studies, also rethinks national security based on environmental conceptions (Nogueira and Messari 2005, 162–85). Realistically, this configuration may, in the future, become a threat to Brazil, and articulating environmental and defense policies may be a means to mitigate this threat. As an example, Brazil's National Defense Policy references the "environment."

The document recognizes that in the future there will be boosted pressure on nature, since natural resources are essential for the prevailing economic development model. Accordingly, policies may generate environmental degradation, leading to increased environmental concerns. Nevertheless, the PND makes a generic diagnosis. The issue must encompass more robust and solid arguments to integrate Brazil's national development objectives and projections effectively.

These issues communicate with each other. At the extremes, we have on one side the thesis that environmental policies, in general, would not represent national interests, being obstacles to national development and therefore a barrier to Brazil's self-determination. This idea stems from the perception that developed countries impose environmental policies on developing countries. There is plenty of evidence that this is the case, that is, the Club of Rome and the history of international norms of treaties and conventions that reduce the autonomy of countries to deal with their territory. On the other hand, there is the thesis that the environmental agenda may become the flagship of Brazilian insertion worldwide.

Between these extremes there is a gradient of possibilities (a gray area): real threats; vulnerabilities resulting from governmental inoperability; conspiracy theories; almost irresponsibly skeptical viewers who would not hold their breaths; and a "Pollyanna," or naïve worldview. Therefore, it is necessary to rescale national security in regard to its link to the environmental agenda.

Biological prospecting, biotechnology, patent registration, scientific production, and the extraction of strategic minerals, among others, are alternatives for adding value to the enormous natural heritage that Brazil possesses. However, trading wood and substituting forests for commodities (grains and meat) is not the most responsive alternative, as there needs to be more added value for the world market. Likewise, leaving mineral wealth underground due to a lack of technical capacity for sustainable exploitation of the resources or lack of investments is the easiest way to maintain the country's state of underdevelopment. Shortage of adequate regulations, little interagency cooperation within the Brazilian state, and unfounded fears of foreign interference threaten Brazil's environmental leadership.

To summarize, in illustrative terms, national objectives in defense (Senado, 2018) need to be interpreted within the framework of a diverse society that presents the challenges of the complexity of a diverse social reality with mega biodiversity. In addition, Brazil faces the challenge of promoting national development in an already preestablished world order of international division of labor. However, alternatives to the Eurocentric model are being presented (Quijano, 2005; Wallerstein, 1992). Finding ways to navigate between the environmental agenda and conceptions of national security can become a viable alternative to project Brazil as a leader in the world order.

The imminent need to weigh the risks justifies this discussion on the world system of economic exchange and Brazil's technological dependence in the face of potential environmental, political, economic, and social catastrophes. It is necessary to reflect on Brazil's current institutional structure (both in the public sphere of government and in the civil society sphere of private activities) that can cope with increasingly challenging scenarios. Thus, it is imperative to evaluate Brazil's institutional capacity to plan the territory's management and promote the social cohesion of the various segments of Brazilian society. This institutional capacity is paramount to develop mechanisms for responding to natural disasters, political radicalization, and economic contingencies.

We start from the following premises: 1) the more transparent the internal confidence, the greater the willingness to sacrifice private resources to achieve national goals; 2) if common goals are fair and collectively shared, the greater the social cohesion to keep the nation secure, and the fairer will the redistribution of dividends progress. The environmental and defensive agendas are the gateways to conceiving the national territory, reflecting environmental geopolitics. In principle, all the government needs is to convince, make people believe, establish alliances, and make power arrangements viable. Managing natural resources implies vocabulary standardization (knowledge) and rules operationalization processes (institutionalization). These processes occur in the specialized state (military and civilian) and nonstate (media, business, NGOs, and social movements) bureaucracies. These specialized bureaucracies establish narratives for the territory, homogenizing the socionatural practices (Medeiros, 2018). The political-institutional elaborations involved in the spectrum of national security (geopolitics) and environmental issues (political ecology) constitute narratives of environmental geopolitics.

CONCLUSION

A restricted language game of antagonism between agendas and public opinion is a trap. As an answer, we can propose a critical analysis that integrates the most diverse socioenvironmental perspectives in a national strategic policy framework in environmental geopolitics. In this sense, we verify the research hypothesis put forth in the introduction of this chapter. Throughout the text, the arguments that Brazil's global projection depends on its ability to harmonize the environmental and national security agendas in order to assume environmental leadership in the concert of nations are evident.

The crucial point is that the environmental agenda can support the achievement of national development interests and, consequently, national security. Simultaneously, the national security agenda can also be a fulcrum for reaching crucial goals in the execution of Brazil's environmental agenda. This outlook does not represent a threat to Brazilian sovereignty. On the contrary, it is a window of opportunity for Brazil to be a protagonist on the world stage. As seen in sections two and three, the indigenous environmental agenda could be the stage for disputes over resources that generate a more significant economic insertion of Brazil in the world, also providing better income redistribution.

In sum, it is noted throughout the chapter that there is little or no relationship between the environmental agenda and the security/defense agenda, consolidated in their legal titles. However, potential convergences point to gains in projecting national power in the economic, diplomatic, multilateral, and transnational spheres. Both the environmental and the security/defense agendas are influenced by foreign economic and military issues, but both the former and the latter are products of Brazilian political and socioeconomic arrangements. The military doctrine and the environmental agenda have little mutual dialogue, which creates the main misconception that needs radical change.

In short, despite internal contradictions, national states plan their actions based on the machinations of specialized bureaucracies that must deal with different contexts, countries, and situations to keep commercial (for their people) and security (for their interests) opportunities under control. In Brazil specifically, there is a constant battle for the mobilization of resources (material and human) to legitimize strategic actions for national development. Nevertheless, Brazilian bureaucracies specialized in national security, diplomacy, intelligence, and environmental policies need to coordinate a minimum consensus to make a common political agenda viable that can mobilize socioenvironmental assets (capital). On the contrary, they dispute hegemonic narratives, which propagate reductionist convictions to obtain more visibility in Brazilian public opinion that legitimizes larger budgets for their portfolios.

Therefore, this chapter suggests notes for a concept of environmental geopolitics. To reconfigure the strategic boundaries between environmental and defense agendas, we can affirm that environmental geopolitics is narrative. Nexuses between the environmental and the national security agendas cohere to integrated strategic calculations to drive the competitive logic for primacy in the concert of nations, giving vent to national development aspirations.

Roughly speaking, environmental geopolitics is the government of nature and people, set in almost all prescriptions of institutional practices (defense terminology, industry, means of environmental protection, legal norms, academic definitions, programs, and projects). To find, within a qualified analysis, the dimension of environmental geopolitics and asymmetric power relations in territorial governance, this chapter had to dismember (in analytical terms) the hermetic fields of knowledge to create a path that would demonstrate the power relations involving the Brazilian territory and external threats. The institutional engagements of the national security and defense apparatuses establish decision-making processes concerning territorial governance that should reflect the objective of Brazil's international projection through environmental leadership and the technological development of persuasive means for development.

The beginning of the twenty-first century shows growing narratives on climate change and Amazon deforestation. Moreover, narratives pervade biopiracy, traditional knowledge appropriation, land conflicts, foreigners' land purchase, the timber industry, and other illegalities. These themes raise debates about sovereignty, geopolitics, environmental practices, and developmental policies. Even though they do not deal directly with internationalization, the issue is latent within them. In the first decades of this century, environmental assumptions became more substantial, and the institutional role of the state in promoting environmental preservation receives more criticism than ever.

The analysis presented serves to understand how practices promote the Brazilian nation's designs. Environmental geopolitics means establishing procedures, analyses, reflections, calculations, and tactics that allow the exercise of a particular and complex form of power, which targets the forests, borders, mineral resources, water, territory, population, new technologies, and space. It also means constituting specific forms of ecological, biological, sociological, diplomatic, economic, strategic, and military knowledge. Hence, we analyzed the integration between agendas, which generates a series of specific apparatuses of territorial government and sets of knowledge to direct alternative understandings, conjugating interests that include a fair and developed country.

NOTES

1. Hybrid warfare is a contested concept and has faced much criticism due to its lack of conceptual clarity. Initially mentioned in 2005 by two US military officials, in a nutshell, this taxonomy refers to the combination of conventional and unconventional strategies, methods, and tactics, as well as the psychological and informational aspects of modern conflicts aimed at exploiting the vulnerabilities of an antagonist and achieve synergistic effects.

2. Geopolitics is a theory of power supported fundamentally on territory and is only valuable if it uses geographical factors in formulating a policy (Miyamoto, 1981, 7). The dynamics of environmental geopolitics is based on a political-administrative thought for governing territory, nature, and people. In this way, the nation is established in historically manufactured practices and categories (Berger; Luckmann, 1973). To deal with the Brazilian territorial complexity, environmental geopolitics explicitly operates practical-symbolic stock of categories previously instituted in the logic of the administration of the national territory (Medeiros, 2018).

REFERENCES

Baer, W. *A economia brasileira: uma breve análise desde o período colonial até a década de 1970*. São Paulo: Nobel, 2002.

Becker, Bertha. *Geopolítica da Amazônia: a nova fronteira de recursos*. Rio de Janeiro: Editora Zahar, 2005.

Becker, Bertha, and Cláudio Egler. *Brasil: uma nova potência regional na economia-mundo*. São Paulo: Bertrand Brasil, 1993.

Berger, P., and T. Luckmann. *A construção social da realidade tratado de sociologia do conhecimento*. Petrópolis: Editora Vozes, 1973.

Birkland, T. A. "Agenda sett ing in public policy." In *Handbook of public policy analysis: theory, politics and methods*, edited by Frank Fischer, Gerald J. Miller, Mara. S. Sidney, 63–78. New York: Taylor and Francis Group, 2007.

Buzan, Barry, Ole Waever, and Jaap de Wilde. *Security: a new framework for analysis*. Boulder and London: Lynne Rienner Publishers, 1998.

Castro, Iná Elias de. *Geografia e política: território, escalas de ação e instituições*. Rio de Janeiro: Bertrand Brasil, 2004.

Castro, Therezinha de. *Geopolítica: princípios, meios e fins*. Rio de Janeiro: Biblioteca do Exército, 1999.

Chang, Ha-Joong. *Chutando a Escada: a estratégia do desenvolvimento em perspectiva*. São Paulo: UNESP, 2004.

Cobb, Roger W., Jennie-Keit Ross, Marc H. Ross "Agenda Building as a comparative political process." *American Political Science Review* 70, nº 1 (March 1976): 126–138.

Costa, Wanderley Messias da. *Geografia política e geopolítica*. São Paulo: Hucitec/Edusp, 1992.

Costa, Wanderley Messias da. "Crise da Integração e Tendências." In *Geografia e Geopolítica da América do Sul: integrações e conflitos*, edited by Wanderley Messias da Costa e Daniel Bruno Vasconcelos. São Paulo: FFLCH/USP, 2019.

ESCOBAR, A. *Encountering development: the making and unmaking of the Third World*. Princeton, NJ: Princeton University Press, 1995.

Fernandes, J. "Da Geopolítica Clássica à Geopolítica Pós-Moderna: Entre a Ruptura e a Continuidade." *Política Internacional* 26, (Outono-Inverno 2002): 161–186.

Foucault, Michel. *As palavras e as coisas: uma arqueologia das ciências humanas*. São Paulo: Martins Fontes, [1981] 2007.

Foucault, Michel. *A verdade e as formas jurídicas*. Rio de Janeiro: Nau, [1973] 2003.

Foucault, Michel. *A Ordem do Discurso*. São Paulo: Edições Loyola, [1978] 1996.

Furtado, C. *Formação Econômica do Brasil*. São Paulo: Ática, 1987.

Giddens, Anthony. *A política da mudança climática*. Rio de Janeiro: Zahar, 2010.

Giddens, Anthony. *As consequências da modernidade*. São Paulo: Editora UNESP, 1991.

Heller, H. *Teoría del Estado*. Ciudad de México: FCE, 1947.

Latour, B. "Para distinguir amigos e inimigos no tempo do Antropoceno." *Revista de Antropologia* 57, no. 1 (2014): 11–31.

Latour, B. *Ciência em ação: como seguir cientistas e engenheiros sociedade afora*. São Paulo: Editora Unesp, 2000.

Le Prestre, P. *Ecopolítica Internacional*. São Paulo: Editora SENAC, 2000.

Leirner, Piero. *O Brasil no espectro de uma guerra híbrida: militares, operações psicológicas e políticas e uma perspectiva etnográfica*. São Paulo: Alameda, 2020.

Lewinsohn, T. *Avaliação do estado do conhecimento da biodiversidade brasileira*. Brasília: Ministério do Meio Ambiente, 2006.

Lovelock, James. "Gaia: um Modelo para a Dinâmica Planetária e Celular." In *Gaia: uma teoria do conhecimento*, edited by W.I. Thompson. São Paulo: Ed. Gaia, 2000.

Marshall, T. H. *Cidadania, Classe Social e Status*. Rio de Janeiro: Zahar Editores, 1967.

Medeiros, R. A. L. *Decodificando a Internacionalização da Amazônia: análise de uma geopolítica ambiental*. Brasília: Trampolim, 2018.

Mialhe, J. L. *Elementos de Direito Internacional Ambiental: Curso de Direito da UNISAL*. Campinas: UNISAL, 2012.

Miyamoto, S. *Geopolítica e poder no Brasil*. Campinas: Papirus, 1995.

Miyamoto, S. *O pensamento geopolítico brasileiro (1920–1980)*. MA Diss., São Paulo University, 1981.

Miyamoto, S. "Os estudos geopolíticos no Brasil: uma contribuição para sua avaliação." *Perspectiva* 4 (1981): 75–92.

Moura, A. *Governança Ambiental no Brasil: instituições, atores e políticas públicas*. Brasília: IPEA, 2016.

Nogueira, J., and N. Messari. *Teoria das relações internacionais: correntes e debates*. Rio de Janeiro: Elsevier, 2005.

Rawls, John. *Uma Teoria da Justiça*. São Paulo: Martins Fontes, 1997.

Rua, M. G. *Políticas públicas*. Florianópolis: Departamento de Ciências da Administração UFSC, 2014.

Sachs, I. *Desenvolvimento sustentável: desafio do século XXI*. Rio de Janeiro: Garamond, 2005.

Scott, J. *Seeing like a state: how certain schemes to improve the human condition have failed*. New Haven, CT: Yale University Press, 1998.

Santos, M. *A Urbanização Brasileira*. São Paulo: Editora HUCITEC, 1993.

Senado Federal. Decree nº 179/2018. Accessed September 14, 2022. https://legis .senado.leg.br/norma/30745258/publicacao/30745550.

Souza, C. "Estado da arte da pesquisa em políticas públicas." In *Políticas públicas no Brasil*, edited by G. Hochman. Rio de Janeiro: Editora Fiocruz, 2007.

Souza, R. *Entendendo a questão ambiental: temas de economia, política e gestão do meio ambiente*. Santa Cruz do Sul: EDUNISC, 2000.

Queiroz, F. A. *Hidropolítica e Segurança: as bacias platina e amazônica em perspectiva comparada*. Brasília: Fundação Alexandre de Gusmão, 2012.

Quijano, A. "Colonialidade, Eurocentrismo e América Latina." In *A colonialidade do saber: eurocentrismo e ciências sociais*, edited by E. Lander. Buenos Aires: Clacso, 2005.

Tanno, Grace. "A Contribuição da Escola de Copenhague aos Estudos de Segurança Internacional." MA Diss., Pontifical University of Rio de Janeiro, 2002.

Tokatlian, J. "La teoría de la interdependencia: Un paradigma alternativo al realismo?" *Estudios Internacionales*, 23, no. 91 (1990): 339–382.

Tundisi, J. G. "Recursos hídricos." *Parcerias estratégicas*, 20 (2005): 689–708.

Wallerstein, I. "La creación del sistema mundial moderno." In *Un mundo jamás imaginado*, edited by L. Bernardo. Bogotá: Editorial Santillana, 1992.

Wu, Tim. *The master switch: the rise and fall of information empires*. New York: Vintage Books, 2011.

Weber, M. "Bureaucracy." In *The Anthropology of the state: a reader*, edited by A. Sharma, and A. Gupta. Malden: Blackwell Publishing, [1968] 2004.

Wither, James K. "Making Sense of Hybrid Warfare." *Connections* 15, no. 2 (2016): 73–87.

Chapter 3

What is Beyond the Amazon Region and the High North?

Geopolitical Perspectives for Brazil in Central America and the Caribbean

Flávio Helmold Macieira

The high north of Brazil has historically and politically stood as a national land's end. However, Brazil has never in its independent history sufficiently extended its influence and projection up north to the Caribbean, and the Central American Isthmus,[1] a dual region, however, that lies intimately close to the Brazilian national territory.[2]

This chapter identifies the reasons for this odd and traditional Brazilian (relative) isolation from its immediate northern neighborhood. The analysis will lead to the assumption that the country's northern coast ceases to stand as a mere territorial and political limit to the Brazilian territory. Instead, it may assume an alternate profile as a connection line through which, or over which, Brazil can naturally strengthen its relationship up north.

The Brazilian high north comprises a natural coastal arch shaped like a smooth crescent, departing from the Brazilian-French Guyana border and reaching the coast of Ceará.[3] State. That coastal line has a unique characteristic: it is the only area of Brazil in which the Amazon rainforest directly touches the ocean. Translating that suggestive circumstance to the language of Brazilian strategic circles, it is the only Brazilian coastal sector along which the so-called Green Amazon—the Amazon jungle biome—directly touches a parcel of the so-called Blue Amazon—the vast extension of Brazilian territorial waters and maritime zone of exclusive economic exploitation.[4] Thus, the high north of Brazil and its smooth coastal bend can be metaphorically

described as a "bi-Amazonian crescent" through which the Brazilian ecosystem remains integrated into a broader natural system encompassing the
Caribbean and the Central American areas. Its geopolitical importance for
Brazil also stems from the fact that it comprises the magnificent estuary of
the Amazon River—a solemn and long-ranging entrance to the Brazilian
hinterland.

Departing from the identification of those geographical characteristics, this
chapter analyzes a handful of political and historical reasons that also press
Brazil to adopt a more assertive diplomatic and multifocused policy in its
relationship with its immediate northern neighborhood.

In order to confirm and stress the geopolitical importance of that
bi-Amazonian crescent, it also recalls that this territorial segment is situated
in an Atlantic zone that can be defined as the entrance to the Caribbean Sea.
That leads to an additional structural premise: considering the bi-Amazonian
crescent location, and especially the Amapá State's[5] coastal line, Brazil can
duly be considered a "Caribbean country."[6] This condition pushes Brazilian
diplomacy to strengthen links and interaction with the countries and territories of the Caribbean and Central America region.[7]

These analytical lines support the final proposal of this text: to bring to
light the importance of the bi-Amazonian crescent coastal line as a Brazilian
active window to the geostrategic zone located in the center of the American
hemisphere.

1. MULTIPLE COUNTRIES AND ONE SINGLE REGION

1.1 History Broadens Distances

As previously stated, the green Amazon meets the blue Amazon in the
Brazilian high north bi-Amazonian crescent coastal line. Brazil's mainland
meets the Caribbean Atlantic in a shared equatorial system frame.

Beyond the geographical dimension, Brazilian-Caribbean human and
sociological affinities are also remarkable. The countries of the Caribbean
basin are inhabited by a similar amalgam of multiple populations mixing
African, Indigenous, and European roots.[8] They share cultural inputs, and
in the social and economic fields, they coincide in struggling to surmount
similar vulnerabilities.

The fundamental question in this context is: Why, despite that set of affinities and their geographic proximity, do Brazil and the whole Central America
and the Caribbean (CAC) region still struggle to build a more complex and
intense relationship?

Historic factors explain the long-lasting relative isolation among the peoples in the region. The first fragmentation and isolation factor was the European model of colonization, which was applied in the New World after the discovery of America in 1492 (1500 for Brazil). In the Americas, colonization was undertaken following a pattern based on locally closed and ill-communicated systems (Spanish, Portuguese, British, French, and Dutch), which as a rule, in colonial times, were able to trade and communicate exclusively with their European metropoles, and never with their neighbor territories connected to different colonial systems.

After the independence of American territories, a new obstacle to creating a culture of interaction in the pan-Caribbean region was interposed by the growth of the North American power of attraction and influence. A dependent economic relationship between CAC and the United States surged. In addition, multiple American direct armed interventions boosted it in the Antilles and Central America.[9] Indeed, since their emancipation from the colonial regime, these regions turned mainly to the north while Brazil concentrated its neighboring interaction primarily in South America.

That practical isolation of Brazil and the whole of South America from the spaces lying immediately north has been indirectly aggravated by historical events in Panama, which became independent from Colombia in 1903. The United States has supported the move, planning to build an interoceanic canal across the Panamanian land strip.[10] Works on the future waterway started one year after the independence of Panama[11] from Colombia. The canal and its margins (the canal zone) became a territory under American administration until the year 2000, which meant the establishment, in practice, of an advanced and operational North American landmark close to the southern edge of Central America.

Despite Colombia's natural resentment of the independence process, and the fact that Panamanian economic links with Colombia were not totally severed after its emancipation, Panama has since successfully consolidated its national sovereignty. Yet understandably, it has always remained cautious in dealing with its southern neighbor. A regrettable consequence of that special relationship has been the noncompletion of the Pan-American Highway, originally planned to link Alaska to Patagonia.

The Carretera Panamericana unites the United States (and all of North America) with the Central American isthmus but does not proceed beyond it. Instead, it stops at the Darién Forest area (known as the Tapón de Darién), which lies as a geographic buffer inside the Panamanian territory, keeping Panama relatively isolated from Colombia.[12] That discontinuity of the emblematic Carretera, added to the lack of an adequate regional freight and passenger maritime transport system in South American countries, including Brazil, keeps them ill-connected by land and sea with Central and North America.

The economic and political consequences of that lack of physical communication are deplorable. Exporters from South America are unable to compete in the Central American consumer markets in the same conditions as their North American competitors, since the latter can directly access these markets by land using the Carretera. Economic isolation generates political distance. As a result, and even though the vast majority of Central and South American countries are parts of the same abstract geopolitical and cultural caucus called Latin America, they have been unable to put in place significant political and institutional schemes of interregional integration and stimulation to fruitful interdependence.

1.2. Interregional Attempts to Fill the Political Gap

That sociohistorical scenery explains in brief why Brazil, since its national independence in 1822 and throughout the twentieth century, remained much more isolated from the CAC region than geography, sociology, and history could require. The creation of the Group of Rio in 1985, and of CELAC (Community of Latin American and Caribbean States) in 2007, would install exceptional moments of increased political interaction in the whole of Latin America and the Caribbean, and Brazil was an active party in both processes. Still, those experiences lost momentum following political changes in member states. Brazil eventually left CELAC and remains apart at the time of this writing. In 2019, it participated in the foundation of an alternative forum—PROSUL (Foro para o Progresso da América do Sul/ Forum for the Progress of South America)—which was established by a group of then liberal-oriented Latin American governments. Almost three years have elapsed since its foundation, but PROSUL is still not institutionally structured. Meanwhile, CELAC remains in place[13] and may eventually resurge as an inclusive Latin American and Caribbean mechanism of dialogue and integration.

It is worth recalling, in this context, that a specific legal disposition pushes Brazil to favor integration initiatives in Latin America. The Brazilian Federal Constitution expressly determines in a single paragraph of Article IV that "the Republic Federative of Brazil will pursue the economic, political, social and cultural integration of the peoples in Latin America, aiming at the formation of a Latin American community of nations."[14]

1.3. Recent Brazilian Move to Approach the CAC
Regions in the Economic Field

As already seen, South and Central Americas have kept a relatively modest profile in mutual economic relationships throughout modern history. Still, a short-lasting exceptional period that is now closed can be regarded as noticeably exceptional:[15] at the beginning of the twenty-first century, the Brazilian economy went through a period of expansion toward foreign markets leading to a boost in exports of goods and services to CAC markets. The surge was especially remarkable in the building services segment. But, as it is well-known, although Brazilian building companies then managed to earn a solid reputation of excellence in the region,[16] their regional market share dramatically shrank following a set of judicial setbacks.

In parallel, Brazilian technical cooperation with the CAC regions also surged at the beginning of the twenty-first century—a drive that has declined following the conclusion of MINUSTAH (the United Nations Stabilization Mission in Haiti) on October 15, 2017.[17]

2. LOOKING NORTH: PLANNING FOR THE FUTURE

2.1. The Case for a New Brazilian Relationship Policy
Toward the CAC Region

This study supports the adoption of a new relationship approach, by Brazil, toward the CAC region. Beyond the region's proximity to the national territory, other fundamental considerations and factors of interest push in that direction:

1. Economic considerations: despite misconceptions and extensive disinformation, Central America and the Caribbean conform a market that Brazilian exporters cannot neglect. That macroregion's population surpasses eighty million people, which is more than the population of any single South American country.[18] The Brazilian offer of consumer products and services[19] is notoriously competitive and seems able to widen its share in that market if a new export-promoting effort is locally undertaken. Furthermore, the importance of the Panama Canal for Brazilian exports must be stressed.[20] Although, in the Panamanian official statistics (see Autoridad del Canal de Panama Statistics, 2020), Brazil does not count as a major canal user, that interoceanic water path is most important for Brazilians' trade with Asia and the American West Coast markets. That fake contradiction can be explained by the fact

that much of the transit of goods through the canal, from and to Brazil, circulates in foreign ships.

2. Transport safety considerations: the Caribbean Sea is crossed by the aerial and maritime routes that communicate Brazil and much of South and North America. This routing system requires a regional union of efforts to guarantee navigation safety.

3. Military considerations: as seen before, the bi-Amazonian Crescent is a highly strategic area for Brazil for three main geopolitical reasons: first, it gives access to the Brazilian hinterland, both directly over the coastline and through the Amazon colossus-river. Second, because of its surrounding continental lands in Amazonia and its contiguous sea-bed—concentrate riches (such as the humid forest, rare and valuable minerals, huge freshwater ways and reserves, fishery stocks, and oil and gas deposits on and offshore) that require protection. Third, due to its geographic position, it faces and gives access to the Caribbean and, further, the outer world. Sociological reasons also significantly add to the strategic importance of the High North as a Brazilian front to the Caribbean, thus justifying a traditional local presence of national military, police, and environment protection units as well as constant action in intelligence, planning and training (including emergencies handling) eventually raising the case for collaboration with similar forces in other CAC countries. Conspicuous examples in this sense are the fight against illicit activities such as drugs,[21] guns, people, animals, or botanic samples trafficking;[22] illegal deforestation and wood exports;[23] illegal mining and goods smuggling.

4. Environmental considerations: environment protection, both in the sea and inland, arises as a thematic priority pushing Brazil to dialogue and articulation of efforts with the countries in the Caribbean basin. In this sense, it is helpful in illustratively recalling: a) the increasing frequency of extreme climate episodes at the CAC region—in particular hurricanes and tempests, as well as seasonal floods or droughts; b) the plague of algae that affected the Mexican Caribbean in 2019; c) the appearance in 2019 of a giant pollution floating "island" in the Atlantic portion around the limits between Guatemala and Honduras;[24] d) the appalling oil leakages that occurred in the Gulf of Mexico[25] (2010) and the Brazilian coast (2019),[26] and the regional threats and fears that they have spread; and e) the sporadic media claims that chemical residues resulting from farming activities flow into the Amazon River and pour into the ocean.[27] These references converge to remind us that the High North and the whole Amazonian region do not conform to a biome in isolation. The opposite is true: this emblematic Brazilian macroregion

is inserted in a much broader regional system, thus being influenced by a whole set of external environmental circumstances.

5. Space research activities consideration: the upper equatorial lands are well-known as a favorable operational area for rocket launching. The High North of Brazil hosts two national rocket launching and monitoring bases.[28] They form a geographic triangle with the French base of Kourou in French Guyana, requiring coordinating efforts on flight monitoring, navigation securing, and readiness of emergency structures during launches.

6. Security consideration: the CAC region plays an important role in the globalization of markets and world production since the Panama Canal assures a global east-west maritime link. North-south air and seaborne flows of people and goods in the region add to its importance as a transit path for the global economy. However, that regional vocation to serve as a global interactive locus embeds the undesirable side effect of hosting hidden illicit activities such as drug and arms trafficking, smuggling, or irregular financial operations. Also, in that particular sector, regional coordination in intelligence and repression efforts remains primarily desirable and constantly urgent.

That set of considerations stresses the strategic importance of the Caribbean and Central American for Brazil and sets the case for a new future Brazilian approach toward that region. Therefore, the second half of this chapter will elaborate on an agenda to strengthen Brazilian interaction northbound. That reflection will encompass two spheres: one internal (referring to actions occurring mostly inside the Brazilian territory and, in particular, in the bi-Amazonian Crescent) and the other external (directly aimed at a strengthened Brazilian interaction with the CAC region).

2.2. An Internal Brazilian Agenda for the Bi-Amazonian Region: Suggested Measures

2.2.1. In the Economic and Logistic Field

1. *Improvement in land and fluvial/maritime internal access to the High North*—with completion and consolidation of rail, road, and waterways uniting the region to the rest of Brazil. That effort in reinforcing the transport infrastructure in the Amazonian region has taken place since the end of the twentieth century. It comprises the establishment or consolidation of multiple paths and modals of transportation in the region (for instance, the federal roads denominated BR-164, BR-158, and BR-364). It is highly recommended that those efforts persist and

intensify—evidently in observance of strict ecologic precautions—as
they decisively contribute to the attainment of the secular Brazilian
objective of achieving adequate national territory integration. In a perspective specifically focused by this chapter, they prepare the regional
scene to support a new pattern of the economic relationship between
Brazil and the CAC region.

2. *Continuous consolidation of ports, terminals, and air operational
    bases in the region.* A strong effort in port upgrading is already under-
    way in the Brazil's North Atlantic front. It responds to the completion
    of internal transport routes allowing to move goods from the produc-
    tion zones in the Brazilian hinterland to northern exports-processing
    areas (in the cities of Manaus, Belem, Santarem, Itaqui, Fortaleza, and
    others) and the northeast of Brazil (mainly in the ports of Recife City).
    The Brazilian soya production chain is particularly keen on using that
    multimodal transport system, since the Panama Canal has been enlarged
    to allow the transit of ships of up to 170,000 cargo tons, thus lowering
    the price of roundup operations of grain exports from the High North
    of Brazil to Asia.[29] Other export products profiting from high logistic
    costs gains in the northern Brazilian ports are iron and manganese ore
    extracted in northern Brazilian states, aluminum products, and oil and
    gas extracted offshore.

3. *Constant upgrading in maritime and aerial navigation equipment,* both
    in the civilian and military spheres since the disposal of transportation
    and vigilance means a clue for a more substantial operational presence
    from Brazil in the CAC region. A bolstering in up-to-date equipment is
    mainly required to assure the effectiveness of military and police forces
    acting on the repression of criminal activities in the High North. It is
    also required to keep the capacity to prevent and cope with emergencies
    in the vast areas concerned.

2.2.2. In the Cultural, Educational, and Technical Fields

1. *Stimulation of social awareness* in the northern region of Brazil and the
    whole country on the need for increased national interaction with coun-
    tries and territories in the Caribbean and Central America. Federal and
    local administrations, as well as local and national parliaments, media,
    universities, business unions, work unions, cultural and civic entities,
    must be mobilized to bring that message to the entire Brazilian society.

2. *Assessment, reorientation, and reinforcement of the academic and
    technical research capacity in the Amazon region,* considering its bio-
    geographical and sociological link to the contiguous maritime areas and
    its geographic proximity to Central America. Academic institutions in

the north of Brazil may improve their links to corresponding institutions in CAC in a move of external projection comprising the exchange of researchers, the sharing of data, and the harmonization of academic curricula.

2.2.3. In the Environment Domain

1. *Reinforcement of environment protection actions from a perspective of sustained development*: ecological preservation and sustainable development in Amazonia are permanent Brazilian governing targets. The necessary conciliation between both goals must evolve in strict compliance with the principle that the Amazonian environment is precious and vulnerable, thus requiring strict and unconditional protection. Furthermore, teaching and research institutions in the Brazilian High North are required to spread the assertion that the local ecosystem is not isolated but lies embedded in a vast regional macrosystem that extends far beyond Brazilian borders.

2. *Reinforcement and expansion of environmental vigilance routines* both in the High North and in the whole Amazon region so as to preserve its forest cover from illegal occupation and logging, as well as to protect the indigenous peoples settled in the region and their land reserves. Vigilance must also comprise efforts to prevent illegitimate appropriation of traditional products, technologies, and discoveries through mechanisms of technological piracy, such as the smuggling of animals or botanic samples for research abroad and attempts to register traditional product names as private international trade brands.

2.3. Suggested Measures to Foster Brazilian Relations with the Foreign Environment above the Bi-Amazonian Coastal Line

A nonexhaustive taxonomy of recommended actions to be taken by Brazil aimed at upgrading its relationship with the CAC region could comprise items such as:

2.3.1. Economic Field

1. *Campaigning for the completion of the Pan-American Highway* in the Organization of American States (OAS) and in Latin American deliberating fora (such as MERCOSUR, the Latin American and Caribbean Economic System (SELA), the Amazon Cooperation Treaty Organization (ACTO), the Regional South-American Infrastructure (IIRSA), and the

Latin American Integration Association (ALADI) looms as the most conspicuous task to be fulfilled since the elimination of north-south economic isolation would undoubtedly inaugurate a new era of complex hemispheric relationship in the Americas with a rebounding effect over the whole Pan-American economic scenery.

In present circumstances, exporters from South America cannot fairly compete in Central American markets with their counterparts from the United States and Mexico that enjoy land access to those markets through the Pan-American Highway. Completing the "Carretera"—one of biggest roads worldwide—would require building a short section (roughly 100 km) through the South Panama Darién Forest and its contiguous areas in Colombia.

In particular, it is essential to persuade the United States to support the completion of the emblematic highway (built following an originally visionary North American conception). After all, in case such a north-south link should be completed, although the exporting economies of South America would certainly improve their sales position in Central American markets (thus competing with the American exporters), a similar result would arise in the opposite sense. The Central American, North American, Mexican, and even Canadian economies would also earn an expanded capacity to access South America markets by land. In brief: a major milestone for true economic integration of the Americas would be put in place.

The idea of undertaking the completion of the Pan-American Highway also requires persuasion work on Panama—the country where the regrettable interruption of the highway occurs. Panama already stands as a global reference in terms of communication and navigation for owning the magnificent interoceanic canal and managing the crossing of over two thousand ships used in international transport networks. Following the proposed road completion, Panama may also become a fundamental hemispheric economic land-born link. Furthermore, Panama shall benefit from much-improved access to the consumer markets in Colombia and Venezuela, which are both vital clients of the Panamanian chain of Free Trade Zones, especially of the Colón Free Trade Zone.

2. *The organization of frequent commercial and investment missions to the region* for fact-finding, product exhibition, and market evaluation. Brazil's use of traditional trade promotion tools in the CAC region is recommended and must be increased. Participation in fairs and the establishment of warehouses[30] and showrooms for Brazilian products are additional tools to complete a new comprehensive Brazilian effort to strengthen positions in CAC markets. The exports promotion sections of the Brazilian diplomatic missions and APEX (Brazilian Exporting

Agency) offices in the area count on an experimented and adequate structure to support corporate market prospecting efforts on an expanded scale.

3. *The creation of freight lines with competitive transport offers* departing
   from the Brazilian High North (and from other national ports) toward
   CAC destinies appears as a clue to enhance Brazilian trade with the
   region. Ports in the High North are equipped to handle a vast range of
   industrial or consumption products suitable to be exported to CAC countries, such as vehicles, machinery, trucks, and tractors, electronic goods,
   building materials, steel components, iron ore, soya beans, processed
   food (such as meat and dairy products), and others.

4. *The establishment of maritime passenger lines (in ferryboats)* linking
   Brazil and the Caribbean and Central America should also be stimulated
   so as to reinforce a culture of human relationships in the area. With the
   advent of this kind of link, road tourism would flourish, benefiting both
   Brazil and the other countries of the macroregion. Such a new passenger
   and car transport service offer could partially compensate for the nonex-
   istent operational road link between Central and South America.[31]

5. *Reinforcement and diversification of Brazilian technical cooperation
   with the pelagic Caribbean and Central American States,* comprising
   granted technical cooperation for development and cooperation sensu
   lato. The CAC region is composed of small countries and territories that
   look at Brazil as a regional actor with no colonial ambitions and with
   important experience in cooperating for development—an image match-
   ing the soft-power concept.[32] From the Brazilian point of view, besides
   favoring the country's international influence, cooperation activities also
   create links between local and Brazilian businesses and working unions,
   thus favoring bilateral trade and productive relations. Being carried out
   under the coordination of the Brazilian Cooperation Agency (ABC)
   and covering a vast range of sectors and programs, Brazilian direct aid
   (meaning the granted assistance modality or cooperation sensu stricto)
   to CAC countries is already a reality. However, it is bound to intensify
   considerably in the frame of the new Brazilian relationship agenda with
   the region proposed herein.[33]

However, cooperation is only sometimes a *granting* operation. sensu lato,
it also means a share of efforts in activities and services of common interest.
In that perspective, the Brazilian-CAC countries may broaden cooperation to
a variety of sectors such as maritime and aerial transport safety; telecommuni-
cations; energy generation and handling; creation of academic or professional
networks on research, knowledge sharing, and teaching—with a particular
emphasis on agricultural, maritime, and forest management subjects.

6. *Signing Free Trade Agreements with integration arrangements in the CAC region.* It results difficult for Brazilian exporters to be commercially competitive in the Central American Integration System (SICA) and the Caribbean Community (CARICOM) markets since those regional arrangements grant exemptions or preferences to Brazil's direct trade competitors in the area: the United States[34] and Mexico. It is highly recommended, then, that Brazil (through MERCOSUR) improve its market access to the CAC region by completing free trade agreements with SICA and CARICOM.[35]

2.3.2. In the Environment, Thematic Cluster

Establish a regular regional dialogue on the environment for sharing information and setting up sovereign cooperation on the field. Similarities and points of contact exist to boost cooperation ties, since the Caribbean Sea and its oceanic extension to the east are inserted in a living space shared by all countries in the region, including Brazil. Likewise, the forest spaces in the Central American isthmus, despite such different size parameters, are surprising due to their similarity to the Amazonian forest in terms of flora and fauna.[36] For that reason, regular dialogue between CAC and the Amazonian Cooperation Treaty Organization (which has five South American Caribbean member countries and already counts on a major network linking national academic institutions: the Association of Amazonian Universities (UNAMAZ)) may also be established.

Oceanic, climatic, and forest studies are academic fields susceptible to inspiring contacts and networking between educational and technological institutes in the region.[37] Such mobilization of the Brazilian Amazonian region's academic structure toward an attitude of epistemological communication with the CAC academic environment would mainly contribute to the consolidation of a basic social awareness of the ecological, economic, political, and strategic importance for Brazil and its relationship with its northern vicinity.

2.3.3. In the Diplomatic Domain

1. *Reinforcement of the Brazilian diplomatic operational capacity in Central America and the Caribbean* through expansion of staff and logistic resources available in the diplomatic postings in the area. The new approach herein proposed is multidisciplinary. A whole set of specialized public organs and private agents (e.g., academy, cooperation and intelligence agencies, security organs, armed forces, trade unions,

investors, etc.) will be required to incorporate and implement parts of it in each specific activity sector mentioned. In that context, the embassies of Brazil in the CAC region[38] are operational units with a unique role to play. Beyond their formal political representation functions, they already develop intense activity in business and trade promotion, technical and educational cooperation, cultural promotion, consular services, protection of Brazilian citizens, and others. Developing on their present status, this chapter proposes their upgrade to the practical status of true representations in neighboring countries.[39] That new approach certainly implies establishing an expanded list of objectives, a new agenda of practical actions, and a reinforced budget, all designed to use Brazil's notorious soft power to support the reinforcement and diversify the profile of Brazil's diplomatic presence in the area.

2. *Approaching specific countries to facilitate the activation of Brazil's relationship with the Central American and Caribbean regions.*

The United States. Considering that the United States has a national front at the Caribbean Sea and detains unmatched operational capacity (political and economic) in the whole of the Mesoamerican region, it is most advisable that the Brazilian administration includes Central American and Caribbean subjects in its permanent dialogue agenda with the North American administration. Although the two countries' strategic interests may vary in emphasis or eventually lead to topic divergences or competition, both have much to gain if working in partnership in the CAC region. This is especially true in the fields of 1) cooperation against drug or gun trafficking, 2) joint repression of illicit financial practices, 3) common actions in defense of the sea environment, 4) joint efforts in securing air and sea routes in that vital transport and communication area, and last but not least 5) coordination on actions and programs of cooperation for development in Central American and in the Caribbean regions. In particular, joining efforts may facilitate the creation of alternatives to the current Chinese bids to execute infrastructure works in the CAC region.

Mexico. A Brazilian diplomatic effort to attract Mexico to joint visions and actions in CAC is advisable, since that country remains a major influence in the CAC region. Brazilian and Mexican regional interests vastly coincide in subjects such as the fight against illicit activities and measures to boost trade and business. Moreover, Mexico leads a "Mesoamerican project," framing its dialogue and cooperation with its CAC neighbors. That allows Brazil to propose something like a Brazilian-Mesoamerican-Mexican (and possibly also North American) dialogue on regional subjects.

Panama. The intensification of the Brazilian dialogue with Panama also seems advisable for Brazil in the national effort to improve its relationship with the Mesoamerican countries. As previously seen, Panama is a vital country concerning land, sea, and airborne transportation of goods and persons, and a significant point of interest regarding the fight against international financial illicit activities and the gathering of trade intelligence information.

Ownership and operation of the interoceanic waterway shape the whole Panamanian economy. Panama also appears as a dynamic center for international trading and goods storage. It is globally reputed as a sales place of logistics hardware and equipment for the oil industry and naval building, as well as a servicing center in shipping in areas such as repair, registration, insurance, catering, and provisioning. Panama also became a hemispheric reference in aerial transport in recent years due to the growing importance of the Tocumen airport hub in Panama City. In addition, the country hosts a central regional financial hub—once plagued by accusations of sheltering money of illegal origins. Recently, that hub has been revising operational patterns to guarantee a thorough fulfillment of international transparency and financial ethics rules.

Colombia, Venezuela, Suriname, and Guyana. Those are the South American states that must also be considered and contacted in the context of the Brazilian effort to upgrade its relation northward. They share with Brazil the same challenge to maintain stronger links with the CAC countries and the same regional security challenges and needs arising from their double condition of South American and Caribbean countries.

Cuba. Cuba remains at the margin of some of the major mechanisms of interaction in the Americas, despite its practical, relational agreement with CARICOM and its membership in ALADI. Notwithstanding, Cuba is an emblematic Caribbean country facing most of the same challenges (in the economic or ecological fields, for instance) that are confronted by the other states of the area. Brazil maintains with Cuba a correct bilateral diplomatic relationship able to fit and favor a new Brazilian agenda for relationship intensification with the CAC countries.

2.3.4. Military and Security Fields

Military and security diplomacy is a fundamental area of contact and exchange of information in the CAC region, considering its strategic importance, thoroughly described in previous sections of this chapter. Moreover, as previously mentioned, the CAC region is supposedly a hotbed for multiple illegal activities. It is therefore highly advisable to build an institutional intelligence-sharing system linking all players in the region, with particular emphasis on the major powers of the area, the United States, Brazil, Mexico, Colombia, Venezuela, and Panama. Additionally, those contacts may open a door for the organization of joint actions to combat illicit activities and missions of vigilance, or joint handling of emergencies whenever required by circumstances.

CONCLUSION

This chapter analyzed the reason why Brazil has long remained relatively isolated, politically and economically speaking, from the Caribbean and Central American regions, despite the proximity of these areas to the national territory.

The text navigated between geography and geopolitics and finally to diplomatic recommendations, then composing a road map for bringing Brazil "closer" to the region. The starting point of the argument was that the Brazilian High North should cease to be seen as a dead limit and start to stand as a strategic platform-oriented northwards. Shaped as a capricious geographical "crescent," its coastline exhibits the unique characteristic of being "bi-Amazonian," therefore looming as a natural and strategic locus of transition between land and sea, south and north, Brazil and its immediate vicinity. Among other measures, it proposes the completion of the physical link between north and south America—the so-called Pan-American Highway—a move that can virtually reshape the whole interaction scheme in the Americas, putting an end to centuries of bizarre and deplorable North-South relative land isolation.

In brief, the arguments presented in this chapter encourage Brazil to look above more attentively at its bi-Amazonian High North coastal line in the twenty-first century, to discover and assume that it is a neighboring country to Central America and that it can even be considered a Caribbean country. Accordingly, it is suggested that Brazil works to establish a renewed partnership and a progressive dialogue with a CAC region that, for all reasons, deserves to climb up positions in the Brazilian scale of geopolitical priorities. As a closing remark, it is worth stressing that, by focusing on the relations between Brazil and its northern neighbors, this analysis ultimately claims for a much deeper and more diversified interaction and integration in the American hemisphere.

NOTES

1. This chapter will frequently refer to the dual region comprising Central America and the Caribbean using the acronym CAC.

2. In contrast with the more active Brazilian attitude prevailing in regard to the country's neighbors in South America, especially at the most meridional latitudes of the continent.

3. Ceará State is located in the northeastern part of the country, on the Atlantic coast, and it is the seventeenth largest Brazilian state by area.

4. "Blue Amazon" is a definition especially cherished by Brazilian military and strategists. It introduces the idea that the Brazilian territorial waters are so valuable that they match, in strategic and symbolic importance, the mainland Amazon region itself. Significantly enough, the "Blue Amazon" expression does not refer solely to the Brazilian sea territories facing the Amazonian coast but to the whole set of Brazilian territorial waters of more than three million square kilometers.

5. Amapá is one of the twenty-seven federative units of Brazil. Located in the far north of the country, it is the second least populous state and the eighteenth largest by area, bordered by French Guiana to the north, the Atlantic Ocean to the east, the State of Pará to the south and west, and Suriname to the northwest.

6. The idea of Brazil as a Caribbean country is a formulation by former Brazilian ambassador to Trinidad and Tobago and Dominican Republican, H. E. Mr. José Marcus Vinicius de Sousa.

7. Not neglecting the fact that across the Caribbean Sea, the United States and Brazil face each other as "neighbors beyond a sea" and share a history of dialogue and economic cooperation. At the time of this writing, both countries remain tied in robust economic relations and rely on the Caribbean and Central America as areas of circulation between them both in the airborne and maritime modalities.

8. With an important presence of people of Asiatic descent in the Guianas and in parts of the Caribbean.

9. Recalling that American interventions also occurred in South America but much less frequently than in Central America and the Caribbean. On the subject, see Marc Becker, "History of U.S. Interventions in Latin America (2020) and John H. Coatsworth, "United States Interventions (2005).

10. After giving up the original idea of locating the interoceanic link in Nicaragua.

11. Building works would last for ten years profiting from the structure left behind by France's previous failed attempt to build the waterway. The works required essential sanitary advances to surmount the obstacle posed by the dreadful Yellow Fever plague. On the building epopee, see the definitive study by David McCullough, *The Path Between the Seas: The Creation of the Panama Canal, 1870–1914* (1977).

12. Carneiro et al., "A rodovia Pan-americana e o Tampão de Darién: integração continental e áreas protegidas em zona de fronteira."

13. After a Mexican mandate that guaranteed its survival after the difficulties caused by the Brazilian withdrawal, Argentina was elected in 2022 for the presidency of CELAC.

14. Brasil, "Constituição Federal." In article no.4: "The Federative Republic of Brazil will seek the economic, political, social, and cultural integration of the peoples of Latin America, aiming at the formation of a Latin American community of nations."

15. The special trade regime between the Panamanian Free Trade Zones and Colombia and Venezuela can also stand as a (peculiar) exception.

16. The leading Brazilian exporter of that kind of service managed, in the first decade of the twenty-first century, to conclude contracts of infrastructure building even in Miami, Florida—significantly enough for this chapter, a Caribbean, though continental, location.

17. Presently, the ABC (Agência Brasileira de Cooperação/Brazilian Cooperation Agency) works on maintaining and intensifying the regular flow of Brazilian technical cooperation with CAC countries.

18. On the production side, the region counts on outputs of oil and gas (on and offshore), metallurgy, agro-industrial activity (with an emphasis on cattle and meat production, dairy products, and coffee), fishery, food preparations, footwear, energy generation, and mining. GNP for Central America was estimated at US$ 376 billion by the USTR in 2019. For the Caribbean, the same source indicates an estimated US$ 150 billion for the same year.

19. ANAC, "Análise de Mercado. Brasil-Caribe."

20. In addition to being the canal operator, Panama emerges as a providing center for logistic material, as well as an international pole in maritime services such as ship registering and insurance—economic activities that derive from the canal operation and benefit from the Panamanian position as a crucial international financial center.

21. Whitehouse, "Global cocaine trafficking."

22. Estado de Minas, "PF prende no Panamá suspeito pelo desaparecimento de 12 brasileiros."

23. Preservation, combined with sustainable economic exploitation, is the legal motto to be observed in any regional policy.

24. BBC, "O gigantesco 'mar de lixo' no Caribe com plástico, animais mortos e até corpos."

25. *New York Times*, "New Estimates Double Rate of Oil Flowing Into Gulf."

26. O Estado de São Paulo, "Estadão no rastro do óleo no Nordeste São Paulo."

27. El País, "Um imenso mar de sargaços floresce no oceano dopado por fertilizantes."

28. Alcântara, in Maranhão State, and Barreira do Inferno in Rio Grande do Norte State.

29. Popov, "Veja os 10 portos brasileiros que mais embarcaram soja em 2019."

30. For instance, in the Colón Free Trade Zone of Panama.

31. Items "c" and "d" require the participation of private agents to be implemented.

32. In a nutshell, soft power is the ability to affect others through the cooptive means of framing the agenda, persuading, and eliciting positive attraction to obtain preferred outcomes.

33. Granted technical cooperation in the area has traditionally covered areas such as agriculture knowledge, social programs, organizational assistance, professional formation, medical social assistance techniques, academic interchange, military training, and others. That whole set of cooperation chapters can be expanded so as to consolidate the welcome Brazilian presence in those countries.

34. USTR, "Free trade Central America summary."

35. Another subject in this regard is the access to the Puerto Rican market, since the United States, through Section 27 of the Merchant Marine Act (known as the Jones Act), determines that the goods transported to the island can only be made by North American ships departing from US ports. This provision could supposedly be discussed in the WTO.

36. A most remarkable illustration in this sense is the presence of the jaguar on the top of the animal chain in both regions—occupying a central position among symbols and references found in the culture of indigenous peoples in Amazonia and Central America.

37. The tradition, size, and expertise of academic and technological institutes in the Northern region of Brazil (such as the Federal Universities of Pará, Amazon State Institutions, and Roraima State Institutions, and also the Instituto Nacional de Pesquisa da Amazônia—INPA) fully entitle them to act as Brazilian focal points in the frame of enhanced academic cooperation with sister institutions in CAC countries.

38. Brazil is diplomatically represented in all the Central American countries and eight Caribbean countries.

39. That is a practical definition based on the fact that Brazil maintains especially active and sizeable embassies in most South American countries.

REFERENCES

ANAC, Agência Nacional de Aviação Civil. "Análise de Mercado. Brasil-Caribe." https://www.anac.gov.br/A_Anac/internacional/publicacoes. Brasília. Brasil. Access: July 14, 2020.

Autoridad del Canal de Panama. "Statistics." Accessed August 29, 2020, https://micanaldepanama.com/wp-content/uploads/2019/10/10-. PrincipalesPaises.pdf.

BBC News Brasil. O gigantesco 'mar de lixo' no Caribe com plástico, animais mortos e até corpos. São Paulo. Brasil. *BBC Brasil,* November 2, 2017 https://www.bbc.com/portuguese/internacional-41853621

Becker, Marc. "History of U.S. Interventions in Latin America." Marc Becker's internet site. Duke University Press, Durham, North Carolinae. Accessed July 20, 2020. http://www.yachana.org/teaching/resources/interventions.html.

Brasil. "Constituição Federal." Accessed September 14, 2020. http://www.planalto.gov.br/ccivil_03/constituicao/constituicao.htm.

Coatsworth, John H. "United States Interventions." *Harvard Review of Latin American.* (Spring/summer 2005). Accessed August, 2020. https://revista.drclas.harvard.edu/book/united-states-interventions.

Carneiro, Camilo Pereira, Reolon, César Augusto, Portela, João Pedro. "A rodovia Pan-americana e o Tampão de Darién: integração continental e áreas protegidas em zona de fronteira." Dossier. *Revista Transporte y Territorio.* Buenos Aires: Universidade de Buenos Aires, 2019.

El País. "Um imenso mar de sargaços floresce no oceano dopado por fertilizantes." *El Pais,* July 5, 2019. https://brasil.elpais.com/brasil/2019/07/04/ciencia/1562219478_533571.html. Access: Jul. 15. 2020.

Estado de Minas. "PF prende no Panamá suspeito pelo desaparecimento de 12 brasileiros." *Estado de Minas*, August 6, 2018. https://www.em.com.br/app/noticia /nacional/2018/08/06/interna_nacional,978405/.

ICIJ, International Consortium of Investigative Journalists. "Giant Leak of Offshore Financial Records Exposes Global Array of Crime and Corruption." *ICIJ,* April 3, 2016. https://www.icij.org/investigations/panama-papers/20160403-panama -papers-global-overview/ Access: June 5, 2020.

Luria, Simon. "The Panama Papers: The Largest Financial Scandal of Modern Times." Createspace Independent Publishing Platform, 2016.

Macieira, Flávio. "A América Central e o Caribe como macrorregião estratégica para o Brasil. Análise e proposta de uma nova agenda regional brasileira." Course diss., Brazilian Defense College, 2020.

Mccullough, David. *The Path between the Seas. The Creation of the Panama Canal 1870–1914*. New York: Simon and Schuster, 1977.

Meyer, Peter J., and Clare Ribando Seelke. "Central America Regional Security Initiative: Background and Policy Issues." *Congressional Research Service*, December 17, 2015. https://sgp.fas.org/crs/row/R41731.pdf.

New York Times. "New Estimates Double Rate of Oil Flowing Into Gulf." *New York Times*, July 14, 2022. https://www.nytimes.com/2010/06/11/us/11spill.html/.

O Estado de São Paulo. "Estadão no rastro do óleo no Nordeste São Paulo." *O Estado de São Paulo*, October 10, 2019. https://sustentabilidade.estadao.com.br/noticias/ geral,estadao-no-rastro-do-oleo-no-nordeste,70003060850. Access July, 14. 2022.

Popov, Daniel. "Veja os 10 portos brasileiros que mais embarcaram soja em 2019." *Canal Rural*, December 11, 2019. https://www.canalrural.com.br/projeto-soja -brasil/noticia/10-portos-que-mais-embarcaram-soja-2019/.

Suape Notícias. "Porto de Suape volta a bater recorde de movimentação de cargas." Accessed April 24, 2020. Brazil. http://www.suape.pe.gov.br/pt/noticias/1308.

Sul21. "Ao menos 57 brasileiros aparecem nos Panama Papers." Published April 4, 2016. https://www.sul21.com.br/ultimas-noticias/politica/2016/04/ao-menos-57 -brasileiros-aparecem-nos-panama-papers/.

USTR. "Free trade Central America summary." Accessed June 14, 2020. https://ustr .gov/about-us/policy-offices/press-office/fact-sheets/archives/2003/december/.

Vinícius de Sousa, H.E. José Marcos. Former Brazilian Ambassador to Trinidad e Tobago and Dominican Republic. Private interview by the author. June 17, 2020. Brasília. Brazil.

Whitehouse."Global_cocaine_trafficking." Accessed June 5, 2020. https://www .whitehouse.gov/sites/whitehouse.gov/files/ondcp/.

Chapter 4

Brazil in the Geopolitics of Amazonia

Reflections on the Construction of an International Regime

Carlos Alfredo Lazary Teixeira, Fábio Albergaria de Queiroz, and Guilherme Lopes da Cunha

The uniqueness of the Amazonia is culturally embedded in Brazilian society as a symbol of greatness, revealing a socioemotional essence, a feeling built on the daring acts of notable pioneers. Among them, there was Euclides da Cunha (1866–1909): historian, engineer, and one of the most prominent Brazilian writers, coming back from a year-long border demarcation mission and crossing the treacherous waters of the Purus River—one of the largest of the Amazon basin—he felt enthusiastic about the vastness and complexity of that remarkable nature.

After sailing approximately 6,400 kilometers (4,000 miles), Euclides provided dense descriptions of what he saw. In a letter to Congressman Artur Lemos in 1905, he said "it is a magnitude that requires the subtle penetration of microscopes and the brief narrow vision of analysts; it is an infinity that must be dosed."[1] He went on to describe the landscape as "the last unfinished page of Genesis."[2] In a nutshell, it illustrates the geostrategic importance of the biome for accentuating global security concerns (Román, 1998; Lovejoy and Queiroz 2018, 688).

Located in the north-central portion of South America, the Amazonian region occupies around 7,800,000 square kilometers (3,011,580 sq m), encompassing territories in Brazil, Bolivia, Peru, Ecuador, Colombia, Venezuela, Guyana, Suriname, and French Guiana (French overseas territory), which

correspond to 40 percent of South America's area. Keeping about one-third
of the planet's genetic stock, Amazonia is the world's largest biodiversity
reserve (Silva, 2005, 67–69).[3]

In addition, with almost 7,000,000 square kilometers (2.702,715 sq m)
from its sources in the Peruvian Andes to its mouth in the Atlantic Ocean, the
Amazon River basin also stands out for its grandeur, the most extensive river
system in the world. Representing almost 20 percent of the world's surface
freshwater, with 25,000 kilometers (15,534 m) of navigable rivers and exceptional hydraulic potential, its strategic geopolitical importance for the economic and social development of all the riparian countries makes Amazonia
a high priority in South American international relations (Procópio, 2005;
Procópio, 2007, 272–73).

Amid the complexity of such a scenario, the classic relational trinomial
that defines geopolitics—space, power, and actors—gains new contours in
the twenty-first century. In this sense, we can verify, in this vital space, the
characteristics of a logic of power in which a collective project such as the
Amazon Cooperation Treaty (ACT) and the Amazon Cooperation Treaty
Organization (ACTO) results both in sovereignty strengthening and in
mechanisms of joint management of a biome whose genetic potential offers
the opportunity to overcome underdevelopment.

This way, Amazonian countries face significant challenges and opportunities by seeking to amalgamate efforts toward the harmonious development
of this strategic space. A fundamental role in this endeavor is attributed to
ACT and ACTO, whose guiding principles are the balance between socioeconomic, scientific, and technological development, besides an active environmental conservation agenda.

In addition, given the complexity of an international context in constant
mutation and whose destinies of its multiple actors and structures are inevita-
bly intertwined, we are urged to reflect on those variables capable of shaping
the Amazonian geopolitical landscape.

A determining step in this process is understanding the meaning that unites
Amazonian countries around cooperative propositions, the effects, and the
institutional mechanisms needed to deal with some of the current multidimensional challenges to the region. In this process—from the analysis of historical prolegomena—we sought to identify geopolitical elements that allow us
to verify the contributions of the ACT/ACTO in constructing an Amazonian
international regime. It emphasizes an actor with a prominent position in this
sui generis political-diplomatic architecture: Brazil.

To accomplish this research proposal, we first seek to explain why and
how countries choose to cooperate by using the conceptual lens of regime
theory. Then, we apply some of its premises to our universe of analysis

Figure 4.1. The Brazilian Amazonia and the Amazon River Basin. Modified from Théry (2005, 45).

after collecting, in a second moment, empirical evidence from the analysis of historical facts that led to initiatives aimed at developing Amazonian multilateralism.

1. EPISTEMOLOGY IN THE CONSTRUCTION
OF REGIMES: AN AMAZONIAN PROPOSAL

From the 1980s onward, several international relations theorists began systematically working on the concept of "regime." These endeavors culminated in developing a broad literature on the subject, leading us to the initial task of defining the most appropriate conceptual parameters to be applied to the Amazonian context.

One of the pioneer definitions and, even today, one of the most important and referenced, was proposed by Stephen D. Krasner (1982), which gravitated around the convergence between actors. Thus, for him, regimes are "principles, norms, rules, and decision-making procedures around which actor expectations converge in a given issue area" (185–86).

Krasner's conceptual framework was decisive for a better understanding of the links between actors who—even being ontologically different and guided by their interests—converge in a system of values. In this context, i) principles are understood as beliefs of facts and causation, ii) norms, as patterns of behavior defined in terms of rights and obligations, iii) rules, as prescriptions or proscriptions for actions, and, finally, iv) decision procedures, as practices for making and implementing collective choices (Krasner, 1982).[4]

Nonetheless, despite its practical usefulness, Román (1998) believes that the current theoretical perspectives, in general, do not satisfactorily explain a regime's maturation process or its results. For the author, these theoretical approaches are mainly concerned with understanding how certain institutions guide international cooperation, resulting in a greater emphasis on institutions and negotiations that take place at the international level and less on the results of cooperation itself. They become, therefore, static concepts incapable of capturing the variant characteristic of the regimes. It is essential to correct this discrepancy to evaluate a regime's effectiveness throughout its development process (Román, 1998, 59).

Converging with these statements, Levy, Young, and Zürn (1995) suggest the existence of conceptual arrangements conceived from the combination of empirical reality with the different effects of regimes over time after their implementation. Moreover, this method made it possible to typify the regimes

Table 4.1 Regime Definitions as to Formality and Expectations

Convergence of Expectations		
Formality	*Low*	*High*
Low	no regimes	tacit regimes
High	dead letter regimes	classic regimes

Source: Levy, Young, and Zürn (1995).

by associating their degree of normative formality with the actors' convergence of expectations that shape them, as shown in the table 4.1.

Thus, by seeking an alternative definition capable of dealing with the limitations mentioned above, Román (1998) proposes that international regimes be defined as "social institutions composed of agreed-upon principles, norms, rules, and decision-making procedures that are intended to govern, or govern, the interaction of actors in specific issue areas" (65).

According to Filho (2005), by adding the expression "that are intended to govern" (52–53), this concept admits the possibility of a regime being established and executed, but without producing the expected results. Moreover, this happens because the negotiation processes at the international level differ from domestic ones, thus leading to discussions that can result in vague or ambiguous decisions.

Considering such conceptual frameworks, in which typology would the Amazonian case be inserted? From different levels of analysis—domestic, regional, and international—which geopolitical variables gave the first contours to an Amazonian regime from the 1970s onward? Looking for answers to these questions as our starting point, we analyze externalities arising from a paradigmatic event: the controversial case of the Amazonian Great Lakes Project.

Headed by Hudson Institute (HI), this initiative was formally presented to the international community at the first Latin American Development Conference, held on October 16–19, 1964. It was based on the proposal of creating a colossal lake system in South America by merging the Andean-Amazonian main waterways toward La Plata basin in the Southern Cone of the subcontinent.

The first pages of an underexplored Brazilian and South American foreign policy chapter were written. Commonly relegated to footnotes, it should not be regarded as a marginal or second-order event. On the contrary, the "Hudson Episode" was a determining variable in explaining how some Brazilian foreign policy initiatives were taken and, in addition, how they led to the country's decision to lead the efforts toward a bold and unlikely project of constructing an Amazonian cooperative regime at that time.

2. HUDSON INSTITUTE, THE GREAT LAKES PROJECT, AND ITS IMPLICATIONS FOR AMAZONIAN MULTILATERALISM

HI was created in 1961 in Croton-on-Hudson, New York, by Herman Kahn with Max Singer and Oscar Ruebhausen. It was originally thought to be a research organization for promoting interdisciplinary studies on US security and defense, including their intersection with international relations, economics, culture, and science and technology.

In Brazil, HI gained significant notoriety in the 1960s when Herman Kahn and Robert Panero—HI representatives assigned to Colombia and Brazil— made public a project that, at the least, could be defined as simply astonishing but which was carefully presented to the audience, without pomp, as a "catalyzing agent of the economic and social development of South America" (Panero, 1968, 44). The core idea within the project was to create several artificial lakes capable of providing conditions of continuous navigability

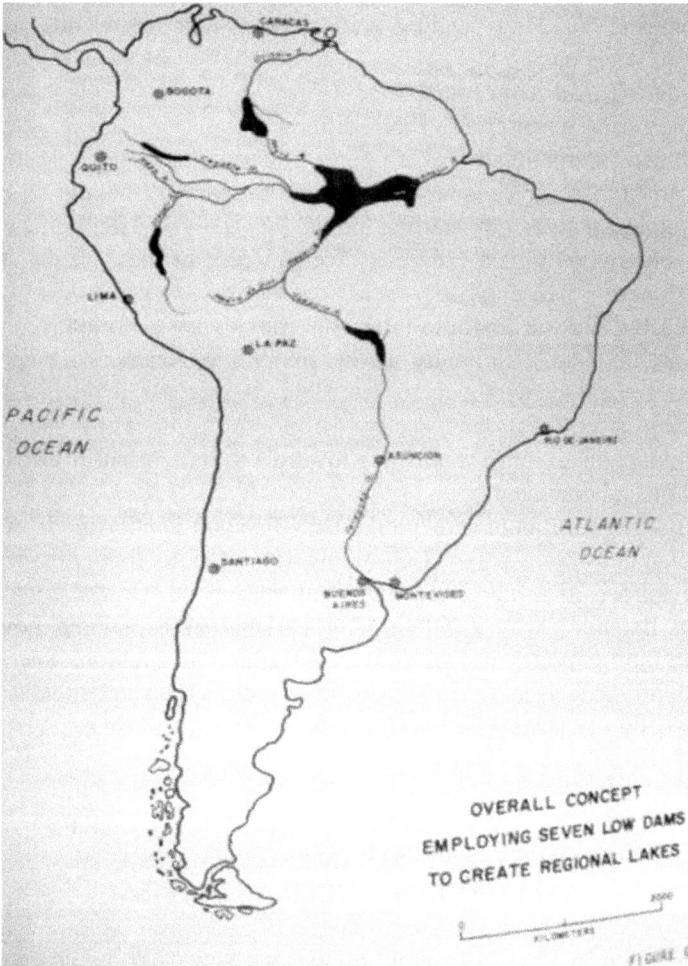

Figure 4.2. Possible Geographical Configuration of South America after the Construction of a "Great Lakes" System as Proposed by Hudson Institute. Panero (1967, 28).

practically all over the South American waterway extension, as well as some other secondary benefits.[5]

Summing up, Panero asserted that more than any other development alternative, the Great Lakes project—in addition to the primary purpose of opening a continuous waterway of continental dimensions—would stimulate 1) trade between the industrial complexes of Buenos Aires (Argentina), Montevideo (Uruguay), and São Paulo (Brazil) and the producers of raw materials from Venezuela, Colombia, Ecuador, Peru, and Bolivia; 2) the development of new large-scale productive activities in the fields of energy and logging; 3) the massive occupation of the surrounding areas around these flourishing trade centers and mineral exploration spots, until then labeled as inaccessible areas.

It was unclear at that moment the precise connection between the primary purpose of HI and the creation of an integrated system of lakes in South America. As a result, in the heat of discussions that took place about the motivations that would have led HI to advance this herculean structural intervention in the Amazon basin, words such as those uttered by the Prussian statesman Otto von Bismarck that "natural resources in the hands of nations that do not want or cannot exploit them, cease to constitute assets and become threats to those who possess them" resonated, for many, with remarkable sharpness.

Undeniably, a decisive voice in the efforts to restrain the project, the Brazilian Ministry of Foreign Affairs—also known as Itamaraty—sent, on September 15, 1967, three diplomats to HI headquarters to gather information in order to get a more accurate assessment of the implications of the South American Great Lakes to national interests. This endeavor resulted in a detailed report that was urgently addressed to the Brazilian president with several cautionary suggestions based on the identified inconsistencies in the project (Cabral, 1968, 149–50).[6]

Figure 4.3.   QR Code. Correio da Manhã (1968, 10–11).

Almost a year after the diplomatic mission, on July 14, 1968, the headline of the Brazilian newspaper *Correio da Manhã*, entitled "Correio reveals the whole truth about Amazonia," highlighted some aspects revealed by Itamaraty's report, such as initiatives forecast in the HI proposal. Among them, the flooding of lowlands in Amazonia to create lacustrine access routes that, in turn, should be capable of fostering regional development through improvements in agriculture and infrastructure projects.

The report also brought forth a series of general considerations about the HI, drawing particular attention to a relevant fact: its close connection with the US government, an observation stemming from the evidence that more than 85 percent of its budget came from official agencies, especially from the Department of Defense. Hence the question raised by the investigative commission: What would have led HI to guide its actions toward an effective occupation of the Amazon region?

One of the considered hypotheses in response to such a query was that, in the logic of the Cold War's dispute, the US strategic-military concern with an integrated regional system of access to Panama and the west coast of South America could be solved with the creation of waterways that would lead to the Amazon basin through the Negro and the Orinoco Rivers.[7] Furthermore, the United States would not be alone in pursuit of this purpose. As for the scenario projected for the Andean Amazonia, the document highlighted Colombia, Peru, and Bolivia as clearly prone to the idea, having even constituted national committees to appreciate the benefits of the projects for their respective territories. At first glance, many advantages with just a few drawbacks.

Thus, some emergency measures to be taken by Brazil were suggested, such as: a) conducting a detailed investigation of the connections between HI and Washington, especially with the Departments of State and Defense; b) mapping the contacts made by HI with the governments of Colombia, Peru, Ecuador, and Bolivia; c) defining a development agenda encompassing the Amazon basin from the perspective of Brazilian interests; and d) assignment of specialized technicians to keep under observation the work developed by HI (RBPI, 1968, 141).

As a result, in 1968, the Brazilian war college, Escola Superior da Guerra, published a report later titled Operação Amazônia / Amazon Operation, classified as secret (Brasil, 1968). It established the guidelines of a security policy for the Amazon region, including improvements in matters of transport and communications aiming, among other objectives, at the welfare of population groupings living in transboundary areas, thus reinforcing the relationship between security and development. Still in this regard, the report proposed alternatives to: a) the implementation of the so-called Amazon Operation to update and give new priorities for development and occupation programs of

Figure 4.4. "Operation Amazonia." Appendix to the Ministerial Report presented to the President of the Republic by the Extraordinary Minister for the Coordination of Regional Organizations. Secret File/Confidential References. Brazilian Ministry of Foreign Affairs Library, Historic Collection Section (1968).

the Amazonian territory; b) the creation of "free trade zones" (*zonas francas*) in the region aimed at stimulating its industrialization; and c) the regulation of tax exemptions and other incentives to foster the development of the Amazon.

Finally, the Amazon Lakes Project stimulated the Brazilian military to recognize the importance of exerting a presence within the Brazilian Amazonia. Results therefrom were the Trans-Amazonian Highway system and the extensive number of hydroelectric projects, some of which have been built, others are still just planned. At the same time, in this context, security-related issues came to be seen as inseparable from the national development project in a complex equation that had as one of its key elements the reaffirmation of

sovereignty not only in the Brazilian Amazonia but in the Hylea as a whole–
this strategic space historically marked by sparse and irregular contacts
between neighbors (Medina, 1983, 261; Caubet, 1984, 804).

3. THE AMAZON COOPERATION TREATY: 1978

In this scenario, under the Brazilian initiative, the idea of institutionalizing
the regional cooperation process through a formal treaty was conceived.
This brought benefits for territories covered by the Amazon Basin, including
those that, due to their geographical, ecological, or economic characteristics,
were closely linked to the same hydrological and socioeconomic dynamics.
According to Ricupero (1984, 186), given the transnational nature of the
basin, nothing is fairer than keeping the exclusive responsibility to decide on
the area's future to the Amazonian countries (i.e., within the regional sphere).

Furthermore, this proposal also served another purpose: to reduce vicinal
suspicions about supposed Brazilian expansionist intentions (Caubet, 2006,
171). Therefore, there was caution in conducting negotiations in order to
maximize the potential for cooperation with minimum risks of constraints,
especially in regard to Venezuela, which observed with great reserve the
growing participation of Brazil in the northern portion of South America, a
region where Caracas had pretensions of exerting influence and a possible
leadership (Cervo, 2001, 8).[8]

Initially, in March 1977, Brazil verified in the chancelleries of each
Amazonian country the reaction that would arouse the conclusion of an
agreement of this type. Once the idea was taken into account, negotiations
followed a detailed schedule. The objections and suggestions raised by the
participants were analyzed and, as far as possible, incorporated into the draft.
To this end, three meetings were scheduled: in November 1977, and March
and May 1978, the first two in Brasília, Brazil, and the last in Caracas,
Venezuela, where, finally, the final text was approved (Ricupero, 1984, 185).

This is how, by Brazilian initiative, in 1978 the eight Amazonian countries signed the Amazon Cooperation Treaty (ACT) in Brasília. Comprising
twenty-eight articles in its definitive version, the ACT can essentially be
qualified as a framework agreement, that modality of treaty that establishes
general directives so that, from then on, the additional mechanisms necessary
for the outlined objectives are achieved. When analyzing the ACT's preamble
it is possible to identify the fundamental principles that shaped the guiding
corollary of Amazonian regional cooperation. They are:

1. The exclusive competence of the countries of the region in the develop-
    ment of the Amazon basin (preamble).

2. The sovereign right of each state in the use and preservation of natural resources, and in the development policy of the Amazon areas in their territories, without interference from third parties, even if they are members of the treaty (preamble; art. IV; XVI).
3. Regional cooperation as a facilitator of achieving these two objectives (preamble, art. XI).
4. The balance and harmony between development and ecological protection (preamble; art. I and VII), a debut theme in international relations at that time.
5. Absolute equality, guaranteed by the application of the unanimity rule for all important decisions to be taken by the member states (art. XXV).
6. The exchange of information, the collaboration in scientific and technological research (including the participation of international organizations as long as it is deemed necessary and convenient), and the sharing of national experiences in terms of regional development and environmental preservation (preamble, Article VII and IX).

By considering such principles it becomes clear that a relevant aspect of ACT is the way its modus operandi was established, that is, with the affirmation of sovereignty preceding cooperation. While, on the one hand, the eight signatories were assured exclusive responsibility for the Amazonian zones located in their respective territories, on the other, the implementation of complementary measures that reinforced actions of common interest was relegated to the area of regional cooperation (and even then, limited to a restricted group of subjects) to be carried out in their territories. In this regard, the priority for national development plans was confirmed.

This perspective results from significant changes to the ACT draft, which was initially conceived by the Brazilian Ministry of Foreign Affairs, also known as Itamaraty, the great architect of the proposal. In essence, this situation pointed out that a close commitment between the parties in sensitive areas, such as, for example, security and defense, was not seen as adequate, probably due to the fear of vicinal interference (especially from Brazil) in issues intrinsically linked to political stability and territorial integrity. Therefore, texts such as "collaboration for the defense and development of the respective Amazonian territories" and "the preservation of the security and prosperity conditions of these territories"—targets of objections that could compromise the outcome of the negotiations—were suppressed (Queiroz, 2012, 330).

After accepting, albeit grudgingly, the rejection of the proposal for regional defense cooperation, Itamaraty's efforts turned to another equally sensitive topic: the physical integration of Amazonia. In a speech given at the opening of the second preparatory meeting of the Amazon Pact, Chancellor Azeredo da Silveira stated that "what is desired is to fill in the gaps and mobilize cooperation in an area that has not yet been considered: physical integration" (Silveira, 1978, 54). According to Silveira, the lack of an adequate infrastructure was the main reason that made the region's development so difficult (Antiquera, 2009, 7).

As expected, due to its breadth and potential implications, this issue was also a reason for objections, mainly from Peru and Bolivia, the first ones to speak out against total commitment to such an inclusive commitment. The priority of these countries, supported by Venezuela, was to promote the physical integration of the Amazonian territories into their respective economies before integrating them with Brazil, a more developed country still seen as a threat (Costa, 1987, 28).

Therefore, texts that presupposed ambitious and equally binding goals such as "the recognition of the parties that physical integration is an indispensable requirement for the process of regional development" were replaced, in this specific case, by "The Contracting Parties agree on the advisability of creating a suitable physical infrastructure among their respective countries, especially in relation to transportation and communications" (art. X), a less covetous (albeit complex) legal provision that, at the same time, demanded a lower degree of commitment (Caubet, 2006, 173).

The analysis of the described scenario allows us to infer that Brazil prioritized the accession of Amazonian countries to the ACT rather than the emphatic defense of its original proposal, which meant renouncing themes that were considered crucial to the country's pretensions, such as cooperation for defense and integration. The words of Brazilian president Ernesto Geisel in this regard are enlightening. In a speech given during the signing ceremony of the ACT, Geisel (1978, 10) emphasized,

> The sovereignty valued and reinforced in the Treaty is not, however, only or mainly the regional one, but before it, the national one, which constitutes its primary and untouchable source. The occupation of Amazonia and the definition of internal development policy will remain, as now, matters of exclusive competence of the national sphere of each country.

Likewise, the minister of foreign affairs, Azeredo da Silveira, sought to reinforce the intention of the Brazilian proposal as devoid of any veiled attempt of imperialism or intrusion into the internal affairs of its Amazonian neighbors. To this end, Silveira (1978, 12) stated:

> On the one hand, we consecrate with meridian clarity that the Treaty does not interfere in any way with the sovereign jurisdiction that each country corresponds to in its Amazonian territories. Nevertheless, on the other hand, in no

way do we intend to replace each State's exclusive right and responsibility to ensure the development of its Amazonian region as an essential and integrated part of its national set.

In these terms, the words of Azeredo da Silveira made it clear that it was a matter of consolidating an Amazonian pillar, repelling interests that were adverse to sovereign assumptions. It was in this context that the spirit that gave foundation to Amazonian cooperation was developed: twenty years later, in Caracas, the Protocol of Amendment to the Amazon Cooperation Treaty was signed, creating the ACTO and opening a new and challenging chapter in the international relations of the "eight Amazonians countries."[9]

As we will see, this mosaic reveals that, in the Amazonian environment, in which identities were being shaped and shared interests crystallized as normative principles, there was room for a framework prone to cooperation, albeit fragile. Moreover, it means that even with the ambiguities and weaknesses identified, the relations between the Amazonian states, perceived as sufficiently positive, promoted situations of mutual advantages capable of reducing vicinal distrust.

4. QUO VADIS, AMAZONIA? WHAT DOES THE EMPIRICAL EVIDENCE ON THE ACTO DEMONSTRATE?

Verifying the trajectory of an Amazonian regime under construction leads us to reflect on the meaning of the different stages of this process. In this sense, it is worth highlighting that, when analyzing the political and institutional trajectory of the Amazon Pact, from its signature to the creation of the ACTO, Aranibar (2003) identified three distinct moments. However, to update his contribution, we believe that it is possible to recognize the fourth phase with the support of literature and official documents.

The first moment, defensive-protectionist, is marked by the signatory countries' quest to express to the international community their absolute and unquestionable sovereign right over the destiny of the Amazonian space in their respective territories. Paradoxically, this is a period notably marked by the inactivity of ACT, a direct result of its institutional fragility (such as the transience of the secretariat[10] and lack of resources). Moreover, the multilateralism of poor results that made the 1980s, in the assessment of Procópio (2005b, 71) and Antiquera (2006, 107–35), led to the lost decade of Amazonian cooperation.

This fragility supports the assertion that, in several diplomacies of the hylea,[11] the so-called circumstantial pragmatism prevailed: casuistic and accommodating the ambivalences arising from the overlapping of private interests. Consequently, this contributed to relegating ACT to the worrying condition of a dead letter regime, incapable of preventing structural inequalities and insecurities that hindered the advances necessary for constructing an Amazonian political face (Procópio 2005b, 67–71). Still, starting in 1988, we see substantive efforts that resulted in the creation of several special commissions.[12]

The second phase in Aranibar's taxonomy, named as a political incentive and strengthening, began in May 1989, with the holding, in Manaus, Brazil, of the First Meeting of Presidents of the Amazonian countries. Thus, it constituted the cornerstone of the political commitment renewal of the Amazonian states with the objectives and principles of ACT. Only in the early 1990s, with the ecological-environmental issue becoming one of the most powerful dimensions of globalization, Amazonia would reappear as a promising means of attracting international financial resources for projects aimed at the region's development, which helps to understand the revaluation that ACT underwent in the period. As pointed out by Román (1998, 274), after the United Nations Conference on Environment and Development, held in 1992 in Rio de Janeiro:

> The fact that the preservation of Amazonia now emerged as a new means to obtain external funding indicated that the role of the Amazon Cooperation Treaty changed. It was in this increasingly clear setting that the Treaty, apart from its original function as an institutional framework protecting the Amazon countries' sovereign right to economic development, could also serve as a platform in global negotiations on environment and development. Furthermore, the apparent effort to extend regional cooperation would, in this case, allow the Amazon countries to appear as environmentally concerned and dedicated.

Therefore, the paradigmatic fact of this period was the joint participation of ACT members as a consensual voice in the UNCED/1992, thus establishing a milestone in the dialogue with developed countries and reinforcing, in addition, the need for a revitalization of the Amazon pact. Taking advantage of the favorable context to put on the agenda the discussion on increasing the degree of institutionalization and strengthening of the ACT—in order to make it operational and more effective in capturing and applying these potential resources—Brazilian diplomacy acted quickly and proposed, in 1993, the creation of an international organization with permanent headquarters, with its own budget and international legal personality.[13]

The acceptance of Brazil's proposal by the other member countries culminated in the signing of the Protocol of Amendment to the ACT in 1998, which in turn created ACTO, and its permanent secretariat, based in Brasília,

Brazil, headed by a secretary general. Upon completion of the protocol ratification process, the new intergovernmental organization began its activities in 2002.[14]

This third phase, institutional maturation, began to take shape in 1994, when the Amazon Cooperation Council, at its VI Meeting, determined the constitution of a committee to study the technical, administrative, legal, and financial implications of installing a permanent secretariat (PS). This lasted until 2002, when studies on the transition from the ACT to the ACTO were completed, thus guaranteeing the new entity a more efficient operational level capable of streamlining the activities carried out in its different areas of interest.

As a result, since the establishment of the PS/ACTO, under the leadership of its first secretary general, Dr. Rosalía Arteaga, former president of Ecuador, several initiatives were launched, supported by strategic partners—the German Government (BMZ/GIZ), the Brazilian Cooperation Agency (ABC), the International Bank for Reconstruction and Development, the UN Environment Programme, the Pan American Health Organization—in the various pillars of the ACT, such as biodiversity, water resources, health, indigenous peoples, forests, among others.

Finally, the fourth phase, as we propose, setting a strategic renewal, begins with the approval, in 2009, of the Amazonian Strategic Cooperation Agenda 2010–2018 (ASCA). It is the main instrument for guiding the work of the permanent secretariat of ACTO. It has its apex with the inauguration of ACTO's new and first permanent headquarters in Brasília, on October 21, 2021, with funds from the German Development Bank.

Within the timeline of this new phase, the Conference of the Parties to the Convention on Climate Change, held in Paris in 2015, indicated to ACTO the advisability of updating the content of the ASCA.

In this regard, at the XIII Meeting of Ministers of Foreign Affairs, held on December 1, 2017, in Tena, Ecuador, it was decided to convene the "I Regional Meeting of ACTO Focal Points for the Review and Updating of ASCA," which took place on April 5–6, 2018, in Bogotá, shortly before the commemoration of the fortieth anniversary of the signing of the ACT, on July 3. Thus, the next step was the approval of the updated version of ASCA, for 2019–2030, at the XXI Meeting of the Amazon Cooperation Council in November 2018 in the city of Santa Cruz de la Sierra, Bolivia.

In short, it is a document based mainly on south-south cooperation and deeply linked to the premises of the sustainable development goals of the 2030 agenda and the commitments of the Paris Agreement on Climate Change, among other international agreements related to the objectives of the Amazon Cooperation Treaty.

A closely related subject is the field of water resources. Looking for the integrated management of the Amazon basin, actions taken have been aimed at setting up and operating the Hydrometeorological and Water Quality Data Network,[15] with more than four hundred automatic measurement and monitoring stations, which will be able, for example, to anticipate extreme events such as floods and droughts. For this purpose, a situation room was created at ACTO's new headquarters in Brasília.

Still, regarding water resources, the activities of a working group were resumed for the adoption of a Regulation for Commercial Navigation in the Rivers of the Amazon Basin.[16] This is the first step toward the future integrated management of the watershed, which will necessarily include the implementation of waterways.

In a broader approach, ACTO obtained resources from the European Union (Euroclima+)[17] for Amazonia to be the first region to comply with the Paris Agreement decision to establish a platform for valuing the knowledge of indigenous peoples and local communities.

Concerning forestry, it is worth noting that ACTO carried out projects to monitor forest cover, financed by the Amazon Fund, formed with resources from Norway and Germany (USD 1.288 billion) and implemented by the Brazilian National Bank for Economic Development.[18] After years of negotiation, such projects facilitated the unanimous approval in 2021 of the Regional Forestry Program and the Memorandum of Understanding on Cooperation and Mutual Assistance for the Integral Management on Fire.

The year 2021 also marked advances in the Amazonia biodiversity agenda. The Regional Biological Diversity Program, unanimously approved, was implemented with the technical support of the Humboldt Institute of Colombia. It convened around 120 academics and specialists, including Indigenous people, to prepare the Rapid Assessment of Biodiversity and Ecosystem Services in Amazonia, based on the Intergovernmental Platform on Biodiversity and Ecosystem Services methodology.

Still, on the biodiversity pillar, it is vital to highlight the Bioamazônia project, financed by the German KFW Development Bank, which aims to protect flora and fauna species threatened by unsustainable trade. The primary reference is the lists annexed to the Convention on International Trade in Endangered Species of Wild Fauna and Flora.

One of the guiding threads of the Amazonia cooperation agenda, highlighted in ACT, is the collection, production, systematization, and dissemination of quality information. The Amazon Regional Observatory,[19] therefore, is the most critical initiative underway at ACTO, as well as a reference center for promoting the flow of scientific-technological information between institutions and intergovernmental authorities of the member countries, linked to the study of Amazonia.

Last but not least, another deed worth mentioning in this phase of ACTO's strategic renewal is the reestablishment of contact with Amazonian legislative branches, since the sustainable development of Amazonia depends on coherent, stable, convergent, and permanent public policies. Based on this inference, in the preparatory phase of Rio 92, coinciding with the first Summit of the Amazon Pact, the Amazon Parliament, aka Parlamaz,[20] was established in Lima, Peru, in 1989, with the mission of engaging the legislative branch on the region's sustainable development agenda.

Parlamaz, after three decades of intermittent operation, was reactivated in 2020, under the leadership of the Foreign Relations Committee of the Federal Senate of Brazil. In 2022, in its first face-to-face meeting, under the presidency of Senator Nelsinho Trad from Brazil, Parlamaz issued a statement urging the chancelleries to initiate the negotiation process of an additional protocol amending ACT, to institutionalize it within the scope of ACTO.

CONCLUSION

Criticism of Amazonian multilateralism is a common ground in political analysis. However, despite these voices, it is worth mentioning that the normative framework verified—resulting from the images that actors present about others and themselves, emphasizing the role played by Brazil—shaped the cooperative structure thought to mediate their mutual interactions. It represents an important step, although limited in its scope and outcomes.

By analyzing the Amazonian case—from the theoretical perspective of Mikael Román (1998) on the construction of international regimes and the typology presented by Aranibar (2003)—it is possible to qualify the initiatives described in this chapter as an essential part of this process. According to Román's proposal, a regime should be understood as a gradual process, subject to what he called "formative moments": those immediate and/or long-term events necessary for a qualitative change to occur.

Therefore, according to this approach, it is feasible to obtain a regime even if the expected results have not been fully achieved. Thus, considering the ontological and epistemological elements presented in this analysis, could we verify relevant advances in terms of normative arrangements complementary to the Amazon Pact capable of validating the case as an operationally effective regime?

In order to test these propositions, it is essential to consider that the situational and structural dynamics of contemporary international politics have led to the emergence of new challenges for Amazonian countries. In addition, the answers to these phenomena require a decision nexus that points to the urgent need to improve cooperation mechanisms to tackle the complex adversities stemming from this scenario. Furthermore, in this case, the mentioned processes, marked by advances and setbacks, resulted in the coordination of plans, policies, and strategies that have witnessed remarkable achievements in a subregional order that values, in the first place, the sovereignty of states, which has constituted the backbone of the Amazonian regime since its origin.

In this sense, the need to improve the ACTO lies in the face of old and new challenges. The old or traditional ones are those identified in the history of the Amazonian countries that continue to exist in different emphases and scales. Among them is biopiracy,[21] drug trafficking,[22] as well as narratives supported by political actors who show sympathy for salvationist discourses, constituting elements of a rhetoric of confrontation.[23]

Among the new challenges—as an update of the "formative moments"—elements of a structural and situational nature can be mentioned. In this context, geopolitical issues are added to the traditional agenda of Amazonian countries, adding new layers of complexity. This perception is confirmed by the intrusion of extraregional actors in South America, which alerts us to the emergence of potential obstacles to the total effectiveness of an Amazonian regime.[24] Therefore, with a precise understanding of the deleterious effects of such a scenario for the Hylea, the necessary Amazonian consensus may avoid hurdles.

Given the variables listed, we can observe the construction of an Amazonian regime containing sui generis characteristics, with Brazil, since its origin, being a prominent actor in the process. Among other elements, the oscillation in the internal priorities of the member countries, the pendular movement of extraregional alliances, and difficulties imposed by the ideological plurality anchored in the emergence of nationalisms, in addition to budget restrictions and limitations, amid sociocultural disparities, show destabilizing elements that hinder the evolution of the Amazon regime.

Therefore, because of the evidence collected, as to regime formality and expectations, we are led to infer that the classical typology best reflects the current condition of the Amazonian case. However, it must be recognized that, in the context of the taxonomy, a persistent mark of incompleteness still stands out: that is, when we revisit the model of Levy, Young, and Zürn (1995), we verify that, in the Amazonian case, a high degree of normative formality is associated to an oscillation in the convergence of expectations of the actors that comprise it. Nonetheless, the latter is an externality that has positively given signs of change in the scope of what we have called ACTO's strategic renewal phase.

NOTES

1. Euclides da Cunha, *Um Paraíso Perdido: Reunião de Ensaios Amazônicos.* Brasília: Conselho Editorial do Senado Federal, 2000, 353.

2. Euclides da Cunha, *Obras Completas*. Rio de Janeiro: Nova Aguilar, 1995, 230.

3. With approximately 4,196,943 square kilometers (1,620,439 sq m), the Amazon rainforest is the largest Brazilian biome, occupying 49.29 percent of the national territory according to official data from the Brazilian Institute of Geography and Statistics (source: http://www.ibge.gov.br/home/presidencia/noticias/noticia_visualiza.php?id _noticia=169).

4. Through their specific rules, international regimes constrain behaviors, affect protagonists' decisions on which issues will integrate their political agendas, determine which activities are legitimate or reprehensible, and influence whether, when, and how conflicts that arise are resolved.

5. In 1952, Brazil and the United States celebrated a military agreement aimed at, among other provisions, establishing cooperation for drawing up aeronautical maps of the Brazilian territory. Notwithstanding the presence of a restrictive clause prohibiting any kind of transferring of the material obtained to other countries, individuals, or companies (art.7, §2), the US government provided III with an inventory revealing the location and extent of mineral deposits in Amazonia, a fact confirmed by one of the engineers involved in the project, which suggests a close connection between the Hudson Institute—despite its private nature—and Washington policy makers. All the information collected, as expected, was widely used in elaborating the Great Lakes project (Cabral 1968, 152; Carvalho 2001, 254).

6. The full report, entitled *The Truth about the Hudson Institute*, was reproduced in the *Brazilian Journal of International Policy* (RBPI), issue 41/42, Mar./Jun. 1968, pp.138–47. The names of the three diplomats assigned to the mission were not revealed in the document.

7. Source: *Brazilian Journal of International Policy* (RBPI), 1968; p. 140.

8. Caubet (2006, 172–73) asserts that several suspicions were raised about the possibility of such a document serving as an instrument that would allow Brazil to interfere in the commercial system created in 1969 by the Andean Pact, since all six signatories of the Cartagena Agreement would also be in the Amazon treaty. In addition, there was the fear publicized by Venezuela of sharing its borders with an "atomic giant" (such discomfort stemmed from the new nuclear cooperation agreement signed between Brazil and the Federal Republic of Germany in 1975). Such barriers were only overcome after Venezuela waved positively in participating in the negotiations of the Amazon treaty. This attitude was decisive because when Caracas came on the scene as a counterweight to Brazilian influence, the other Andean countries felt more comfortable and safer participating in the negotiating phase.

9. In December 2002, an agreement between the Brazilian government and ACTO was signed, establishing the headquarters of the organization's permanent secretariat in Brasília. It is worth noting that, to date, ACTO is the only multilateral international organization headquartered in Brazil.

10. In the ACT, a structure was chosen in which the secretariat functions would be performed pro tempore by the party in whose territory the next ordinary meeting of the Amazon Cooperation Council was scheduled to be held (art. XXII), a point commonly referred to as one of the reasons for its institutional fragility (Caubet, 2006, 181; Antiquera, 2006, 4–5; Procópio, 2007, 238).

11. Hylea is the name given by the German naturalist Alexander von Humboldt (1769–1859) to the great humid equatorial forest that extends from the Andes through the Amazon valley to the Guianas.

12. These special commissions were created to address topics such as: the environment (CEMAA); science and technology (CECTA); health (CESAM); Indigenous affairs (CEAIA); transport, infrastructure, and communications (CETICAM); tourism (CETURA), opening space for a new phase of the organization.

13. Despite being officially formalized in the Brazilian proposal, the topic of the ACT institutional strengthening appeared for the first time on the agenda of the Third Meeting of Ministers of Foreign Affairs, held in 1989, in Quito, Ecuador.

14. As the host country, Brazil has committed itself to making possible the transfer of physical facilities to the ACT secretariat.

15. Alexandra Moreira, "Amazon Treaty Cooperation Organization." Accessed November 15, 2022. https://unece.org/sites/default/files/2021-03/4_session_3_ Moreira.pdf.

16. Amazon Cooperation Treaty Organization, "Amazonian countries resume negotiations of the Regulation on Commercial Navigation in the Amazonian Rivers."

17. Euroclima, The Amazon Cooperation Treaty Organization (ACTO), the European Union, and Euroclima+ meet in the first working session to formulate the work plan of the project. "Creation of the Amazon Regional Platform on Indigenous Peoples and Climate Change."

18. Amazon Fund, "Donations."

19. Amazon Cooperation Treaty Organization, "Amazon Regional Observatory."

20. Amazon Cooperation Treaty Organization, "In historical session the Amazonian Parliament is reactivated after 10 years."

21. Although the Nagoya Protocol is important in creating rules for accessing genetic resources and sharing benefits through the ABS System (Access and Benefit Sharing), biopiracy is a recurrent practice. See Abreu (2018) and Cunha, Queiroz, and Martinez (2020).

22. Luiz Vassallo and Fausto Macedo, "Crime organizado é responsável pelo desmatamento da floresta amazônica, afirma Raquel," Estadão September 2, 2019. https: //politica.estadao.com.br/blogs/fausto-macedo/crime-organizado-e-responsavel-pelo -desmatamento-da-floresta-amazonica-afirma-raquel/.

23. These narratives are exemplified by Souza (2019) and Walt (2019).

24. On the presence of extraregional powers in the region—more specifically China, Russia, and Iran—and their externalities, see Andrade (2020), Teixeira Júnior (2019), and Coutinho (2017 and 2018).

REFERENCES

Abreu, Gustavo de Souza. *Amazônia: o enigma da segurança*. Curitiba: Editora Prisma, 2018.

Andrade, Gabriel. "Iran's Advances in Latin America." *Middle East Quarterly* (Fall, 2020):1–10.

Andrioni, F. S. "Quando a história também é futuro: as concepções de tempo passado, de futuro e do Brasil em Herman Kahn e no Hudson Institute (1947–1979)." PhD diss., São Paulo University, 2014.

Antiquera, Daniel de Campos. "Amazônia e a política externa brasileira: análise do Tratado de Cooperação Amazônica (TCA) e sua transformação em organização internacional (1978–2002)," MSc diss., São Paulo State University, University of Campinas, and Pontifical Catholic University of São Paulo, 2006.

Amazon Cooperation Treaty Organization. *Ata da Primeira Reunião de Ministros da Defesa sobre Defesa e Segurança Integral da Amazônia*. Brasília: OTCA, 2006.

Amazon Cooperation Treaty Organization. *Declaração de Belém*. Brasília: OTCA, 1980.

Amazon Cooperation Treaty Organization. *Declaração de Iquitos*. Brasília: OTCA, 2005.

Amazon Cooperation Treaty Organization. *Declaração de Lima*. Brasília: OTCA, 2010.

Amazon Cooperation Treaty Organization. *Declaração de Manaus*. Brasília: OTCA, 2004*b*.

Amazon Cooperation Treaty Organization. "Amazon Regional Observatory." Accessed November 14, 2022. http://otca.org/en/wp-content/uploads/2021/11/livretoORA_en_digital.pdf.

Amazon Cooperation Treaty Organization. *Plano estratégico da Organização do Tratado de Cooperação Amazônica (2004–2012)*. Brasília: OTCA, 2004.

Amazon Cooperation Treaty Organization. "Amazonian countries resume negotiations of the Regulation on Commercial Navigation in the Amazonian Rivers." (January 10, 2021). http://otca.org/en/amazonian-countries-resume-negotiations-of-the-regulation-on-commercial-navigation-in-the-amazonian-rivers/.

Amazon Cooperation Treaty Organization, "In historical session the Amazonian Parliament is reactivated after 10 years." (May 19, 2022). http://otca.org/en/in-historical-session-the-amazonian-parliament-is-reactivated-after-10-years/.

Amazon Fund. "Donations." Accessed November 14, 2022. http://www.amazonfund.gov.br/en/donations/.

Aranibar, Antonio. "La OTCA, algunas claves de su evolución histórica." *Relatório de Consultoria*. Brasília: OTCA, 2003.

Brasil. Operação Amazônia. Project classified as secret by the Brazilian Government, no.18 (1968). The Ministry of Foreign Relations Library, Historic Collection Section, Brasília. File consulted April 8, 2022.

Cabral, Bernardo."O Grande Lago Amazônico e o Hudson Institute." *Revista Brasileira de Política Internacional* 11, no.41 (op.cit. Speech, the Brazilian Chamber of Deputies, Ordinary Session, 12 February, 1968):148–165.

Carvalho, Leonardo Arquimino de. "Internacionalização da Amazônia Legal? Aspectos político-históricos e neo-colonialismo expropriatório." *Cena Internacional* 3, no.2 (2001):247–268.

Caubet, Christian G. "Le Traité de Coopération Amazonienne: regionalisation et développement de l'Amazonie." *Annuaire Français de Droit International* 30 (1984): 803–818.

Caubet, Christian G. *A Água Doce nas Relações Internacionais.* São Paulo: Manole, 2006.

Cervo, Amado Luiz. "A Venezuela e seus vizinhos." *Cena Internacional* 3, no.1 (2001): 5–24.

Costa, Gino F. *Las relaciones económicas y diplomáticas del Brasil con sus vecinos de la Cuenca Amazónica, 1974–1985.* Lima: Centro Peruano de Estudios Internacionales, 1987.

Coutinho, Leonardo. "Turning the tables: how Brazil defeated an ISIS Threat." *Global Dispatch* 5 (2017): 1–13.

Coutinho, Leonardo. *Hugo Chávez, o espectro: como o presidente venezuelano alimentou o narcotráfico, financiou o terrorismo e promoveu a desordem global.* São Paulo: Vestígio, 2018.

Correio da manhã. "Correio revela tôda a verdade sobre a Amazônia." *Correio da Manhã*, July 14, 1968. Brazilian National Library Collection, Digital Newspaper Library. http://memoria.bn.br/DocReader/Hotpage/HotpageBN.aspx?bib=089842 _07&pagfis=93748&url=http://memoria.bn.br/docreader#.

Cunha, Euclides da. *Obras Completas.* Rio de Janeiro: Nova Aguilar, 1995.

Cunha, Euclides da. *Um Paraíso Perdido: Reunião de Ensaios Amazônicos.* Brasília: Conselho Editorial do Senado Federal, 2000.

Cunha, Guilherme Lopes da, Queiroz, Fabio Albergaria de, and Martinez, Monica Montana. "Biodiversidade, Biotecnologia e Poder: a Amazônia em meio a estratégias de desenvolvimento na América do Sul." In *Economia de Mercado e Políticas Ambientais na Amazônia: Sustentabilidade Socioeconômica dos Povos Indígenas*, edited by Sandra Buenafuente, and Marcelo Gantos, 142–160. Boa Vista: EDUFRR, 2020.

Euroclima, The Amazon Cooperation Treaty Organisation (ACTO), the European Union and Euroclima+ meet in the first working session to formulate the work plan of the project. "Creation of the Amazon Regional Platform on Indigenous Peoples and Climate Change." Accessed November 14, 2022. https://www.euroclima.org/en /recent-events/en-news/1705-the-amazon-cooperation-treaty-organisation-acto-the -european-union-and-euroclima-meet-in-the-first-working-session-to-formulate -the-work-plan-of-the-project-creation-of-the-amazon-regional-platform-on -indigenous-peoples-and-climate-change.

Filho, Armando Gallo Yahn. "Conflito e Cooperação na Bacia do Prata em relação aos cursos d'água internacionais (de 1966 a 1992)." MSc diss., São Paulo State University, University of Campinas, and Pontifical Catholic University of São Paulo, 2005.

Geisel, Ernesto. "Discurso do presidente Ernesto Geisel por ocasião da solenidade de assinatura do Tratado de Cooperação Multilateral na Amazônia." In *Resenha de Política Exterior do Brasil* 18. Brasília: Ministério das Relações Exteriores, 1978.

Krasner, Stephen D. *"Structural Causes and regime consequences: regimes as intervening variables," International Organization* 36, no.2 (Spring 1982): 185–205, https://doi.org/10.1017/S0020818300018920.

Levy, Marc A., Oran R. Young, and Michael Zürn. "The Study of International Regimes." *European Journal of International Relations* 1, no.3 (September 1995): 267–330.

Medina, Maria Elena. "Alguns aspectos políticos no processo de integração." In *El universo amazónico y la integración latinoamericana*, edited by Bolivarian Republic of Venezuela, pp-pp. Caracas: Universidad Simón Bolívar, 1983.

Moreira, Alexandra. "Amazon Treaty Cooperation Organization." Accessed November 15, 2022. https://unece.org/sites/default/files/2021-03/4_session_3_Moreira.pdf.

Panero, Robert. *Un sistema de 'grandes lagos' para Sur America*. Croton-on-Hudson: Hudson Institute, 1967.

Panero, Robert. "Um Sistema Sul-Americano de Grandes Lagos," *Revista Brasileira de Política Internacional* 11, no. 41 (March / June 1968): 33–50.

Panero, Robert, and Herman Kahn. "Novo enfoque sobre a Amazônia." *Revista Brasileira de Política Internacional* 11, no.41(March / June 1968) 1968): 51–64.

Procópio, Argemiro. *Destino Amazônico*. São Paulo: Hucitec, 2005a.

Procópio, Argemiro. "O multilateralismo amazônico e as fronteiras da segurança." In *Os excluídos da Arca de Noé,* Edited by Argemiro Procópio, 67–162. São Paulo: Hucitec, 2005b.

Procópio, Argemiro. *Subdesenvolvimento Sustentável*. Curitiba: Juruá, 2007.

Queiroz, Fábio Albergaria de. *Hidropolítica e Segurança: As Bacias Platina e Amazônica em perspectiva comparada*. Brasília: Fundação Alexandre de Gusmão, 2012.

Queiroz, Fábio Albergaria de; and Thomas. E. Lovejoy. "The Amazon as a low-cost arena in the Cold War's game of power? The case of the Amazonian Great Lakes Project (1964–1968)," *Revista de Estudos e Pesquisas Avançadas do Terceiro Setor* 5 (2018): 682–710, http://dx.doi.org/10.31501/repats.v5i1.10019.

RBPI - Revista Brasileira de Política Internacional [Brazilian Journal of International Politics]. (1968). Ano XI, n.° 41/42, Mar./Jun., 219 p.

Ricupero, Rubens. "O Tratado de Cooperação Amazônica." *Revista de Informação Legislativa* 21, no. 81 (jan./mar. 1984):177–196.

Román, Mikael. *The implementation of international regimes: the case of the Amazon Cooperation Treaty*. Uppsala: Uppsala University, 1998.

Silva, Américo Luís Martins. *Direito do Meio Ambiente e dos Recursos Hídricos*, vol. 2. Sao Paulo: Editora Revista dos Tribunais, 2005.

Silveira, Antonio Azeredo da. Discurso no Palácio Itamaraty por Ocasião do Encerramento da II Reunião Preparatória sobre Cooperação Multilateral na Amazônia, em 31 de março de 1978. In: *Resenha de Política Exterior do Brasil* 16 (jan/fev/mar 1978).

Souza, Renato. "Macron convoca o G7 para discutir Amazônia: 'Nossa casa queima,," Correio Brasiliense, Acessed August 22, 2019, https://www.correiobraziliense .com.br/app/noticia/brasil/2019/08/22/interna-brasil,778616/presidente-da-franca -chama-g7-para-discutir-queimada-na-amazonia.shtml.

Teixeira Junior, Augusto W. M. "Geopolítica e Postura Estratégica da Rússia na Crise da Venezuela." *Análise Estratégica* 14, no.4 (2019): 21–41.

The Brazilian Institute of Geography and Statistics. "News." Accessed April 22, 2022. http://www.ibge.gov.br/home/presidencia/noticias/noticia_visualiza.php?id _noticia=169.

Théry, Hervé. "Situações da Amazônia no Brasil e no continente." *Estudos Avançados* 19, no. 53 (2005):37–49.

Walt, Stephen M. "Who will save the Amazon (and how)?," *Foreign Policy*, August 5, 2019. https://foreignpolicy.com/2019/08/05/who-will-invade-brazil-to-save-the -amazon/.

Vassallo, Luiz, and Fausto Macedo. "Crime organizado é responsável pelo desmatamento da floresta amazônica, afirma Raquel," Estadão September 2, 2019. https: //politica.estadao.com.br/blogs/fausto-macedo/crime-organizado-e-responsavel -pelo-desmatamento-da-floresta-amazonica-afirma-raquel/.

Chapter 5

The Amazon

Global Change, Environmental, Economic, and Geopolitical Interests of Brazil

Everton Vieira Vargas

We are living in times for which we have no consensus to define: some speak about structural changes., others about global threats of multiple natures, and others yet sustain that we are amid deep crises at domestic and global levels. These crises could give way to different sorts of phenomena: political, economic, and social transformations expressed in military confrontations, poverty, hunger, environmental degradation, juxtaposition of cultures and of social organizations, or advancements in science and technology, innovation, better use of natural resources, more economic efficiency and productivity; all of them with deep impacts on populations, economy, and nature itself.

Changes have been part of the journey of mankind on earth and have shaped history according to the circumstances experienced by societies. The great navigations brought about and consolidated a novel perception about the dimensions of the earth, imposing a new concept for distance and time, as noted by Hannah Arendt.[1] The arrival of Columbus and other explorers to the coast of what became known as America added a whole new world to those parts of the earth known since time immemorial. As J. M. Roberts writes, "There was a striking change in world history after 1500 and it was quite without precedent. Never had one culture spread over the whole globe." Spanish and Portuguese conquests were not only the result of a search for new territorial domains, but also for natural resources: minerals, plants, animals were at the core of expeditions during the modern age. Spain and Portugal acquired large geographical areas, which were added to the trade with India, as they provided crops and animal species, beginning "the greatest reshaping of ecology ever to take place."[2]

America and the land of the Amazons were European inventions. They were the result of the dogged perseverance of Spain and Portugal to strengthen their power at a moment of profound change in Europe. The expansion of their territorial control was rooted in a double objective: to substitute the commercial route to Asia lost to the Turks in the fifteenth century; and, in alliance with the pope, ensure the territorial gains and propagate the Catholicism. From the point of view of the construction of a national identity, it was a representation of the heroic and messianic ideal of the Crusades and of the wars that led to the expulsion of the Arabs from the Iberian Peninsula.

From the economic perspective, the endeavor of the conquest aimed at supplying scarce essential natural resources in Europe.

Resource exploitation and contact with Indigenous peoples provoked a radical change in economics, in the notion of how diverse mankind is. The bloody fights involving sailors and soldiers from the European powers against the original occupants of the new world challenged prevailing political and social conventions. It was perhaps the biggest and the most unequal clash of cultures in history. Big losses in lives by the power of firearms, poisonous spears and arrows, and the contagion of diseases changed the fortunes of both conquered and conquerors.

Since the first explorers arrived at the coast of what is now known as the Amazon, Portugal and Spain realized the strategic importance of securing access to its territory and its potential wealth. Officials in the courts of Madrid and Lisbon reported on Vicente Yáñez Pinzón's voyage, in 1500, and the discovery of what he named as "Mar Dulce," certainly did not discard that the mouth of the great river should be the gate to new territories.

Pinzón's trip, and Diego de Lepe's in the same year, marked the beginning of the struggle of Indigenous peoples for survival: Pinzón took thirty-six Indians with him to Spain; De Lepe faced an attack by the same people, months later, and retaliated with firearms, killing and imprisoning several in what was the first mortal confrontation between Europeans and Indians in the land. Violence and exploitation were the first salvos in Amazonian history.

These events associated to legends and fantasies, which inspired dreams and imagination among Europeans about an "El Dorado," had a lasting impression in the memory of the colonial settlers and especially among the native peoples. At home, the feats of both sailors were rewarded by the Spanish Crown with titles that gave them the right to explore the resources believed to exist in the new lands.[3]

The first inroads by foreigners forced Lisbon and Madrid to reinforce their presence in the region, building a series of military installations, fortresses, and ports to defend their domains. For decision-makers in both capitals, a consistent policy of defense and occupation should be at the heart of their action to prevent any scramble of the territories. Time proved them right. The dimensions and the risks of the undertaking, however, would introduce variables that were far beyond their calculations. Knowledge, methods, language and social barriers, greed and national interests clashed even during the Iberian union, when Portugal and Spain were under the same Crown.

Portugal was determined to ensure adequate command and control of operations, in such an inhospitable environment, to roll back incursions by foreigners (French, Britons, Irish, and Dutch). That meant ignoring the 1494 Treaty of Tordesillas, which divided the lands situated at one hundred leagues west of the coast of Cape Verde between Portugal and Spain.[4]

This chapter aims at reflecting on how the saga of the occupation of the Amazon projects itself in contemporary concerns about the region and the role it plays in the development of Brazil and South America, as well as the possible environmental effects of carelessness in the maintenance of its forests, rivers, and biodiversity on peoples and the on global climate. The struggle to occupy and defend the region is, from the very beginning, at the heart of the geopolitical concerns of Brazil. A key point in the analysis is how the geographical integrity of the Amazon has been at risk in view of policies adopted by different national governments. Such policies intended to secure the sovereignty over the vast area, but put at risk the design of defense, economic, and developmental and environmental policies for the region. Most of all, why were the negative consequences of those failed strategies that victimized the original inhabitants of the Amazon not considered upfront?

Climate change, sea level rise, deforestation, change in rainfall, land degradation, reduction in essential crops, increase in the propagation of viruses and diseases, pressure on institutions to protect human health and predatory agriculture and livestock farming are some of the threats associated to human behavior or the lack of political will to restrain it.

Changes in power and military capabilities, reduction in economic perspectives, or the capacity of nations to manage their internal challenges and respond efficiently to a growing need for international cooperation are an important part of the negative effects of those phenomena. They are powerful enough to put the world at risk, increasing the sense of vulnerability within societies. But, unfortunately, the urgent and necessary measures to counter those negative effects are either not taken or insufficient.

Since the United Nations Conference on Environment and Development, held in Rio de Janeiro in 1992, global efforts are underway to promote international cooperation to preserve the environment involving governments at all levels, civil society, local communities, Indigenous peoples, business, academia, and other stakeholders. Notwithstanding their legal and political commitments at national, regional, and global levels, their actions are much behind agreed goals and targets. Environmental change is being progressively dealt with as a matter of national security by today's great powers. Their discourse presents the prospect of climate change and, to that effect, the devastation of the Amazon rainforest as a close existential danger. But the quality and intensity of their actions are not in line with the pressing threats, as well as with measures to mobilize the best available knowledge and financial and technological cooperation to redress the emergencies in the region and in adjacent areas.

This should be a central concern among the countries that share sovereignty over the Amazon region. Strategies that recognize distinctive biomes, economic situations, and prospects for development need to be adopted to enhance national capabilities.

1. THE UNIQUENESS OF THE AMAZON

Location, population, national power, neighbors, sea routes, national integration, and natural resources are among the key elements to determine a country's position in the world. Nicholas Spykman wrote, "The policy of a state does not derive from its geography, but it cannot escape that geography."[5] Geography informs strategic and political decisions at home and in relation to a country's immediate circumstances. As a source of state policies, geography encapsulates constraints and opportunities. The role of a country or region is influenced by its regional or global location. External influences and pressures originated either in its vicinity or much further away, like wars, economics, and political decisions, are sometimes determinant of the course followed by a government. Geography also plays a role in relation to the well-being of a population, in particular the access to health and education, preservation of culture and identity, and to the development of science and technology, and communications. Science, better communications, and free access to education and knowledge have produced major changes. The findings of science on the importance of environmental protection and the climate crisis witnessed in different parts of the world are impacting geography. Besides its effects on weather patterns, climate change plays a key role in eroding the resilience of natural resources, and in the very survival of low-lying coastal areas.

Geography plays an important role in the design and definition of Brazilian domestic policies as well as in shaping its relations in South America. With a territory that comprises most of the subcontinent and covers different cultural identities, climates, biomes, landscapes, and types of agricultural lands, Brazil is a country where policies require consideration of multiple aspects of its natural, political, and socioeconomic features.

The Amazon shapes South America prominently and has a unique profile in the Brazilian map. It is a huge space that projects itself over three of the five geographical regions of the country—north, southeast, and center-west—comprising an area of 5.019 million square kilometers, 58.9 percent of the Brazilian territory.[6] It is home to more than twenty-nine million people, among them 180 Indigenous groups, as well as several isolated groups (known, but not yet contacted). It is a very diverse territory, part of a bigger land mass, known as Pan-Amazon, which spreads over eight other South American countries: Venezuela, Guyana, French Guiana, Suriname, Colombia, Ecuador, Peru, and Bolivia.[7] Such diversity is reflected in the uniqueness of the region compared to other areas in the world.

The Amazon is in the humid tropics, a swath that comprises 10 percent of the earth's area (equivalent to 1,500 million ha). The rich vegetable cover associated with its characteristics is intensified by the rainforest and tropical savannahs. The rainforest is the largest area and attracts more attention due to its huge biological diversity. Among the world's three largest rainforests—the African, the Indo-Malaysian, and the South American—the latter is the largest, covering the Orinoco and the Amazonas basins, making up one-third of the entire humid tropics. High levels of insolation and abundance of humidity generate high productivity of vegetable biomass in these tropics.[8] Its main features are the dense tropical forest, the world's biggest river basin, and the huge cornucopia of plants, animals, insects, viruses, minerals, among other natural products.

The equatorial climate and the dense rainforest have also played a crucial role in other regions of Brazil and in Amazonian countries. The rainfall regime has been vital for the living conditions and production of commodities in the center-west and southeast of Brazil. Such a regime is the result of a complex interaction between the forest, the rivers, and the levels of humidity. This has been closely observed by scientists, authorities, and local communities because of the negative effects that "the intensive use of natural resources, both renewable and non-renewable may generate in precipitation rates maintained by moistures flows from evaporation in the tropical Atlantic Ocean and by forest evapotranspiration recycling."[9]

The geographical and historical circumstances of the Amazon are in the predominance of forest and water.[10] The territory attracted the attention of explorers, even before the arrival of the Portuguese at the Brazilian coast in 1500. Fantastic dimensions associated to the mythology about the Atlantic would inspire its first narrators. Their discourse about physical and cultural characteristics of the land helped reinforce certain myths and tales with great impact in Europe. Those fantasies would be explained by the first visitors by means of a simple and direct analogy to what was then known. As the first settlers established themselves, they had to face the challenges of understanding and representing the reality of this new world. As Anthony Pagden points out, "The European observer (. . .) was not equipped with an adequate descriptive vocabulary for his task and was beset by an uncertainty about how to use his conceptual tools in an unfamiliar terrain.:[11]

2. COLONIAL EXPERIENCE

The British, French, Dutch, and Spaniards visited the region on behalf of their sovereigns and tried to establish contact with the Indians. These travelers produced very detailed geographical information to facilitate navigation. They created several hamlets, particularly in the eastern Amazon, worrying the Portuguese who established themselves there in the sixteenth century. In expelling the foreigners, the Portuguese greatly benefitted from the knowledge and experience of La Ravardière, who had been the commander of the French forces that had occupied Maranhão between 1612 and 1615. The strategy of the governor general of Brazil, Gaspar de Sousa, to combat the foreigners ignored the 1494 Treaty of Tordesillas, according to which Portugal only had jurisdiction over a small fraction of the Amazon. He instructed his troops to occupy the Amazon River that was under the jurisdiction of Spain. This was the moment of the Iberian Union (1580–1640), when the king of Spain was also the king of Portugal, a critical juncture for Portugal and Spain. In 1637, Pedro Teixeira sailed through the Amazonas River to make a detailed reconnaissance of the rivers that would lead to Quito. The trip occurred without major mishaps. He was well received by the Spanish authorities and by the missionaries, staying there for a year. On his return, Teixeira carried out the secret instruction he had received when he departed for his mission: he took a handful of soil and cast it into the air and took possession of the whole area, rivers, and trade on behalf of King Felipe IV to the Portuguese Crown. This act was the very beginning of Portuguese colonial rule of the huge Amazonian area, as well as the devastation of its mythic and pluricultural universe.[12]

"The Amazon is a subcontinent, where, since the sixteenth century, an unrelenting march towards the nation-state has taken place, derived from the same European phenomenon," points out Márcio Souza (2019), author of the *Historia da Amazônia: do período pré-colombiano aos desafios do século XXI*. Such change, argues the author, has led to the formation of societies that championed the monopoly of the use of legitimate political force in that huge, new, and virtually empty space. To control the territory—or part of it—the Europeans had to overcome several obstacles: from the physical realities of the region to the interaction with local people who had lived there for ages.

Antagonism is the word that summarizes this challenging endeavor. Overcoming obstacles significantly influenced the occupation of the Amazon. This undertaking was marked by ethnic friction between the Indigenous peoples and Europeans. Darcy Ribeiro refers to this process as "ethnic transfiguration," by which the natives tried "to preserve themselves as ethnic entities through successive changes in their biological substrate, in their culture and in their forms of relation with the involving society." This change, according to Ribeiro, goes beyond the cultural dimension. The aborigines were forced to adopt or rearrange economic ways to be incorporated in the economic system generated by the European occupation.[13]

The use of force and the ruthless exercise of power enabled domination of the area and submission of the original inhabitants. Portuguese colonial rule in Brazil was, in economic terms, mainly one of exploitation rather than colonization. Lisbon's priorities concentrated on the coastal areas or on the banks of waterways and large rivers that provided a strategic advantage for both communications and defense. Therefore, the Portuguese knew hardly anything about the backlands of the colony.[14]

In the mid-seventeenth century, the Brazilian Amazon became a colonial state—known as Grão-Pará (Greater Pará)[15]—directly linked to the Portuguese Crown. Grão-Pará was an autonomous political entity with no political relation with the State of Brazil until the independence of the latter in 1822. The colonization of both states was different because of the policies implemented by Portugal. The colonial society in Brazil prevailed over the Indigenous populations with the use of violence and the institutionalization of slavery. In the Amazon, the colonial society was mainly indigenous, even if most of that population had suffered a process of detribalization. The indigenous presence was hegemonic for a long time compared to the other ethnic groups in the region, notwithstanding the westernization of the local society.[16]

The political separation from Lisbon (1822) took place before the consolidation of national unity (1840–1850). In Brazil, like in other Latin American countries, the state preceded the national identity. The struggle for political independence was not a result of nationalist or revolutionary movements, but rather the consequence of an accord among the ruling class of landowners.

The region started to be a part of Brazil in August 1823, when the news of independence arrived in Belém, with the so-called submission of Pará, a deal reached with Belém's political class forced to submit to the Brazilian empire under the threat of bombardment and blockage. This negotiation was consistent with the political arrangement that led to independence: it was made without the people having a say.[17] It was much more an engagement between the "national elite," the Portuguese Crown, and England.[18]

The two centuries of the two-state coexistence led to a pair of societies that were very different from one another in the first half of the nineteenth century. For the empire, securing sovereignty over the Amazon was the antidote against the precedent set by the Dutch occupation of the northeast of the country between 1630 and 1654. Uniting the territory was also a way to prevent the division that marked the end of Spanish colonization in the rest of Latin America. Incorporating Grão-Pará was, however, a challenging political task. The ineptitude of the province's presidents[19] sent by the empire, and the negligence of the people's demands by Rio de Janeiro led to revolts that strengthened social and political conflicts, increasing political instability. Moreover, the Brazil's independence coincided with a severe economic crisis in Grão-Pará and Rio Negro (which corresponds to the western Amazon today). Integrating the Amazon was a brutal process that led to more impoverishment and reduction of population, ending only in 1840 with the Cabanagem, a civil war that encompassed Grão-Pará and Rio Negro. It took more than thirty thousand lives and coincided with the political turbulence that followed the abdication of Emperor Peter I in 1831. The bloody conflicts in the Amazon led to the breakdown of the colonial project. This, however, did not mean better times for the region: the rebellions were usually provoked by powerful local groups that prevailed over the masses to secure their private interests. According to Márcio Souza, the dominance of the privileged "inaugurated an awkward tradition in the Amazon, by which the people are always left in a limbo of the major decisions, paralyzed by stopgap measures The political frailty of the region led the people to support a neocolonial relationship imposed by the central power.[20]

3. FOREIGN INTERESTS AND THE AMAZON

The frequent presence of foreigners in the Amazon during colonial times (even though the region was closed to the outside world during the colonial period), the social conflicts and its difficult integration after independence, certainly had a decisive weight on how the Amazon came to be seen by the Brazilian empire and subsequent governments. Those were not the only factors to condition the views of the government in Rio de Janeiro. Others were equally important, like its geographic scale, its demographic emptiness, the obstacles to affirm and defend Brazil's sovereignty, the plain territory beginning in the Andes (where the Amazon River headwaters lie) and extending itself to the Gulf of Marajó, at the mouth of the great river, the enormous basin that favored the penetration by the Portuguese (and forces of rival powers) well beyond the line of Tordesillas and, by the same token, resulted in bloody conflicts with the Indigenous peoples.

The foreign policy of the empire was deeply influenced by England. London was a forceful supporter of independence. Its economic, financial, and political advantages, earned with the signature of unequal treaties with Rio de Janeiro, would be considered iniquitous in Brazil, during the entire nineteenth century and beyond. The British benefitted from favorable taxes for the entry of their products in Brazil, and the dependence of the empire on their financial support was used to interfere in the domestic politics of the country. From the first trade agreements between both countries, Britain exerted heavy pressure on Rio de Janeiro to abolish the slave trade. Traffic was the only economic activity that remained under the control of Portuguese merchants. The failure of the empire to stop the slave trade increased repression from England against slave ships. The tension reached its apex in 1845, with the adoption of the Aberdeen Bill by the British Parliament authorizing open repression by the Royal Navy against those ships and a clear intervention within Brazilian territorial waters.

All this pressure led to the adoption, by the Brazilian Parliament, of the Eusébio de Queiroz Law, in 1850, that abolished the traffic of slaves to Brazil. But the negative effects of the Aberdeen Bill, on relations with Britain, remained until it was revoked in 1869.[21] The immediate consequence was the lack of workers in Brazilian farms and the decision of slave owners in the north and northeast of Brazil to "sell" their slaves to the coffee growers in the south and southeast of the country.[22] At the same time, European immigrants started to come to Brazil to work in the farms, particularly in the south and southeast. Their arrival and the laws that started to restrict or prohibit slavery in some cases changed the economy and the social fabric.

British influence reflected a Weltanschauung whose center was in Europe as part of a bigger economic and strategic system including the Americas and the Indian Ocean.[23] In Latin America, notwithstanding the Monroe Doctrine, announced by the US government in 1824, the British were a constant presence. The Monroe Doctrine was viewed by the United States as a justification for the annexation of territories without limits, keeping European powers at bay. As Lars Schoultz writes, "Much of Britain's ubiquity was interpreted as the result of Latin American's incompetence." People in the recently emancipated countries of the Western Hemisphere were seen as unwilling or unable to defend themselves and there was also "a belief that a deep gulf separated the Anglo and Hispanic American character."[24]

The Amazon was at the center of a controversy with the United States in the nineteenth century due to the closing of the Amazonas River to international shipping. Pressure from Britain, France, and mainly the United States, forced the Brazilian government to reconsider the issue. The discussion in the State Council was framed from the perspective of a commercial opening of the river as written in the legal opinion, prepared by the rapporteur José Antonio Pimenta Bueno (Marquis of São Vicente), in response to a message from the emperor. In 1867, this communication was submitted to the

State Council and endorsed by the rapporteurs Paulino José Soares de Sousa (viscount of Uruguay) and Franciso Jê Acaciaba de Montezuma (viscount of Jequitinhonha).[25]

The extension of US borders, because of the war against Mexico (1846–1848), worried Brazilian authorities. US expansionism after 1850 led to a crisis in the slave economy and the Amazon could be a possible solution for this. After the Civil War in the United States, a plan was considered to create a colony of former slaves in America and settlers to produce rubber and cotton in the Amazon.[26] In the nineteenth century, a rapid change occurred in the region with increasing scientific and imperial interests in terms of knowledge and resource espionage. Susanna Hecht notes,

> Nineteenth century Amazonia resided at the intersection of ambitious dreams of empires and new republics; it was embedded in old mercantile commodity circuits as well as an emergent globalized capitalism that relied on tropical raw materials for machinery, medicine, and industrial outputs for new markets of mass consumption.[27]

The document endorsed by Soares de Sousa and Montezuma highlighted the risks that could be faced by the Imperial Government in contrasting the interests of Brazil vis-à-vis those of the riverain countries and of the international powers. The rapporteur did not believe Brazil was prepared to defend its national interests if the Amazonas was opened to international shipping. Furthermore, he believed that ensuring some rights of navigation in rivers in Peru and Ecuador was more relevant to national interests. American practices, like border policies, oriented toward demographic settlements, provocation, conflict, and annexation, were seen as a threat to the integrity of the region within the empire. Pimenta Bueno recommended that the opening of the Amazonas River should occur, but it should not be put into force immediately. The possibility of navigation by neighboring countries should be established via bilateral agreements and would not be extended to the tributaries nor to military ships. Ships from other countries would also be allowed according to bilateral agreements.

According to Márcio Souza, the empire saw the Amazon strictly in geopolitical terms. The economy was neglected: no investments were made in the region and the trade of commodities was controlled in order to protect the interests of more influential provinces, like Bahia, Pernambuco, and Rio de Janeiro.[28]

The geographical complexity of the region and the freedom of navigation and international trade were kept at bay until the second half of the nineteenth century. The massive use of rubber made from the latex of *Hevea brasiliensis* confirmed that the flora was the biggest source of wealth of the Amazon. This gave rise to a radical change about the perspectives of the region, which were based on plants, not minerals.[29] The Amazon became an important geopolitical spot, as the latex industry was the main driver of regional exports.

When the Amazonas was open for commercial navigation a whole set of issues related to boundaries, sovereignties, and information came to the fore. Despite the trips by explorers and scientists, the ambiguity of the treaties, knowledge about the extension and limits of the land, as well as about its resources, was precarious. The scientific discourse was part of an offensive to extend limits of European possessions in the north of South America to justify future territorial gains up to the margins of the Amazonas River. "Science confused and imperialism acted," according to Luís Cláudio Santos, biographer of Rio Branco.[30]

This was a particularly sensitive issue for the Imperial Government, which would remain at the center of concerns even after the coup that led to the installation of the Republic in 1889. As Susanna Hecht says,

> Brazil's boundaries involved over twelve thousand kilometers from Rio de la Plata north to the Amazon basin in some of the remotest and least documented parts of the planet, where the DNA could involve extinct empires, ecclesiastical lands, the assertions of ex-colonies, distant republics, new utopias, financial speculations, and modern imperia.[31]

At the twilight of the nineteenth century, industrial use of latex and the discovery of gold in British Guyana turned the Amazon into a convulsive land, over which local authorities had no control. Borders were fluid and very loosely defined. In the beginning of the twentieth century, the definition of the borders of Brazil gained special emphasis with the tenure of the Baron of Rio Branco[32] as foreign minister (1902–1912). His previous experience as the head of Brazilian delegation in negotiations about Palmas, Amapá, and Acre induced him to put the solution of the impending border issues with neighboring countries at the top of his agenda. "The Baron," as he is referred to by Brazilian diplomats to date, was a pragmatist: he mixed his encyclopaedical knowledge of history, geography, and international law with the political concepts and practices prevailing at the time of the dispute. For him, physical occupation of a territory meant sovereignty.[33] He was adept at bilateral negotiations considering a practical sense of reality, as observed by Rubens Ricupero. The decision by the king of Italy in the arbitration in the case of the border with British Guyana, convinced him that this method should be an exception, agreed only when no other alternative could be adopted with the other side. Rio Branco put into question the validity of the treaties of limits reached during colonial times, in view of the lacunae that existed about the extent of the territories in dispute and the exact location of the border demarcation.[34]

4. VULNERABILITIES AND CONCERNS

The diplomatic triumphs of Rio Branco did not assuage concerns about foreign interests in the Amazon. Despite the dynamics of the latex economy in the last quarter of the nineteenth century and beginning of the twentieth century, competition brought about by the smuggling of seeds of *Hevea brasiliensis*, in the 1870s, by a British citizen, and the development of huge and more efficient plantations in Southeast Asia, provoked economic and social havoc in the whole region, particularly in Brazil and Peru.[35] Such an act of biopiracy (it is estimated that seventy thousand trees were illegally subtracted from Brazil) accentuated the frailties of the extractive economy in the Amazon and the vulnerabilities associated with the weak presence of the Brazilian state.

The intensity of rubber production until the industry breakdown, in the beginning of the twentieth century, led to its integration into modern commodity circuits.[36] The latex economy was based on abundance of manpower and very low salaries. Its high productivity increased the global demand for rubber, without improving earnings or the quality of life of the rubber tappers. It also gave rise to an enormous social problem that affected several thousand migrants who left northeast Brazil, at that time suffering the terrible effects of the longest drought ever recorded (1877–1879), to work under miserable conditions in the Amazon, when the region had worldwide monopoly of latex.

The profits in the rubber sector derived mainly from unequal "exchange and commerce, localized trade monopolies produced by private steam vessels, 'captive' rivers, and manipulation of markets, information, speculation on the latexes."[37] The vulcanization of rubber, invented by Charles Goodyear in 1839, gave traction to technological developments that resulted in the transportation revolution, railroads, and electricity, among other radical changes in life and production.

The opening to international trade and the development of cities, particularly Manaus and Belém, attracted people from different parts of the world, like Jews, Syrians, Lebanese, Americans, Italians, Japanese, and Portuguese. All of them left important contributions to the economic, social, and cultural life in the Brazilian Amazon.

The decision to open the Amazonas River to international shipping boosted the rubber trade. Commercial ties between industrial powers and the Amazon blossomed. However, such links matured without full participation of the Brazilian state. Local business stakeholders developed more trading and investment links with New York and Liverpool than with Rio de Janeiro or São Paulo.[38] This created an illusion, emulated by the political and cultural ingredients of Europe, that led to a breach with colonial habits and an atmosphere of isolationism as well. This was concretely reflected in the architecture of the *sobrados*, theaters, and other buildings in Belém and Manaus. Márcio Souza writes that the rich estate owners of the extractive industry seemed to wish to give away a national definition by aspiring to a status of world citizens.[39]

The collapse of the latex economy also mirrored the challenges of governing the Amazon without robust institutions and the perpetuation of the wide gulf between those living in opulence and those mired in misery. Underlining this deep divide was the distance between the rubber tappers and landowners. The poor were important agents in the development of the extractive industry, but they were unable to be a transformational factor of their own lot.

Such situations fitted into Amartya Sen's notion that poverty is more than low income. It includes "deprivation of basic capabilities," highlighting the lack of freedom of choice as a result of labor bondage with indebtedness.[40] Part of this was due to the weak relationship of the region with Rio de Janeiro and the rich states in the south. Looking from an investment perspective, Fragoso and Teixeira da Silva note that in few economic ventures was the action of the big capital as visible as in the rubber exploitation. This also led to direct investments by Britain in infrastructure, like ports and energy. France was the source of credits and became the largest creditor of the Amazonas state in the beginning of the twentieth century. US firms had strong interest to displace old European powers from the hegemonic situation they enjoyed in the Amazon.[41]

At the same time, Brazil was in political and economic turmoil. Such conflicts were part of the slow process of construction of the nation-state. This delay in the process was due to the absence of the Brazilian state and the deep social, economic, and political asymmetries among the administrative units that became autonomous with the proclamation of the republic. The war against Paraguay, between 1864 and 1870, was very costly and destroyed imperial finances; the presidents of the provinces,[42] as the governors were called, lacked cohesion. The central government faced considerable social demands because of the abolition of slavery in 1888. Changes in the world economy with the advent of industry and increase in capital availability gave incentive to investments in infrastructure and public services in countries like Brazil. Such changes, however, were not strong enough to crumble structural permanencies, like the dominant role of agriculture in the economy, the concentration of land property, and their political effects.

This situation was not even altered by the beginning of industrialization in Brazil. The lack of liquidity and credit stimulated using foreign loans as a privileged mechanism to finance public expenditure. The decline in international prices of coffee, Brazil's main export in 1890, and the 1894 recession in Europe deeply affected the US economy, Brazil's main importing market. The friction between the interests of a nascent bourgeoisie with those of an entrenched agrarian sector within a weak civil society worked together[43] in the sense that "[i]f we want things to stay as they are, things will have to change," like in Lampedusa's novel *The Leopard*.

Amin points out that the Amazon is an important vital area in the quest for strategic natural resources that are crucial for the continuous expansion of the economy in the most powerful countries, both in military and civilian terms. The rubber boom coincided with the acceleration of industrial production in Europe and the United States. The latex economy put the Amazon among the critical regions for the intensive production of strategic raw materials needed for the global transformation spurred by industrialization. Such materials produced strong impacts on the economy and in the geopolitical importance of the regions and countries where those resources were located. The negative consequences caused by the start of production in Southeast Asia were partially mitigated during World War II due to the conquest of that region by Japan preventing the Allies from using the rubber produced there.[44]

The entry of the United States into World War II led to significant changes in the management of its economy. Strategic resources, among them rubber, were essential for the war effort. The Amazon was again viewed as the region that could restore rubber supply. In 1940 and 1941, the United States pressed Brazil to interrupt the provision of strategic resources to Germany and give Americans exclusive rights to purchase strategic material, including rubber. The pendular diplomacy of the Getúlio Vargas government, between Germany and the United States, was frowned upon by the Roosevelt administration. The Vargas administration wanted to modernize military equipment and designed a plan to promote "the development of a Brazilian industrial sector, at the heart of which was a major steel plant."[45] The interest of the German company Krupp in the business alarmed Washington. At the same time, the United States Steel Corporation avoided participating in the bid for the construction of the steel mill.

The US engagement in military operations, after Pearl Harbor, led Washington to control all aspects of the American economy to enhance national security. This government intervention not only subordinated the interests of business and trade unions, but also mobilized government programs and agencies to promote the increase of rubber production in the Amazon.[46] The 1942 Washington Accords between Brazil and the United States provided assurances that "the price of Brazilian rubber would be increased, and production would also expand in the Amazon region."[47] The agreement on rubber meant maintaining the bilateral trade relation based on raw materials. The interest on the Brazilian rubber was underlined by Roosevelt during his meeting with Vargas in January 1943, on the return of the former from the Casablanca conference.

Those accords, however, may be seen as a first step in building the strategic role of the Amazon in contemporary Brazilian foreign policy. In spite of the shift by Rio Branco in favor of a rapprochement with the United States, in the beginning of the twentieth century, the memory of how the Americans acted in defense of their national interests in previous dealings with Brazil had not gone away. A central aspect was the awareness, like in the decision to open the Amazonas River to commercial shipping, of the limits of Brazilian national power. Brazilian leaders looked askance at maneuvers by Washington that could influence the decision-making of states about the use of their territory.

The increasing importance of raw materials, many of them essential for a significant number of processes and products, like forest, water, minerals, and biodiversity, led to a new understanding about the role of the Amazon in the regional and global orders. The Amazon also became a reference in the strategic planning of rich countries.[48]

5. THE AMAZON AND CONTEMPORARY ISSUES

Contemporary concerns about the Amazon still have as reference the intentions of imperial powers between the first news about the land and their concrete interests, whether in terms of land occupation, or appropriation of its resources.

The geopolitical doctrine on the Amazon was mainly a formulation by the Brazilian military. Army officer Mário Travassos, published a book in 1935, *Projeção Continental do Brasil*, that would become the synthesis and key reference of classical geopolitical thought in Brazil. For the first time, a strategy was planned regarding the relations of Brazil with its South American neighbors in the following decades.

Travassos argued that geography is crucial in the organization of the dynamics of geopolitics, as means or barriers to access different zones. He identified these zones as antagonists among themselves in South America: Pacific, Atlantic, the Amazon region, and the Rio de la Plata. The rivers serve as borders and as a line of communication that facilitate exchange and give identity to a region.[49] According to him, the Amazon has a natural centripetal force strengthened by the rivers shared with neighboring countries and provide access to the Pacific via passes or junctions in the Andes. Those rivers provide an extraordinary geographical advantage for Brazil. The Amazon basin is central not only for South America, but it may also be used by foreign powers in search of oil and rubber. Travassos's perspective is contradicted by other geopolitical analysts who considered the Amazon a peripheral space. For him, the Amazon was a key asset in the interest of neutralizing Argentina, considered as the key competitor of Brazil for influence in the continent.[50]

One of Travassos's main concerns was the increasing American presence in Panamá, with the administration of the canal zone, and in the Caribbean. The Panamá Canal would provide rapid and easy access to both coasts of the United States and would facilitate access to the Madalena and Orinoco basins (and to the huge oil wealth of the latter) and, therefore, to the Amazon basin through the natural canals that connect it to the Orinoco. For Travassos, the Amazon basin is not only central for South America, but also for the access of foreign powers searching for natural resources. In his view, Brazilian foreign policy should work closely with its neighbors to guarantee its geopolitical advantages in the Amazon vis-à-vis Argentina and the United States.[51]

Travassos's concerns about the integrity of the region were not consensual in the armed forces and suffered the erosion of time and circumstances after his book was published. There are nuances in the understanding about the role of foreign powers, in particular the United States. Travassos saw American interest and possible penetration into the region as a direct threat to Brazilian interests that should be opposed, notwithstanding the disproportionality of forces. On the other hand, Golbery do Couto e Silva—another military and influential thinker during the military regime (1964–1985)—writing during the Cold War, does not consider a direct threat by the United States to Brazil, but an indirect threat to the United States, in the context of the rivalry with the USSR, that could renew an alliance between Brazil and the United States. The Amazonas River and the northeast coast were valuable assets for Brazil during the Cold War as strategic points in the transit of the South Atlantic. Golbery did not see foreign presence searching for natural resources in the Amazon as foreign greed. His focus was the integration of the Amazon to the national development process and an immediate defense structure of vulnerable points at the borders with neighboring countries.[52]

The Amazon is a huge territory with the world's largest equatorial forest and endemic in biodiversity and great differentiation of species between areas. The greatest diversity of organisms by area, diversity of trees, thousands of plants, most of which with some medicinal and nutritive properties and as producers of oils, greases, waxes, varnishes, aromas, tannin, condiments, etc. show the high value of the forest. At the same time, minerals and energy resources are widely distributed, like gold, bauxite, coal, manganese, iron, kaolin, and zinc.[53]

The huge potential of the stocks of those resources, essential for technological innovations, development of bioeconomy and energy use, among other applications, has enhanced foreign interest in the Amazon. There is a growing concern, nationally and internationally, about the effects of policies at national and state levels aiming at the conservation and sustainable use of those resources.[54]

This vast wealth awakens interest not only of countries, but also of the private sector. Concerns about the consequences of climate change, deforestation, and the loss of biodiversity have led to mounting pressures on the Brazilian government based on doubts about the ability of the country to effectively respond to the global challenges in the Amazon. Such interests are sometimes openly expressed in the sense that the Amazon should be submitted to an international regime to ensure its preservation. A case in point was the comment made by the former prime minister of France, Michel Rocard, in 1989, to the head of the Delegation of Brazil at the Hague Conference on Environmental Protection, that "Brazil was not capable of taking care of the Amazon."[55] At that same event, former president François Mitterrand championed the idea of an international authority for the environment. In his view, "This would be translated in a waiver by some countries of part of their sovereignty." And he added, "This is necessary. We have made concessions in the European Community and even in other international issues. What is important is to go ahead."[56]

Aware of the geopolitical weight of the Amazon, the Brazilian government promoted, at the end of the 1970s, the negotiation of the Amazon Cooperation Treaty (ACT) involving the other seven countries of the basin. According to Rubens Ricupero, a key Brazilian negotiator of the agreement, the participation of Venezuela and Peru was instrumental to overcome delicate political hurdles, like border disputes that were still pending between some countries of the basin. The agreement signed in Brasília, on July 3, 1978, provided great potential for stimulating regional cooperation in areas such as scientific research and environment.[57] The treaty is a privileged diplomatic instrument for dialogue, development of joint policies, and cooperation projects, as well as of common norms for the protection of the environment, use and conservation of biodiversity, forest, and water. The mitigation of climate change, in particular combatting deforestation and forest fires, is a topic where common policies may be carried out.

Technological changes during the second half of the twentieth century and the beginning of the twenty-first, together with global challenges, derived from processes that take place at different geographical scales and inform multiple interpretations and actions, have ted ambiguous and conflicting interests at different levels, as remarked by Bertha Becker:

At the global level, the Amazon is a frontier perceived as a space to be preserved for the survival of the planet. In this perception, legitimate environmental interests coexist, as well as economic and geopolitical interests expressed in a process of nature marketing and appropriation of the decision-making power of states over the use of their territories. At the national level, where diverse interests also coexist, the dominating interests and perceptions still assign the condition of a resource frontier to the Amazon, that is, an area of expansion of human occupation and of the national economy, which should guarantee Brazil's sovereignty over its huge territory.[58]

External problems, pressures, and challenges influence the internal decision-making process aiming at the establishment of parameters for behavior and deals by both domestic and international actors. Domestic behavior and pressures strongly influence national responses to mitigate negative effects by public and private actors. On the other hand, retaliations, such as restrictions for access of forest and agricultural products to international markets, weigh in the definition of those responses and the design of a strategy with repercussions in foreign policy. The increasing value of the forest as a source of development of the Amazon's bioeconomy, its utilization as a carbon sink and for environmental services, such as the regulation of the rainfall in the center-west and part of the southeast of Brazil, are opening new options for investment, jobs, and more income for the populations that live in the hinterland of the region. This requires the integration of public and private actions aimed specifically at the challenges and opportunities in region.

Bioeconomy is a key element in the strategy of combatting climate change. It also encompasses social and health benefits and their environmental services. As stated by Joaquim Levy, a former finance minister of Brazil, "The value of avoided emissions today is bigger than that of tomorrow."[59] According to Carlos Nobre, one of the leading climate scientists working on the Amazon, savannization in the region is not a hypothesis anymore. The longer drought season in the south and southeast of Brazil, less water recycling and higher surface temperatures in pasture areas, and less evaporation from the forest in the southern Amazon are signals that the forest is losing its capacity to absorb CO_2. This means less rain in areas adjacent to the Amazon, like the center west (the breadbasket of Brazil) and São Paulo. Most concerning is that all those effects—longer drought season, less rainfall, and warmer climate—give rise to higher mortality of trees typical of the humid climate. This encompasses Bolivian and Peruvian Amazon and reaches the south of the Brazilian Amazon until Amapá and French Guyana.[60]

Becker identifies the emergence of a new geopolitics anchored in "technological progress" and "planetary circulation." These two elements allow nations with technology-based economies and robust private sectors with financial means to live in a symbiosis of interests with their private sectors about where to invest and exploit resources beyond their national jurisdiction. The countries that share sovereignty over the Amazon face challenges to implement their national or provincial policies as a result of the asymmetries between them and those nations where firms or other private entities have their headquarters. Alerts about the internationalization of the Amazon are a recurring argument among military thinkers and some civilian experts.

Among the hallmarks of "new geopolitics" is the "internationalization of social movements with their own geopolitics," adding to the complexity of the international system.[61] These social movements, whose roots are in civil society, encompass NGOs, academic and scientific institutions, churches, Indigenous peoples and traditional communities, business, and press, among others. Myrian D'Allonnes observes that these movements give emphasis to the social as a nonpolitical dimension, which is a sociological, economic, anthropological, and conceptual subversion of what is to be seen as political.[62] The work of some of these entities is frequently controversial because of their financial dependence on developed countries, allowing donors to condition their support to an agenda that reflect their views of the issues.

It must be stressed that these movements also include activities by organized crime (terrorism, money laundering, violation of indigenous rights and lands, drug trafficking, smuggling, illegal logging and mining, land grabbing, among others). The presence of criminal groups using heavy weapons in the Amazon is one of the single most important obstacles to implementing sustainable development. This is a new security challenge for the Brazilian state. It strengthens the hand of illegal land grabbing and illegal mining. Part of this situation is due to the long and porous borders in the region, a condition that remains even with the increase in Brazilian military presence. Organized crime is currently a significant threat not only to policy implementation but also to national security, maintenance of public order, and upholding sovereignty. Combatting illegal actions is a key challenge to the government inaugurated on January 1, 2023.

CONCLUSION

The history of the Amazon has been marked by the challenge of controlling its huge territory. The struggle for survival by its original populations, since the arrival of the Europeans, has been a permanent feature with frequently negative repercussions in its occupation and in the relationship between man and nature. The establishment of the borders at the end of the nineteenth and beginning of the twentieth century defined its geography and the location of enormous wealth. Internal balance and regional harmony depend on stable borders.

The Amazon matters and it will be a primary determinant in regional and national decision-making. The design and adoption of a strategy is the missing tool to reconcile action on technical issues (e.g., climate change, land regularization, conservation of biodiversity, availability of technical and technological means) and management of social and political issues (like cooperation at all levels of government and with foreign actors, quality of information, sensitivity to local and national challenges, coordination of policies, and relations with civil society). Transparency and accountability of the various actors is also important.

Since the 1950s, a fast industrialization process and, since the 1970s, a rapid transformation of its agriculture with high productivity, have made Brazil a major trading partner. In the Amazon, the concentration of industrial plants close to Manaus helped minimize the destruction of the forest in Amazonas State. On the other hand, huge farms and ranches, some of them still without land property titles, have been at the forefront of deforestation.

Economic change in the Amazon, produced by the effort to integrate it with the rest of Brazil and reinforce its security, started with the building of roads like Belém-Brasília in the 1950s and the Transamazônica in the 1970s. These roads and others served to transport production and signaled the presence of the state. They also helped establish projects to occupy the region and access new areas. This occupation has generated high rates of deforestation, intensification of social and environmental problems, and high economic, social, and environmental costs for other interventions such as hydroelectric dams or mining.[63]

The parameters that have informed Amazon development throughout the past seventy years need to be reconfigured by the above-mentioned strategy. The social, economic, and political significance of the region will be enhanced with the development of infrastructure, growth of cities, better education, forest regeneration, intensification of contacts between populations living at the borders, growing participation of Indigenous peoples, traditional communities, and civil society together with the increase in access to technologies, especially communication technologies and promotion of innovation. Better connectivity is key to increasing economic possibilities and ensuring better effectiveness for dialogue and knowledge access with other centers of the country. This dialogue should be oriented toward reinforcing production chains, developing a robust understanding about solutions that are in harmony with nature and the region, and responding to urgent basic needs of the people, like healthcare, education, sanitation, credit, and fresh water.

Infrastructure and sustainability must go hand in hand in the Amazon. Forest and agriculture must be exploited bearing in mind the challenges of climate change and loss of biodiversity. In order to achieve the full potential of bioeconomy, it is necessary to invest in knowledge, productivity, and markets. Universities, laboratories, and technical schools play a central role in this domain and in the training of more and better human resources. Research and development must be jointly supported by the state and the private sector. Bioeconomy has been practiced for ages in the Amazon. Innovation is crucial to enhance bioeconomy initiatives and increase productivity. Industry and consumers are increasingly checking policy safeguards to avoid becoming compromised with unsustainable patterns of production.[64]

Modern technology has revolutionized the economic development of the last decades. Most of these technologies use natural resources, like iron ore, manganese, niobium, titanium, diamonds, chromium, copper, and nickel, all present in the Amazon. The state of Pará is the biggest mineral province in Brazil. However, mining is still a challenge, since illegal activities associated with it have produced pollution and other social distortions.

Companies and investors of the world's five big economies are interested in securing opportunities for investments in the region. This increases the geopolitical importance of the Amazon as a pivotal space to explore those resources, which should be used in the development of both civilian and military hardware. In the chapter on water, the huge basin of the Amazonas River is certainly a key asset in terms of transportation, fisheries, and maintaining biodiversity. It must also be highlighted that the largest aquifer of Brazil, that of Alter-do-Chão, with a volume of water of 86 thousand cubic kilometers, lies beneath the states of Pará, Amazonas, and Amapá.

The Amazon Cooperation Treaty Organization (ACTO) should be strengthened. Brazil should play a key role mobilizing financial resources and its institutions to cooperate with the member states. It should serve as a locus for regional coordination and as an interface for multistakeholder projects, particularly those with the participation of more than one international agency. National and international institutions need to understand the Amazon and generate concepts and proposals that can transform reality. The state should use its purchasing power to stimulate entrepreneurship and establish a specific policy for industrialization for the region.

Environmental change is a new factor in political and economic foreign relations, not only because it is new, but also because of considerable uncertainty about its medium- and long-term effects. The accelerated consumption and the degradation of natural resources, increased by their uncontrolled exploitation, by greedy economic affluence, as well as social and political inequality have given rise to global problems, and have globalized problems that previously had local or regional impact.[65] Today, the concept of what is global involves values, behaviors, rules, interests, and power. Neither globalization nor development will be sustainable with the prevailing levels of inequality and asymmetries. A review of the economic equation prevailing in the Amazon is urgent.

Brazil is a country under construction. But contrary to what Travassos and Golbery write, the geopolitical importance of the Amazon is no longer to neutralize Argentina. Despite its challenges, it is integrated with Brazil, and it is no longer a peripheral space. The Amazon is a region with a very delicate environment. Many people live in a situation of vulnerability. The repercussion of domestic decisions and actions at the international level demand public policies, planning, and robust institutions to coordinate federal and local efforts, as well as mobilization of the private sector and civil society to preserve and sustainably exploit Amazonian wealth. The Amazon is under Brazilian sovereignty, but what happens there concerns all those worried about the planet and who care for future generations.

NOTES

1. Hannah Arendt, *The Human Condition* (Chicago: The University Press of Chicago, 1989),
250–51.
2. J. M. Roberts, *The New Penguin History of the World*, 5th edition, updated and revised by Odd Arne Westad (London: Penguin Books, 2007), 630.
3. Auxiliomar Silva Ugarte,"Margens Míticas: A Amazônia no Imaginário europeu do Século XVI." In *Os Senhores dos Rios*, ed. Mari del Priore e Flávio Gomes (Rio de Janeiro: Elsevier, 2003), 5–6."
4. In 1506, the line of demarcation was extended to 270 leagues (about 1,500 km or 932 m), giving Portugal sovereignty over a swath east of Brazil, including the mouth of today's Amazon River. Available at https://education.nationalgeographic .org/resource/treaty-tordesillas.
Access on October 26, 2022.
5. Nicholas J. Spykman, "Geography and Foreign Policy." *The American Political Science Review* 32, no. 2, (April 1938): 213–36.
6. Source: IBGE. These numbers may be different according to the methodology used to calculate the area and the proportions of national surface occupied by the region. If calculated with SIG methodology, using sinusoidal projection, meridian –60°, and adjustment to referential limits between countries, the area of the Brazilian Amazon is 5.238 million square kilometers, corresponding to 61.8 percent of the national area (Source: Amazônia sob Pressão, 2020, São Paulo: Instituto Sócio-ambiental, 2021).
7. This analysis will be restricted to the Brazilian Amazon. Possible references to the Amazon region in other South American countries will be for explanatory or illustrative purposes.
8. Emílio F. Morán, *A Ecologia Humana das Populações da Amazônia*. Petrópolis, RJ: Vozes 1990.126–28.
9. Carlos A. Nobre et al., "Land-use and climate change risks in the Amazon and the need of a novel sustainable development paradigm." In *Proceedings of the National Academy of Sciences (PNAS)* 113, no. 39 (September 27, 2016): 10760.

10. Brigitte Thiérion, *Prefácio*. In *História da Amazônia: do período pré-colombiano aos desafios do século XXI*, edited by Márcio Souza. Rio de Janeiro e S. Paulo: Editora Record, 2019, 15.

11. Anthony Pagden, *The fall of the natural man: The American Indian and origins of comparative ethnology* (Cambridge: Cambridge University Press, 1986), 11.

12. Márcio Souza, *História da Amazônia: do período pré-colombiano aos desafios do século XXI.* 2ªedição. Rio de Janeiro e S. Paulo: Editora Record, 2019, 103–04.

13. Darcy Ribeiro, *Os Índios e a Civilização: a integração das populações indígenas ao Brasil moderno.* Petrópolis: Vozes, 1977, 13.

14. Sergio Buarque de Holanda, *Raízes do Brasil; prefácio de Antônio Cândido.* 21ª edição. Rio de Janeiro: José Olympio, 1989, 73–74.

15. The name Amazonia would be adopted in the nineteenth century.

16. Julyan M. Ramos, "Incorporação e Integração da Amazônia: perpetuação da colonialidade." In *Amazônia Latitude Review* (12ª edition). Access on June 26, 2022. https://amazonialatitude.com/?s=incorpora%C3%A7%C3%A3o+e+integra%C3%A7%C3%A3o.

17. Caio Prado Jr., *Evolução Política do Brasil: colônia e império.* São Paulo: Brasiliense, 1999,
52–53.

18. José Murilo de Carvalho, *Cidadania no Brasil: o longo caminho.* 26ª edição. Rio de Janeiro: Civilização Brasileira, 2010, 32.

19. This was the title of the provincial governors during the empire.

20. Souza, *História da Amazônia,* 186, 195, 207.

21. Ruben Ricupero, *A Diplomacia na Construção do Brasil: 1750–2016.* Rio de Janeiro: Versal, 2017,163.

22. Adriana Lopez and Carlos Guilherme. *História do Brasil: uma interpretação.* 2ª edição. São Paulo: Editora Senac, 2008, 458–59.

23. Adam Watson, *A Evolução da Sociedade Internacional: uma análise histórica comparativa.* In Américo Alves de Lyra Jr. *Política Externa do Brasil Império: a abertura do rio Amazonas à navegação internacional.*" *Anais do XXVI Simpósio Nacional de História (ANPUH).* São Paulo, julho de 2021. Accessed June 28, 2022. http://www.snh2011.anpuh.org/resources/anais/14/1300853062_ARQUIVO_POLITICAEXTERNADOBRASILNOIMPERIO_ANPUH_Final.pdf.

24. Lars Schoultz, *Beneath the United States: a history of the U.S. policy toward Latin America.* Cambridge, Mass: Harvard University Press, 1998, 66.

25. Watson, *A Evolução da Sociedade Internacional.*

26. José Viegas Filho, *Diplomacia do Brasil: de Tordesilhas aos nossos dias.* Belo Horizonte: Editora Forum, 2015, 72–73.

27. Susanna B. Hecht, *The scramble for the Amazon and the "Lost Paradise" of Euclides da Cunha.* Chicago: The University of Chicago Press, 2013, 88.

28. Souza, *História da Amazônia,* 201–02.

29. Eduardo Bueno, *Brasil: uma história: cinco séculos de um país em construção.* São Paulo: Leya, 2010, 166.

30. Luís Cláudio Villafañe G. Santos, *Juca Paranhos, o barão do Rio Branco.* São Paulo: Companhia das Letras, 2018, 211.

31. Hecht, *The scramble for the Amazon*, 89.

32. Title of José Maria da Silva Paranhos Jr.

33. Hecht, *The scramble for the Amazon*, 101, 100.

34. Ricupero, *A Diplomacia na Construção do Brasil*, 303

35. Peru, together with Brazil, was the country that made the most efforts to integrate its portion of the Amazon into the national territory. See Souza, *História da Amazônia*, 271.

36. Hecht, *The scramble for the Amazon*, 261.

37. Idem, *op. cit.*, 266.

38. Xenia Vunovic Wilkinson, *Tapping the Amazon for Victory: Brazil's "Battle for Rubber" of World War II.* Ph.D. diss., Georgetown University, 2009, 50. Accessed July 9, 2022. https://repository.library.georgetown.edu/bitstream/handle /10822/553116/WilkinsonXeniaV.pdf?sequence=1&isAllowed=y.

39. Souza, *História da Amazônia*, 245–50.

40. Amartya Sen, *Development as Freedom*. New York: Anchor Books, 1999, 18–30.

41. João Luís Fragoso and Teixeira da Silva, "A Política no Império e no Início da República Velha: dos barões aos coronéis." In *História Geral do Brasil*, edited by Maria Yedda L. Linhares, Rio de Janeiro: Campus, 1990, 200.

42. After the installation of the Republic the provinces started to be called states.

43. João Luís Fragoso, "O Império Escravista e a República dos Plantadores, Parte A: Economia Brasileira no Século XIX: mais do que uma plantation escravista—exportadora." In *História Geral do Brasil*, edited by Maria Yedda L. Linhares. Rio de Janeiro: Campus, 1990.

44. Mario Miguel Amin, "The Amazon in World Geopolitics of the Strategic Resources of the Twenty-first Century." *Revista Crítica de Ciências Sociais* 107 (September 2015): 17–38.

45. Niell Lochery, *Brazil: The Fortunes of War: World War II and the making of modern Brazil.* New York: Basic Books, 2014, 60.

46. Wilkinson, *Tapping the Amazon for Victory*, 86–93.

47. Lochery, *Brazil*, 136–37.

48. Amin, The Amazon in World Geopolitics.

49. Felipe Garcia de Barros, "O Pensamento Geopolítico de Travassos, Golbery e Meira Mattos para a Amazônia," *Revista Brasileira de Estudos Estratégicos* 13, no. 25 (2021): 83. The notion of Argentina as a rival of Brazil in South America permeated the thinking of military, academic, and diplomatic establishments as a result of the conflicts between both countries during the empire. With the end of the military dictatorships during the 1980s, and the presidential diplomacy conducted by Presidents José Sarney and Raúl Alfonsín, the idea of rivalry was set aside, and a series of agreements was negotiated. This political rapprochement strengthened economic relations and created conditions for the negotiation of the Treaty of Asunción of 1991 that created MERCOSUR.

50. Nilson Fraga et al., "Geopolitics in Amazon Geographic System in XXI Century." *Global Journal of Human Science: Political Science* 14, no. 7 (2014):22.

51. Barros, "O Pensamento Geopolítico de Travassos," 86–87.

52. Barros, "O Pensamento Geopolítico de Travassos," 92–93.

53. Commission on Environment and Development for Amazonia, *Amazonia without Myth*, 15.

54. Amin, "The Amazon in World Geopolitics of the Strategic Resources of the Twenty-first Century."

55. The head of the delegation was Ambassador Paulo Tarso Flecha de Lima, secretary-general of external relations. See André Correa Lago, *Stockholm, Rio, Johannesburg: Brazil and the Three United Nations Conferences on the Environment*. Brasília: Instituto Rio Branco; Fundação Alexandre de Gusmão, 2009, 143.

56. See https://www.elysee.fr/francois-mitterrand/1989/03/11/conference-de -presse-de-m-francois-mitterrand-president-de-la-republique-sur-la-protection-de -lenvironnement-la-haye-samedi-11-mars-1989, Access on 07/09/2022.

57. Ricupero, *A Diplomacia na Construção do Brasil,* 530–31.

58. Bertha Koiffman Becker, *Amazônia: Geopolítica na virada do III milênio*. Rio de Janeiro: Garamond, 2009, 21. Bertha Becker (1930–2013) was a Brazilian geographer and a leading specialist on the Amazon.

59. Joaquim Levy, Speech at the World Circular Bioeconomy Forum, Belém 2021.

60. Daniella Chiaretti, "Savanização da Amazônia está mais próxima, diz Nobre." *Valor Economico*, February 5, 2021. https://valor.globo.com/brasil/noticia/2021/02 /05/savanizacao-da-amazonia-esta-mais-proxima-diz-nobre.ghtml.

61. Bertha K. Becker, *Geopolítica da Amazônia,* in Estudos Avançados 19, no. 53 (January/April 2005): 2.

62. Myrian Revault D'Allonnes*Le Dépérissement de la Politique: généalogie d'um lieu commun.* Paris: Aubier, 1999, 97–98.

63. Ricardo Abramovay, *Infraestrutura para o Desenvolvimento Sustentável da Amazônia,* São Paulo: Elefante, 2022, 11.

64. Izabella Teixeira, *Speech at the World BioEconomy Forum*, Belém, October 2021.

65. Nazli, Choucri "Politics of global environmental change: a conceptual framework." Conference Paper, XVth World Congress of the International Political Science Association, 1991. Commission on Environment and Development for Amazonia. *Amazonia without Myths.* 2001, 1–2.

REFERENCES

Abramovay, Ricardo. *Infraestrutura para o Desenvolvimento Sustentável da Amazônia*. São Paulo: Elefante, 2022.

Amin, Mario Miguel. "The Amazon in World Geopolitics of the Strategic Resources of the Twenty-first Century." *Revista Crítica de Ciências Sociais* 107 (September 2015): 17–38.

Arendt, Hannah. *The Human Condition.* Chicago: The University Press of Chicago, 1989.

Barros, Felipe Garcia de Barros. "O Pensamento Geopolítico de Travassos, Golbery e Meira Mattos para a Amazônia," *Revista Brasileira de Estudos Estratégicos* 13, no. 25 (2021):81–100

Becker, Bertha Koiffman. *Amazônia: Geopolítica na virada do III milênio.* Rio de Janeiro: Garamond, 2009.

Becker, Bertha K. *Geopolítica da Amazônia,* in Estudos Avançados 19, no. 53 (January/April 2005): 71–86

Buarque de Holanda, Sérgio. *Raízes do Brasil; prefácio de Antônio Cândido.* 21ª edição. Rio de Janeiro: José Olympio, 1989.

Bueno, Eduardo. *Brasil: uma história: cinco séculos de um país em construção.* São Paulo: Leya, 2010.

Carvalho, José Murilo de. *Cidadania no Brasil: o longo caminho.* 26ª edição. Rio de Janeiro: Civilização Brasileira, 2010.

Chiaretti, Daniella. "Savanização da Amazônia está mais próxima, diz Nobre." *Valor Economico,* February 5, 2021. https://valor.globo.com/brasil/noticia/2021/02/05/savanizacao-da-amazonia-esta-mais-proxima-diz-nobre.ghtml.

Choucri, Nazli. "Politics of global environmental change: a conceptual framework." Conference Paper, XVth World Congress of the International Political Science Association, 1991.

Commission on Environment and Development for Amazonia. *Amazonia without Myths.* 2001.

D'Allonnes, Myrian Revault. *Le Dépérissement de la Politique: généalogie d'um lieu commun.* Paris: Aubier, 1999.

Filho, José Viegas. *Diplomacia do Brasil: de Tordesilhas aos nossos dias.* Belo Horizonte: Editora Forum, 2015.

Fraga, Nilson et al."Geopolitics in Amazon Geographic System in XXI Century." *Global Journal of Human Science: Political Science* 14, no. 7 (2014):21–29.

Fragoso, João Luís, and Francisco Carlos Teixeira da Silva. "A Política no Império e no Início da República Velha: dos barões aos coronéis." In *História Geral do Brasil,* edited by Maria Yedda L. Linhares, Rio de Janeiro: Campus, 1990.

Fragoso, João Luís. "O Império Escravista e a República dos Plantadores, Parte A: Economia Brasileira no Século XIX: mais do que uma plantation escravista—exportadora." In *História Geral do Brasil,* edited by Maria Yedda L. Linhares. Rio de Janeiro: Campus, 1990.

Hecht, Susanna B. *The scramble for the Amazon and the "Lost Paradise" of Euclides da Cunha.* Chicago: The University of Chicago Press, 2013.

Lago, André Correa do. *Stockholm, Rio, Johannesburg: Brazil and the Three United Nations Conferences on the Environment.* Brasília: Instituto Rio Branco; Fundação Alexandre de Gusmão, 2009.

Levy, Joaquim. Speech at the World Circular Bioeconomy Forum, Belém 2021.

Lochery, Neill. *Brazil: The Fortunes of War: World War II and the making of modern Brazil.* New York: Basic Books, 2014.

Lopez, Adriana; Motta, Carlos Guilherme. *História do Brasil: uma interpretação.* 2ª edição. São Paulo: Editora Senac, 2008.

Morán, Emílio F. *A Ecologia Humana das Populações da Amazônia*. Petrópolis, RJ: Vozes 1990.

National Geographic. *Jun 7, 1494 CE: Treaty of Tordesillas.* Accessed October 26, 2022. https://education.nationalgeographic.org/resource/treaty-tordesillas.

Nobre, Carlos A. et Al., "Land-use and climate change risks in the Amazon and the need of a novel sustainable development paradigm." In *Proceedings of the National Academy of Sciences (PNAS)* 113, no. 39 (September 27, 2016): 10759–10768.,

Pagden, Anthony. *The fall of the natural man: The American Indian and origins of comparative ethnology.* Cambridge: Cambridge University Press, 1986.

Prado Júnior, Caio. *Evolução Política do Brasil: colônia e império.* São Paulo: Brasiliense, 1999.

Ramos, Julyan M. "Incorporação e Integração da Amazônia: perpetuação da colonialidade." In *Amazônia Latitude Review* (12ª edition). Access on June 26, 2022. https://amazonialatitude.com/?s=incorpora%C3%A7%C3%A3o+e+integra%C3%A7%C3%A3o.

Ribeiro, Darcy. *Os Índios e a Civilização: a integração das populações indígenas ao Brasil moderno.* Petrópolis: Vozes, 1977.

Ricupero, Rubens. *A Diplomacia na Construção do Brasil: 1750–2016.* Rio de Janeiro: Versal, 2017.

Roberts, J.M. *The New Penguin History of the World.* 5th edition, Updated and revised by Odd Arne Westad. London: Penguin Books, 2007.

Santos, Luís Cláudio Villafañe G. *Juca Paranhos, o barão do Rio Branco.* São Paulo: Companhia das Letras, 2018.

Schoultz, Lars. *Beneath the United States: a history of the U.S. policy toward Latin America.* Cambridge, Mass: Harvard University Press, 1998.

Sen, Amartya. *Development as Freedom.* New York: Anchor Books, 1999.

Simai, Mihaly. *The future of Global Governance: Managing risk and change on the international system.* Washington D.C.: Endowment of the United Sates Institute of Peace, 1994.

Souza, Márcio. *História da Amazônia: do período pré-colombiano aos desafios do século XXI.* 2ªedição. Rio de Janeiro e S. Paulo: Editora Record, 2019.

Spykman, Nicholas J. "Geography and Foreign Policy." *The American Political Science Review* 32, no. 2, (April 1938): 213–236.

Teixeira, Izabella. *Speech at the World BioEconomy Forum*, Belém, October 2021.

Thiérion, Brigitte. *Prefácio.* In *História da Amazônia: do período pré-colombiano aos desafios do século XXI*, edited by Márcio Souza. Rio de Janeiro e S. Paulo: Editora Record, 2019.

Ugarte, Auxiliomar Silva. Margens Míticas: A Amazônia no Imaginário europeu do Século XVI. In *Os Senhores dos Rios,* edited by Mari del Priore e Flávio Gomes. Rio de Janeiro: Elsevier, 2003.

Viegas Filho, José. *Diplomacia do Brasil: de Tordesilhas aos nossos dias.* 1ª edição. Belo Horizonte: Fórum, 2015.

Watson, Adam. *A Evolução da Sociedade Internacional: uma análise histórica comparativa.* In Américo Alves de Lyra Jr. *Política Externa do Brasil Império: a abertura do rio Amazonas à navegação internacional. Anais do XXVI Simpósio*

Nacional de História (ANPUH). São Paulo, julho de 2021. Accessed June 28, 2022. http://www.snh2011.anpuh.org/resources/anais/14/1300853062_ARQUIVO _POLITICAEXTERNADOBRASILNOIMPERIO_ANPUH_Final.pdf.

Wilkinson, Xenia Vunovic. *Tapping the Amazon for Victory: Brazil's "Battle for Rubber" of World War II.* Ph.D. diss., Georgetown University, 2009. Accessed July 9, 2022. https://repository.library.georgetown.edu/bitstream/handle/10822/553116/ WilkinsonXeniaV.pdf?sequence=1&isAllowed=y.

PART II

Brazilian Geopolitical Perceptions for Antarctica

Chapter 6

Antarctica in the Brazilian Geopolitical Thinking

Guilherme Lopes da Cunha, Paulo E. A.
S. Câmara, Fábio Albergaria de Queiroz,
and Ana Flávia Barros-Platiau

Antarctica, the "frozen continent," one of the last frontiers to be conquered and the only uninhabited continent, seduces by the sheer magnitude of its numbers: 14 million square kilometers, the size of the combined territories of Brazil, Argentina, Chile, Uruguay, Peru, and Bolivia. The ice volume is equivalent to 70 percent of all freshwater available on the planet. It also holds colossal mineral deposits of enormous importance, such as uranium, gold, silver, iron, and coal. So, no wonder Antarctica is a burning issue in world politics.

In this context, Brazil has been a successful polar player for more than forty years. The geopolitical importance of Antarctica has been recognized even before that. Nevertheless, Brazil did not have a clear interest in Antarctica prior to the 1970s (Silva, 2020), and most of the facts related to Brazilian concerns in Antarctica remain primarily unpublished. This becomes foggier the further we move back in time, since most of the old documents were classified for many years. Even after the opening and release of these documents, most of them still needed to be explored. Therefore, Brazilian history is gradually but slowly recovered, and this chapter aims to contribute to highlighting the polar geopolitics in Brazil.

In order to verify the geopolitical content in the Brazilian approach to Antarctica, this chapter proposes to verify how current policies and trends find their rationale in initiatives built since the 1950s. The chapter starts with a brief background on the Antarctic Treaty and Brazilian interests and activities. Then, it sheds light on the yet-unknown history of early interests in Brazil and demonstrates how Antarctica—defined as part of the country's strategic surroundings in 2013—was inserted into Brazilian geopolitics.

In broad terms, Antarctica has been predominantly absent from Brazil's cultural identity. Physically immersed in the core of a tropical environment, Brazilian people have historically seen themselves as citizens with little to no connection to polar regions whatsoever. As a result, despite the current critical importance of Antarctica in the central Brazilian scientific and strategic policies, there need to be more references in textbooks, college curricula, and basic academic knowledge.

Moreover, the Brazilian Antarctic Program (PROANTAR) has remained one of the most successful scientific programs in the country. Focusing on national decision-making processes, it reveals a perspective related to the interaction of army officers, diplomats, and representatives of the epistemic community, as presented by Câmara et al. (2020). The authors have recognized the place of Antarctica in Brazilian strategic thinking since 1975 and stress the crucial role of the navy and other institutions that have fostered Antarctic science in Brazil.

Looking outward and based on official documents found in military and diplomatic archives, we divided our analysis of Antarctica into three phases. Initially, from the end of World War II to the Brazilian signature of the Antarctic Treaty in 1975, the main driving question has been: Why should Brazil invest in Antarctic diplomacy and geopolitics? Subsequently, in a second phase that goes up to 2020, when the new Antarctic scientific station was inaugurated. Finally, after 2020, we analyze whether Brazil should participate as a mere observer or as a stark norm shaper in Antarctic-related issues.

Considering some scientific achievements within this timeline, we investigate how to spur scientific development, produce innovation, and overcome financial restraints to participate effectively in Antarctica's governance. Nevertheless, before reflecting on these three phases, let us prepare the roadmap for this journey by bringing back some underexplored aspects of Brazilian history to the spotlight.

1. BRAZILIAN ANTARCTIC THINKING: THE UNTOLD STORY

Literature usually asserts that Brazilian interest in Antarctica goes back as far as 1975, when Brazil decided to accede to the Antarctic Treaty. However, there was virtually no information prior to this landmark. There are two main reasons for this: 1) the lack of interest from Brazilian historians and researchers and 2) the high level of classification given by the government to most of the early documents. In this context, Cunha et al. (2022) and Câmara et al. (2020) present some relevant events and documents that allowed us to map the evolution of Antarctic geopolitical thinking in Brazil.

There is no exaggeration in saying that Antarctica was not a subject of interests to the Brazilian government or its people until the early 1950s. The first known official document concerning Antarctica dates from 1955 and was a report produced by Army Lieutenant Colonel Wladimir Bouças, where he suggests that Brazil should pose a territorial claim to Antarctica (Bouças, 1956). This document was sent to the upper echelons of the army staff. Nevertheless, it did not result in any action and was shortly set aside.

According to a classified file produced by the Brazilian War College (Brazil, 1956, 5), the first official involvement came to Brazilian attention almost by chance. It succeeded when India decided, in 1956, to present a motion for the pacific use of Antarctica at the United Nations General Assembly meeting, in which Chile and Argentina protested. The issue was eventually moved out of the agenda. Nevertheless, the situation forced Brazil to discuss the matter to express itself. India would unsuccessfully try the same motion again the following year, and Brazil was once more urged to look into the issue to take a stand. This succession of events was officially the starting point of Brazilian interest in the subject.

Realizing its limitations and lack of knowledge in Antarctica-related issues, and also in order to avoid getting caught by surprise (and unprepared) again, the Brazilian Ministry of Foreign Affairs ordered a study about Antarctica to the Brazilian War College (ESG),[1] and in 1956 a document was produced containing important insights and acknowledgment of the lack of information and interest in Antarctica from the Brazilian government. In order to fulfill this gap, a second study was soon produced by ESG in 1957 that assumed notable importance, as it was officially considered the position of the Brazilian General Staff of the Armed Forces on this subject and related issues for many years to come.

Comprising a sixty-page document labeled by the authorities as "sober and realistic" (Brazil, 1957), it is the first multidisciplinary study on Antarctica ever made in Brazil, containing information ranging from climate to geopolitics. It was widely shared with Brazilian embassies across the globe, and for many years it was the only existing study on the subject. Somehow, its findings still influence Brazilian Antarctic thinking. Probably most of the policy and decision-makers in charge of running Brazilian polar policies are still influenced by the ideas of this document (and most likely, they never even heard about it). In short, the study highlighted sensitive aspects such as:

a. the strategic influence that the lands of Graham and its neighboring Antarctic regions would have in the defense of the hemisphere, due to its dominant position in the Drake Passage;
b. the possibility of using these regions as bases for self-propelled projectiles intended for attacks on South America;
c. the economic possibilities for the Antarctic continent, whose ore extraction could become economically viable with the development of proper technology;
d. the absence of a legal basis supporting the rights of countries exploring Antarctica at that time.

This paradigmatic study triggered intense political mobilization. On February 24, 1958, the confidential file n. 09-0-40, from the chief of staff of the Air Force to the general secretary of the Ministry of Foreign Affairs (Brazil, 1958a), recommended governmental authorities recognize claims on Antarctica to any country and eventually accept only international administration without declining national interests for the future. A few weeks later, on April 16, 1958, the confidential file n.18-B[2] recommended propaganda, studies, and expeditions to Antarctica (Brazil, 1958b). Additionally, the study was classified as confidential and forwarded, on April 18, 1958, to the minister of foreign affairs, José Carlos de Macedo Soares, by General Octávio Saldanha Mazza, chief of staff of the armed forces.[3]

These considerations were crucial for Brazil's engagement in an autochthonous approach to Antarctica. Analyzing the roots of this conceptual framework, Brazilian diplomat Lindolfo Collor (1956) compared the geostrategic situations of the Arctic and Antarctic at that time, highlighting similarities and differences. In doing so, Collor (1956, 3) cited Canadian senator Pascal Poirier's sector theory,[4] inspiring an academic version of Brazilian claims, although the government has never proposed an official one.

During those years, the so-called defrontation theory became part of the repertoire of Therezinha de Castro. Commonly attributed to her, this theoretical approach is tied to the sector theory. In 1957, it was admitted in an article republished under Castro (1958, 49), where she argues the following:

> Let us claim our share in Antarctica! If they appealed to history, let us appeal too. Let us unite with the South American countries, Argentina, Chile, Ecuador, Peru, and Uruguay around the right of defrontation or the Polar Sectors, idealized by Canadian Senator Pascal Poirier in 1907 when he dealt with the sharing of the North Pole.[5]

It is worth mentioning that these ideas reverberated in the years to come. It was the case of the confidential memorandum from the Ministry of Foreign

Affairs' head of the South America Division to the assistant secretary-general for American affairs. It was sent on December 29, 1967, warning about a telegram sent by the Brazilian embassy in Buenos Aires, Argentina. It mentioned that "Brazil's eventual claim to a sector in Antarctica, as advocated in the study developed by the Brazilian War College (. . .) based on the Theory of Defrontation would conflict, among others, with Argentine territorial claims on the southern continent" (Brazil, 1967b, 17).[6]

Complementarily, classified as urgent and secret, the "DAM-I" (South America Division-I) telegram of August 4, 1978, issued by the Brazilian embassy in Montevideo, Uruguay, reported that matters concerning Brazilian policy to Antarctica were surrounded by absolute secrecy at the highest levels of the Uruguayan government. Nonetheless, with regard to the theory of fefrontation, the document pointed out that it was "unreasonable to encourage the study of a territorialist theory" (Brazil, 1978, 1).

On the other hand, voices in the Brazilian Parliament, such as Eurípedes Cardoso de Menezes, emphasized proactive participation in Antarctica, as notably expressed in a text published in 1971 in the *Military Club Magazine* (*Revista do Clube Militar*) on "the Rights of Brazil in Antarctica." According to Menezes (1971, 5–8):

> We can very well make an official Declaration regarding our legitimate claims. It would not be absurd to issue a decree of the annexation of the part of Antarctica between the meridians of Arroio Chuí and Martim Vaz, by the principle of defrontation, adopted in the division of the North Pole and accepted by Australia, South Africa, and New Zealand. (. . .) If it was considered in the Arctic, why not in Antarctica? Especially since it will be the only way to resolve the issue peacefully. Otherwise, there will be disagreements and friction. (. . .) After the decree, let us occupy what must be ours, and through our Embassy to the United Nations, let us assert our right, sovereignty, and desire for justice and peace.

In this case, one can see how a possible Brazilian territorial claim in Antarctica was based mainly on the defrontation theory. However, it was adapted to the context of the South Pole by Therezinha de Castro and Carlos Miguel Delgado de Carvalho from the Brazilian Institute of Geography and Statistics (IBGE). For them, Antarctica should be divided by the extreme meridians of countries in the Southern Hemisphere, which meant that Brazil would have the right to revindicate part of the Antarctic territory.[7] Therefore, notwithstanding Collor's (1956) proposition on an effective occupation through a naval operation, the version according to Castro and Delgado de Carvalho became more substantial and more coherent, through which Brazil should occupy what belonged to it by right of defrontation, as illustrated in figure 6.1.

To understand the political environment at the time, in 1880, in Austria-Hungary, studying Antarctica gained impetus. It soon resulted in the realization of the Polar Year of 1882/83, repeated half a century later, with the advent of the International Geophysical Year (1957–1958), with thirty-seven nations, including Brazil, which had immense impact on the advancement of polar science. In this paradigmatic episode, it was established that the criterion for participating in the conference to give rise to the Antarctic Treaty was to carry out significant research on that continent during the International Geophysical Year.

Figure 6.1. Antarctica According to the Theory of Defrontation (1956). Carvalho & Castro (1956).

Twelve countries met this criterion and, therefore, were the original signatories. As for Brazil, the country did not participate in research activities in Antarctica and has never sent any expedition to the region during the referenced period. Therefore, the country was not invited to attend the conference. However, the Ministry of Foreign Affairs presented protests without success in its purpose.

Interestingly, shortly before, on March 23, 1955, the general staff of the army sent a report to the secretary of the National Security Council defending the possibility of Brazil's territorial claim over Antarctica. The theme was even highlighted in national newspapers: among others, in Revista da Semana, on April 30, 1955, under the headline "A Piece of Antarctica Belongs to Brazil,"[8] and *O Globo*, on February 9, 1956, with the headline "We Also Have the Right to Antarctica."[9]

2. FIRST PHASE: WHY SHOULD BRAZIL BE CONCERNED WITH POLAR DIPLOMACY AND GEOPOLITICS?

After World War II and with the rise of the Cold War, Antarctica, a place that has remained so far out of any international interest, became one of the focal points within the international politics chessboard. From a strategic point of view, relevant international sea routes are interconnected with Antarctica, such as the Drake Passage and the Cape of Good Hope. Also, the region impacts several global processes, mainly the atmospheric dynamics, oceanic flows, and, therefore, the entire climate system with sensitive consequences for agribusiness and fisheries (Souza, 1967; Simões et al., 2011; Simões 2020).

According to Colacrai (2004), Ainley et al. (2009), and Câmara and Melo (2018), there are vast reserves of strategic ores and freshwater. Moreover, Thorp (2012) states that in the waters of the Ross and Weddell Seas, there are more than fifty million barrels of oil, which is comparable to the reserves in Alaska. Nevertheless, this was not the priority of the geopolitics agenda in the aftermath of the Second World War since scientific knowledge was scarce.

Instead, there was fear that it could attract the tensions of the Cold War to the region and an undesirable weaponization and occupation by significant powers. Some countries had already started to claim sovereignty rights over juxtaposed areas, and even an armed conflict happened in the region (Câmara and Gonçalves 2022). Increasing the potential conflicts, the United States launched the most extensive polar operation so far, Operation High Jump (1946–1947), involving more than four thousand military personnel and thirteen navy warships. At the same time, the former Union of Soviet Socialist

Republics (USSR) launched its flotilla Slava (1946) to Antarctica. Soon after, the United States launched operations Deep Freeze I (1955–1956) and Deep Freeze II (1956–1957).

Parallel to this, the Arctic was being gradually weaponized as military activities increased, initiatives known as cold weather warfare or winter warfare. The Arctic was strategically important because of the past contest for resources and the future, since receding polar ice should reduce the cost of operations (Smith, 2022). In the face of that situation, the major Antarctic players around 1950 decided to call for a mutual understanding to resolve the matters peacefully. In a way that would benefit all, this was the genesis of the Antarctic Treaty.

Initially, as previously pointed out, the treaty was conceived and signed only by twelve countries in 1959 (Argentina, Australia, Belgium, Chile, France, Japan, United Kingdom, New Zealand, Norway, South Africa, USSR, and the United States) and entered into force in 1961. This unique and successful international instrument is now known as the basis of the Antarctic Treaty System (ATS) due to the incorporation of other later legal instruments. However, Antarctica is still the only continent where sovereignty is not yet resolved, since all those territorial claims have not been recanted, but only "frozen" for future decisions, according to Article IV, as follows:

1. Nothing contained in the present Treaty shall be interpreted as:
    a. (a) a renunciation by any Contracting Party of previously asserted rights of or claims to territorial sovereignty in Antarctica;
    b. (b) a renunciation or diminution by any Contracting Party of any basis of claim to territorial sovereignty in Antarctica which it may have whether as a result of its activities or those of its nationals in Antarctica, or otherwise;
    c. (c) prejudicing the position of any Contracting Party as regards its recognition or non-recognition of any other State's rights of or claim or basis of claim to territorial sovereignty in Antarctica.
2. No acts or activities taking place while the present Treaty is in force shall constitute a basis for asserting, supporting or denying a claim to territorial sovereignty in Antarctica or creating any rights of sovereignty in Antarctica. No new or enlargement of an existing claim to territorial sovereignty in Antarctica shall be asserted while the present Treaty is in force.

The ATS has fifty-five members nowadays. However, only twenty-nine are the consultative parties bearing voting rights. According to the ATS, the top legal condition to become a voting member is to conduct substantial scientific research. Article IX, 2 states that:

Each Contracting Party which has become a party to the present Treaty by accession under Article XIII shall be entitled to appoint representatives to participate in the meetings referred to in paragraph 1 of the present Article during such times as that Contracting Party demonstrates its interest in Antarctica by conducting substantial research activity there, such as the establishment of a scientific station or the despatch of a scientific expedition.

Brazil is one of the parties with the right to vote in the annual Antarctic Treaty Consultative Meetings (ATCM), with equal voting rights to the most powerful states on the planet, including all the United Nations Security Council permanent members (Câmara and Melo, 2018). Accordingly, scientific research is paramount for countries willing to influence the future of Antarctic governance. Therefore, science is the geopolitical tool of excellence in the ATS (Mattos and Câmara 2020).

In 2048, ATS members will have the opportunity to propose revisions relating to some key points of the treaty, such as the natural resources exploitation ban now in effect (Coburn, 2017) and the ATCM voting system, changing to a majority instead of the consensus. Although the system has proved stable and efficient, geopolitical shifts will likely occur, even before 2048 (Allen et al., 2020). It is crucial to note that in a context where the ice sheet continues to melt, global demand for oil and minerals may grow, and mining technologies will become more viable (Chown et al., 2022). Nevertheless, historical territorial claims over the "white continent" remain.

3. THE ANTARCTIC TREATY AND BRAZIL: THE WELL-KNOWN STORY

In this context, scientific research is the basis of the Antarctic system. Inspired by this sense of geopolitics, in 2021 Brazil celebrated fortieth anniversary of its first scientific expedition to Antarctica. On November 22 and 23, 2021, the Brazilian Ministry of Foreign Affairs promoted the seminar titled "Brazil in Antarctica: Balance of Four Decades,"[10] congregating researchers and former operational personnel for discussing historical and current challenges. This scientific approach has granted the country the status of a consultative party since 1983, after having launched PROANTAR, one of the most successful scientific programs in the country, lasting more than forty uninterrupted years, a pretty unusual situation when it comes to Brazilian science, as observed by Câmara et al. (2020).

Brazilian interest in signing the Antarctic Treaty started with the 1970s oil crises. Those crises forced Brazil to rearrange its positions. It was a decade marked by turbulence from a multidimensional perspective. Some sectors

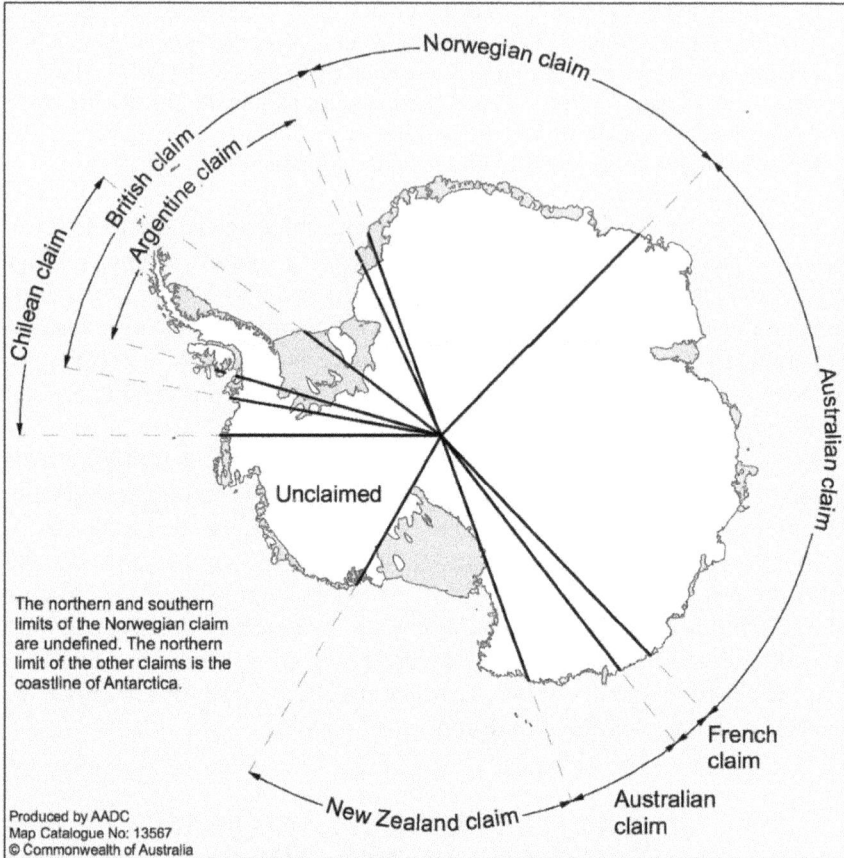

The northern and southern
limits of the Norwegian claim
are undefined. The northern
limit of the other claims is the
coastline of Antarctica.

Norwegian claim

British claim

Argentine claim

Chilean claim

Australian claim

Unclaimed

French claim

New Zealand claim

Australian claim

Produced by AADC
Map Catalogue No: 13567
© Commonwealth of Australia

Figure 6.2. National Claims to Antarctic Territory. https://www.antarctica.gov.au/about-antarctica/people-in-antarctica/who-owns-antarctica/#group-3.

affected are energy, finance, military engagement, and emerging environmentalist order. Hence, Brazil searched for alternatives in the energy supply sector, which finally contributed to the accession to the Washington Treaty in 1975.[11]

Nonetheless, in the 1970s, there was a second wave in favor of the defrontation theory. In this context, parliament representative Euripedes Cardoso de Menezes produced a series of influential speeches at the Brazilian House of Representatives justifying the presence of Brazil in Antarctica and again supporting a territorial claim.[12] Therezinha de Castro and Menezes were fundamental in these efforts to research and discuss Antarctic matters in Brazil. Their influence should not be taken lightly, and they are somehow responsible for Brazil acceding to the treaty in 1975.

Both Castro and Menezes were in favor of territorial claims. This frequently posed discomfort among other countries, especially Argentina and Chile: it was not rare for the Brazilian Ministry of Foreign Affairs to have to write notes on the subject to appease other countries' complaints (Ferreira, 2009). In the end, Brazil never posed a territorial claim in Antarctica. However, Castro and Menezes influenced Brazil into acceding to the treaty in 1975 and creating the Brazilian Antarctic Program (PROANTAR), on January 2, 1982, designed to promote scientific research to understand phenomena affecting national territory, and guarantee the condition of the consultative member of the Antarctic Treaty.[13]

The Brazilian fleet admiral Maximiano Eduardo da Silva Fonseca also had a crucial role in Brazilian Antarctic engagement. As head of the Brazilian Navy from 1979–1984, he created this scientific program focused on Antarctic research. On this occasion, the decree creating the National Commission for Antarctic Affairs (CONANTAR) was signed, as well as a document allocating the responsibility of designing the project to implement PROANTAR to the Interministerial Commission for Resources of the Sea (CIRM).

In addition, under Admiral Maximiano's leadership, the Brazilian Navy bought a polar vessel, undertook the first scientific mission, and built an Antarctic station. The vessel acquired was a second-hand Danish polar ship, *Thala Dan*, then renamed *Barão de Teffé* (H-42).[14] On December 20, 1982, this oceanographic vessel (NApOC) left the city of Rio de Janeiro and sailed south toward Antarctica, arriving on January 4, 1983 (Câmara et al., 2020); in 1983, Brazil launched its first expedition to Antarctica, the Antarctic Operation I (OPERANTAR), alongside the ship N/Oc. Professor W. Besnard, from the Oceanographic Institute of the University of São Paulo (USP).[15] In 1984, a research station was built (Estação Antártica Comandante Ferraz-EACF), and in 1986 it became permanent, meaning that it has operated year-long ever since.

4. SECOND PHASE: BRAZIL AS A MERE OBSERVER OR A NORM SHAPER? THE NEW DEAL IN THE BRAZILIAN POLICY NETWORK

In 1992, as part of Brazilian renewed interests in Antarctica, a deal was made between the navy and the science and technology secretariat. According to this, the armed forces would be responsible for all logistic support (including financing the EACF and the polar vessels), and the science secretariat would be in charge of conducting and financing all of the Antarctic science. This successful agreement has remained effective until now. As a result, there has been no gap in scientific expeditions in the last forty years, even when the EACF was destroyed by a fire in 2012 (Pedone and Hernandez, 2020).

In addition, scientific research is also done on polar vessels and at camp sites. Hence, researchers did not rely exclusively on the station. An exception occurred in the summer of 2020/2021 when, due to the COVID pandemic, research was restricted to the labs in Brazil: it was the only time when PROANTAR scientists did not carry out fieldwork. However, it is essential to note that research did not cease, as the vast majority of polar science in Brazil is done at public universities and research centers. Therefore, it is important to remember that without them, besides all of PROANTAR's relevance, Brazil would have virtually no Antarctic science.

Notwithstanding favorable conditions, Brazil still faces hurdles. The two significant challenges for Brazil are: 1) political, in the sense that Brazilian authorities must keep in mind how Antarctica is important for strategic diplomacy before 2048, in which stable financial support in Brazil has always been a significant concern (Câmara et al., 2020), and 2) scientific and technical, which implies that Brazilian researchers must constantly struggle to reinforce connections with other research teams, including Chile and Argentina, which means that international cooperation is of utmost importance for future research in strategic areas.

In this sense, well-defined, long-term Brazilian interests could find budgetary, administrative, and diplomatic obstacles. Three elements may undermine the Brazilian Antarctic undertaking: 1) regular financial support, 2) logistical neglect (intensifying dependence on Chile and Argentina), and 3) redesign of the administrative sector. Challenges include the lack of regular financial support and the high turnover in strategic positions in the political-bureaucratic structures that deal with the matter (Secretariat of the Interministerial Commission for the Resources of the Sea, SECIRM, and Ministry of Foreign Affairs, for instance). Dangerously combined, these factors have contributed to placing the topic as secondary on the Brazilian political agenda.

Nonetheless, the results of a study carried out by Boyadjian et al. (2020) demonstrate that Brazil has the potential to be better positioned in the Antarctic research ranking for two reasons. First, according to the gross domestic product (GDP), Brazil has conditions to be in the top ten, as it happens when countries are ranked according to this indicator. Furthermore, countries with high GDP have shown stable funding, which is likely correlated with their scientific production in terms of quality and quantity, while stability is not the case in Brazil. Second, Brazil is a Southern Hemisphere country with two neighbors with territorial claims over Antarctica: Argentina and Chile. Without claims, Brazil could be an essential interlocutor for Antarctic issues.

4.1 The New Antarctic Station

Built in 1984, the new Antarctic station EACF has undergone significant expansions and renovations throughout its history. It served generations of scientists until it was almost destroyed by fire in 2012, with the sad loss of two lives. In 2013, a temporary station was already operational at the exact location until a new station was built and inaugurated in January 2020. With 4,500 square meters, it is the biggest station on the Antarctic Peninsula and also the most modern, comprising seventeen newly built labs, with the potential to give Brazilian Antarctic science a big boost if properly funded.

Equipped with state-of-the-art labs, Commandant Ferraz Antarctic Station is located at the same site as the former station, but it is larger than the first version: it has the potential to carry on science year-long, including winter, and its size, architecture, and labs have attracted the attention of other nations, sending an important geopolitical message concerning permanent Brazilian interests in the region and its understanding of the pivotal role of science as the main political tool in the Antarctic Treaty System.

Research is a condition for the right to vote in the annual meetings of the countries that signed the treaty, so the station, according to Simões (Apud Pierro, 2020), has critical geopolitical content. For Câmara et al. (2019), geopolitics for Antarctica in the twenty-first century is more complex because it involves threats of an unconventional nature, such as extreme weather events, sea level rise, and impoverishment of technological diversity. In addition, there are growing challenges concerning territorial appropriation and access to biological resources, showing a geopolitical board that needs to include cyberspace and disruptive technologies. Commenting on Brazilian botanists' works, Câmara and Carvalho-Silva (2020) believe Brazil has a

Figure 6.3.   Comandante Ferraz Antarctic Station Project. https://www.defesaaereanaval .com.br/naval/estacao-antartica-comandante-ferraz-eacf.

Figure 6.4. First Brazilian Scientific Crew at the New Comandante Ferraz Antarctic Station: Flag Day Celebration, 19th November, 2021. Paulo E. A. S. Câmara (2021). Personal archive.

golden opportunity to make the required contributions and play a central role in developing the next generation of international Antarctic science.

Every 3 to 4 years, the Ministry of Science, Technology, and Innovation (MCTI) opens calls for receiving proposals destined to support Antarctic science.[16] Through its funding agency, the National Council for Scientific and Technological Development, CNPq, usually supports about twenty proposals, including diverse areas such as atmosphere, oceanography, marine biology, terrestrial biology, glaciology, edaphology, sea and wind currents, among other fields. The state-of-the-art labs in Ferraz Station associated with human capital corroborate to provide an optimistic scenario for Brazilian Antarctic science soon.

5. THIRD PHASE: HOW TO EFFECTIVELY MAXIMIZE SCARCE BRAZILIAN RESOURCES TO PARTICIPATE IN POLAR GOVERNANCE

The maximization of Brazilian efforts can be felt in initiatives of different natures. The first step is raising awareness and putting polar diplomacy on the radar. On the one hand, as part of an Antarctic mentality, administrative actions have been improving the normative structure that galvanized perennial engagement, demonstrating that both the Brazilian state and scientific community are committed to going forward in making Brazil an Antarctic scientific power. Nevertheless, on the other hand, the results of this state policy are blooming and gaining weight, as can be seen through scientific stations, labs, modules, and vessels that can be interpreted as a symbol where science is the chief source of geopolitical clout.

Brazil has continuously implemented efforts to modernize institutional mechanisms. Decree No.1.791 from January 15, 1996, created CONAPA, the National Committee on Antarctic Research (Brazil, 1996), led by the Coordination for Ocean Affairs and Antarctica, in MCTI (Ministry of Science, Technology, and Innovations). CONAPA was redesigned by Decree No.10.603 on January 20, 2021 (Brazil, 2021). It enhanced normative structures to deal with national guidelines, advisory committees, and domestic and international institutional relationships with Brazilian bodies and SCAR, Research, through representatives of national ministries and the scientific community.

Under the MCTI's secretariat of research and scientific formation competencies, CONAPA is the coordinator for managing and spurring governmental actions in Antarctica (Brazil, 2021). Among other tasks, two of them may be highlighted: 1) the verification of measures undertaken under the initiative named Antarctic science to Brazil: an action plan from 2013–2022 and 2) the launching of the next Antarctic science ten-year plan from 2023–2032, according to recent meetings (Brazil, 2022).

Despite its lethargic engagement in Antarctic affairs, the ten-year plan initiative demonstrates that Antarctica is inserted in Brazil as a state policy. The first ten-year action plan (2012–2022) resulted in the Antarctic science program, whose aim is to develop research on Antarctica and its connections with the Atlantic Ocean and South America, covering six subjects: climate change, cryosphere, geodynamics, biocomplexity, atmospheric dynamics, and emerging themes.

A second Antarctic science ten-year plan (2022–2032) confirms the commitment and corroborates that results reaped and scientific emphasis are paving the way for Brazilian interests. In this sense, Rosa (2022) asserts that the ten-year plan is based on the SCAR agenda; for him, it is designed under the leadership of the Coordination for Ocean Affairs and Antarctica, CONAPA, its branch, prepares the document submitted for public consultation, including experts on Antarctica, whose opinions, suggestions, and corrections return for adjustments. Among other issues, this ten-year plan promises to innovate, contemplating climate change and the scientific insertion of Brazil in the Arctic, a topic debated emphatically as a burning issue in current Brazilian society.

5.1 The New Polar Vessel

Based on the Brazilian scientific perspective of geopolitics, developing the new Antarctic polar vessel (NAPAnt *Admiral Saldanha*) is a relevant tool for expanding capabilities.[17] Barreira (2022) asserts that the Brazilian Navy expects to commission the ship in late 2025 under the consortium between Estaleiro Jurong Aracruz (EJA) and Sembcorp Marine Singapore, signed in October 2021 plans.

Working with the current vessels NApOc *Ary Rongel* (H44) and NPo *Admiral Maximiano* (H41), the vessel is the primary logistics resource and an important means for scientific production. According to Almeida (2019), due to the vessel's five labs, Brazil develops around 40 percent of its scientific production: it is conducted aboard, in areas such as glaciology, meteorology, biology, and climatology, among other fields.

With NAPAnt *Admiral Saldanha*, PROANTAR will operate further south than it has been operating in the last forty years. Also, it should allow for more extended periods of stay, hence allowing for an earlier start of operations and a later end for the austral summer seasons. This will give Brazilians a much bigger wind during summer operations in Antarctica. The ship will displace approximately 5,880 tons for a length of 93.9 meters, a width of 18.5 meters, a draught of 6 meters, a cruising speed of 12 knots, an endurance of 70 days, and a crew of 95, including 26 researchers:

Also, three lightweight twin-engine multipurpose Airbus helicopters, H135s (UH-27 in the Brazilian Navy), were acquired to complement the operational structure. Planned to operate with Brazilian vessels in Antarctica,

Figure 6.5.   Antarctic Polar Vessel (NAPAnt Almirante Saldanha) Project. https://www.defesaaereanaval.com.br/naval/iniciada-a-construcao-do-navio-de-apoio-antartico-napant.

the second-hand H135s were bought in 2019 from Helibras, the Brazilian division of Airbus helicopters, to replace squadron Aguia, the AS355F2 Écureuil (UH-13 in the Brazilian Navy). They are appropriate for troop and cargo transport, surveillance, and evacuation: two were delivered in 2020 (Brazilian Navy, 2020) and the third one in 2021 (Barreira, 2021).

5.2 The Cryosphere modules

Brazil operates Latin America's southernmost scientific module in Antarctica, Cryosphere 1 (84°S), enabling the presence and expansion of Brazil in mainland Antarctica. More than 2,000 kilometers away from the EACF, the Cryosphere 1 automatic module has operated since 2012, and very success-fully. Under a partnership between researchers from the State University of Rio de Janeiro (UERJ), the Federal University of Rio Grande do Sul (UFRGS), and National Institute for Space Research (INPE), it monitors climate and atmospheric chemistry (Marcher et al., 2022). On September 28, 2022, the Automated and Sustainable Laboratory "Cryosphere 2," part of PROANTAR, was shipped to Antarctica.[19] Furthermore, it was set up by the Polar and Climate Center of the Federal University of Rio Grande do Sul (UFRGS).

They are supported by the Financier of Studies and Projects (FINEP), with resources from the National Fund for Scientific and Technological Development (FNDCT). In the second module, eight researchers participated in the installation under Professor Jefferson Simões: Cryosphere 2 prioritizes national technology, dedicating research on climate change, climatology, and glaciology, and ice shelves that affect the South Atlantic. The goal is to improve the understanding of climate variation in Antarctica and how it affects cold fronts, extratropical cyclones, and extreme events, in addition to supporting glaciological research.

5.3 The 2022 National Policy for Antarctic Affairs

Brazil presented to the public, through Decree No. 11.096, of June 15, 2022, the update of the National Policy for Antarctic Affairs (POLANTAR), whose first and outdated version dates from 1987. As previously pointed out, POLANTAR is the primary document that presides over Brazilian Antarctic policy and activities. This new version was designed to handle the contempo-rary challenges stemming from the international context properly and to put forward new perspectives on the Brazilian presence in Antarctica.

Considering that changes within the treaty may happen in 2048 (or even before that), it is crucial for Brazil to start discussing its role in the ATS and the future of Brazilian participation. Above all, in a context where threats that emerge with the capacity to impact Antarctica have become more diffuse and bring disruptive risks. This is the case of the emergence of new poles of power, climate change, exponential loss of biodiversity, or the scarcity of strategic natural resources. From a geopolitical perspective, with the factors listed above, among others, there is ground to strengthen Antarctica as a first-priority strategic issue.

Conclusion

Despite Brazil being the seventh closest country to Antarctica, Brazilians are used to considering their country as tropical, with little or no relation to any polar region. However, the facts described and analyzed in this chapter point out that geopolitical priorities eventually forced decision-makers and strategists to start thinking differently in the mid-1950s. As seen through the analysis of some paradigmatic documents, Antarctica is just too big and too close to Brazil to be ignored.

A careful study of these documents reveals a slow but constant increase in Brazilian interest in Antarctica. Initially concerned with the possibility of avoiding problems with neighboring countries such as Argentina and Chile, Brazil later realized the region was increasingly linked to a wide range of strategic issues. It means food security, biosphere integrity, global hydrological cycle, and climate change.

Today, Brazil faces a potentially exciting new phase, with good possibilities for expansion and increased scientific activities to highlight its role as a relevant polar actor. In a nutshell, the inferences listed throughout these pages show that, between advances and setbacks, Brazil is increasingly aware of the impending challenges in Antarctic geopolitics and has been part of the most important mechanisms of polar governance. In this sense, for instance, possible connections between climate change in Antarctica and variations in the incidence of cold fronts that reach South America demonstrate complex relationships that need to be understood comprehensively, and Brazil has the potential to play a vital role in this endeavor.

Thus, considering the findings mentioned above, through initiatives such as the inauguration of the new Antarctic scientific station and the cryosphere modules, it seems that Brazil is also achieving its goals in paving the way to be a protagonist in the contemporary political arena in the Anthropocene. It constitutes a turning point that puts humanity in a new context of uncertainties and unpredictable consequences, including for Antarctica.

Therefore, Sánchez (2018) reminds us that Antarctica is more fragile than ever. This way, recognizing the uniqueness of the frozen continent, Brazil's National Defense Strategy established as one of its strategic defense actions (AED n.51) the importance of "increase[d] participation in decisions about the fate of the Antarctic region" (Brazil, 2016), as often asserted in this chapter, a trend that facts have confirmed.

NOTES

1. In Portuguese, Escola Superior de Guerra (ESG).

2. Classified document sent by the chief of staff of the armed forces to the minister of foreign affairs. Subject: Brazilian interests in Antarctica.

3. The original document appeared to be the only existing copy and was found in the MRE archives. In 2022, it was published by Alexandre de Gusmão Foundation (FUNAG) and is available for download, in Portuguese, at https://funag.gov.br/biblioteca-nova/produto/1-1191.

4. On February 20, 1906, the sector theory was debated in Canada's Senate. It was a means to justify its rights over the Arctic domains. Poirier (1906, 271) addressed in his speech that "in future partition, of northern lands, a country whose possession today goes up to the Arctic regions, will have a right, or should have a right, or has a right to all the lands that are to be found in the waters between a line extending from its eastern extremity north, and another line extending from the western extremity north. (. . .) This partition of the polar regions seems to be the most natural because it is simply a geographical one."

5. Castro (1958, 49) defined the expression *Defrontação*, in Portuguese, as a synonym for Polar Sectors, evoking Senator Poirier's speech of February 20, 1906. Despite the absence of the word "defrontation" in the English language's formal lexical, as Brazilian academia adopted Castro's taxonomy, we consider the relevance of using the neologism "defrontation."

6. The memorandum mentions a telegram issued by the Brazilian embassy in Buenos Aires on August 16, 1958. Furthermore, this situation would hamper Brazilian efforts to send scientists to the region for many years. It is one of the reasons why PROANTAR historically operates with Chilean support rather than Argentine.

7. Based on this theoretical perspective, Brazil would claim the sector of Antarctica located between the meridians of Arroio Chuí and the island of Martim Vaz.

8. Vinícius Lima, "Um pedaço da Antártica pertence ao Brasil." *Revista da Semana*, April 30, 1955. Brazilian National Newspaper Library. Accessed November 1, 2022. http://memoria.bn.br/DocReader/docreader.aspx?bib=025909_05&pasta=ano%20195&pesq=Antártida&pagfis=16314.

9. O Globo, "Também temos direito à Antártica." *O Globo*, February 9, 1956. https://acervo.oglobo.globo.com/consulta-ao-acervo/?navegacaoPorData=195019560209.

10. Brazilian Navy, "Seminário O Brasil na Antártica: balanço de quatro décadas."

11. The country soon realized that exploiting natural resources was both economically unfeasible and illegal, as established by the Madrid Protocol of 1991.

12. See Menezes (1971).

13. Brazilian Navy, "Programa Antártico Brasileiro (PROANTAR)." Accessed October 7, 2022. https://www.marinha.mil.br/secirm/pt-br/proantar/sobre.

14. For information provided by the Directorate of the Historical Heritage and Documentation of the Navy, see Brazilian Navy (2022).

15. Later, Brazil acquired the NApOc *Ary Rongel* (H-44), also known as the "Red Giant," built in Norway and commissioned to the Brazilian Navy in 1994.

16. Every ten years MCTI elaborates a ten-year plan that organizes and directs how science and funds shall be used. Proposals must be in line with such documents to get funds.

17. Brazilian Navy, " "Assinado o contrato de construção do Navio de Apoio Antártico." *Agência Marinha de Notícias*, June 13, 2022. https://www.marinha.mil.br /agenciadenoticias/assinado-o-contrato-de-construcao-do-navio-de-apoio-antartico.

18. Universidade Federal do Rio Grande do Sul, "Criosfera 2 embarca rumo à Antártica." Accessed September 29, 2022. http://www.ufrgs.br/ufrgs/noticias/ criosfera-2-embarca-rumo-a-antartica-1.

REFERENCES

Ainley, David, Peter Barrett, Robert Bindschadler, Andrew Clarke, Pete Convey, Eberhard Fahrbach, Julian Gutt, Dominic Hodgson, Mike Meredith, Alison Murray, Hans-Otto Pörtner, Guido di Prisco, Sigrid Schiel, Kevin Speer, Colin Summerhayes, John Turner, Cinzia Verde, and Anne Willems, "The Antarctic Environment in the Global System." In *Antarctic Climate Change and the Environment*, edited by John Turner Robert Bindschadler Pete Convey Guido di Prisco Eberhard Fahrbach Julian Gutt Dominic Hodgson Paul Mayewski Colin Summerhayes, 1–32. Cambridge: The Scientific Committee on Antarctic Research, Scott Polar Research Institute, 2009.

Allen, John R., Nicholas Burs, Laurie Garrett, Richard N. Haas, G. John Ikenberry, Kishore Mahbubani, Shivshankar Menon, Robin Niblett, Joseph S. Nye Jr, Shannon K. O'Neil, Kori Schake, and Stephen M. Walt. "How the world will look after the coronavirus pandemic." *Foreign Policy*, March 20, 2020. https://foreignpolicy.com /2020/03/20/world-order-after-coroanvirus-pandemic/.

Almeida, Maurício. "Navio Almirante Maximiano transporta pesquisadores na Antártica." *Agência Brasil*, November 8, 2019. https://agenciabrasil.ebc.com .br/geral/noticia/2019-11/navio-almirante-maximiano-transporta-pesquisadores-na -antartica. Accessed on 30/9/22.

Arpi, Bruno, Jeffrey McGee, Andrew Jackson, A. J. (Tony) Press, Tim Stephens, Lynda Goldsworthy, and Marcus Haward. "The Antarctic Treaty System in 2021 Important Anniversaries but Challenges for Consensus Decision-Making." *Polar Perspectives* 9 (2022): 1–8.

Barreira, Victor. "Brazil signs contract for Antarctic support ship." *Janes* (June 15, 2022). https://www.janes.com/defence-news/news-detail/brazil-signs-contract-for -antarctic-support-ship.

Barreira, Vitor. "Brazilian Navy accepts final H135 helicopter." *Janes* (December 22, 2021). https://www.janes.com/defence-news/news-detail/brazilian-navy-accepts -final-h135-helicopter.

Bouças, Wladimir F. "Antártida: uma reivindicação brasileira." *Mensário de Cultura Militar do Estado-Maior do Exército* VIII, no.90–91 (January-February 1956):1–13.

Boyadjian, Alain, Paulo Eduardo Aguiar Saraiva Câmara, Fábio Albergaria de Queiroz, and Ana Flávia Barros-Platiau. "Grand Challenges in Brazilian Scientific Research in Antarctica." In *Conservation of Living Resources in Areas Beyond National Jurisdiction: BBNJ and Antarctica*, edited by Ana Flávia Barros-Platiau and Carina Costa de Oliveira, 191–212. Rio de Janeiro: Editora Lumen Juris, 2020.

Brazil. World Panorama of International Politics: United Nations Organization. Didactic material classified as reserved by the Brazilian Government, Higher Course of War, General Staff of the Armed Forces, Presidency of the Republic. No. I-05–561 (1956). The Ministry of Foreign Relations Library, Historic Collection Section, Brasília. Consulted April 5, 2022.

Brazil. II Working Group, International Conjuncture, Brazilian War College. Composed by Col Felipe Augusto Short Coimbra, Col Antonio Henrique Almeida de Moraes, Col Av Armando Serra de Menezes, 2nd Secretary Frederico Meira de Vasconcellos, Col José de Ribamar Maciel Campos, Bachelor Milton Monteiro Moutinho, Engineer Luiz Romeiro Silva, no. TD-09–57 (1957). The Ministry of Foreign Relations Library, Historic Collection Section, Brasília. Consulted August 10, 2020.

Brazil. Telegram is classified as confidential by the Brazilian Government, from the Chief of Staff of the Air Force to the General Secretary of the Ministry of Foreign Relations. no. 09-01-40 (February 24, 1958a) The Ministry of Foreign Relations Library, Historic Collection Section, Brasília. Consulted August 10, 2020.

Brazil. "Brazilian interests in Antarctica." Telegram classified as confidential by the Brazilian Government, from the Chief of Staff of the Armed Forces to the Minister of Foreign Affairs, no. 18-B, (April 16, 1958b). The Ministry of Foreign Relations Library, Historic Collection Section, Brasília. Consulted August 10, 2020.

Brazil. "Charter of Consul Mário da Costa Lobo, Argentina and the Malvinas and Antarctica problems, Jurisdiction of the Brazilian Consulate in Bahia Blanca." Telegram, classified as confidential by the Brazilian Government, signed by José Marcus Vinícius de Souza (December 13, 1967a). The Ministry of Foreign Relations Library, Historic Collection Section, Brasília. Consulted August 10, 2020.

Brazil. "DAM Work Plan 1968." Memorandum, classified as confidential by the Brazilian Government, to the Assistant Secretary-General for American Affairs, signed by Espedito de Freitas Resende, Head of the South America Division. (December 19, 1967b) The Ministry of Foreign Relations Library, Historic Collection Section, Brasília. Consulted August 10, 2020.

Brazil. "Antarctica, Documentation, Theory of Defrontation." Telegram, classified as secret and urgent by the Brazilian Government, from the South America Division to the Brazilian Embassy in Montevideo, no.1068 (August 4, 1978). The Ministry of Foreign Relations Library, Historic Collection Section, Brasília. Consulted August 10, 2020.

Brazil. "Decree n.1791. Law," establishing the National Antarctic Research Committee, CONAPA. (January 15, 1996). http://www.planalto.gov.br/ccivil_03/decreto/1996/D1791.htm.

Brazil. "National Defense Policy." Law (1996). Consulted at the Library of Brazilian Presidency. http://www.biblioteca.presidencia.gov.br/publicacoes-oficiais/catalogo/fhc/politica-de-defesa-nacional-1996.pdf/view.

Brazil. "Decree n.10603." Law, presenting the National Antarctic Research Committee (January 20, 2021). http://www.planalto.gov.br/ccivil_03/_ato2019-2022/2021/decreto/D10603.htm.

Brazil. "O Comitê Nacional de Pesquisas Antárticas avaliará plano de ação científica brasileira na região." *Boletim diário MCTI*, May 2, 2022. https://repositorio.mctic.gov.br/bitstream/mctic/4272/1/2022_05_02_boletim_diario_mcti.pdf.

Brazilian Navy. "Aeronaves UH-17 do 1o Esquadrão de Helicópteros de emprego geral realizam primeiro voo na Antártica." Published November 26, 2020. https://www.marinha.mil.br/noticias/aeronaves-uh-17-do-1o-esquadrao-de-helicopteros-de-emprego-geral-realizam-primeiro-voo-na.

Brazilian Navy. "O Brasil na Antártica: balanço de quatro décadas." Accessed September 29, 2022. https://www.marinha.mil.br/secirm/proantar/noticias/seminario-mre.

Brazilian Navy. "Assinado o contrato de construção do Navio de Apoio Antártico." *Agência Marinha de Notícias*, June 13, 2022. https://www.marinha.mil.br/agenciadenoticias/assinado-o-contrato-de-construcao-do-navio-de-apoio-antartico.

Brazilian Navy. "Programa Antártico Brasileiro (PROANTAR)." Accessed October 7, 2022. https://www.marinha.mil.br/secirm/pt-br/proantar/sobre.

Câmara, Paulo Eduardo Aguiar Saraiva, and Renato Batista de Melo. "Brasil na Antártica, os próximos 30 anos." *Revista da Escola Superior de Guerra* 33, no. 68 (2018): 64–8.

Câmara, Paulo Eduardo Aguiar Saraiva, Ana Flávia Barros-Platiau, Luiane Magalhães Dias, Igor Magri de Queiroz, Isabella Monteiro Valentim, and Elaine Sampaio de Barros. "Potências Polares na Antártica e a Diplomacia Estratégica Brasileira." *Annals of the XVI Academic Congress on National Defense*, Naval War College, 2019.

Câmara, Paulo Eduardo Aguiar Saraiva, Ana Flávia Barros-Platiau, Israel de Oliveira Andrade, and Giovanni R.L. Hillebrand. "Brazil in Antarctica: 40 years of science." *Antarctic Science* 33 (2020): 30–38.

Câmara, Paulo Eduardo Aguiar Saraiva, and Micheline Carvalho-Silva. "180 years of botanical investigations in Antarctica and the role of Brazil." *Acta Botanica Brasilica* 34, no.2 (2020): 430–436.

Câmara, Paulo Eduardo Aguiar Saraiva, and Joanisval Brito Gonçalves. "O Incidente da Baía Esperanza: possibilidades de confrontação militar na Antártica." *Revista Marítima Brasileira* 144 (2022): 159–164.

Cunha, Guilherme Lopes da, Paulo Eduardo Aguiar Saraiva Câmara, Fábio Albergaria de Queiroz, and Ana Flávia Barros-Platiau. "O Pensamento Antártico Brasileiro e as Instituições de Defesa." *Revista da Escola Superior de Guerra* 37, no.81 (September / November 2022): 58–73.

Carvalho, Carlos Delgado de, and Therezinha de Castro (1956). "A questão da Antártica." *Revista do Clube Militar* 142 (April / July 1956): 502–506.

Castro, Therezinha de. "Antártica—o assunto do momento." *Boletim Geográfico* 16, no. 142 (January / February 1958): 42–49.

Chown, Steven L., and Rachel I. Leihy, Tim R. Naish, Cassandra M. Brooks, Peter Convey, Benjamin J. Henley, Andrew N. Mackintosh, Laura M. Phillips, Mahlon C. Kennicutt II, Susie M. Grant. *Antarctic Climate Change and the Environment: A Decadal Synopsis and Recommendations for Action.* Cambridge: Scientific Committee on Antarctic Research, 2022.

Coburn, S. "Eyeing 2048: Antarctic Treaty System's mining ban." *Columbia Journal of Environmental Law* 42 (2017): 1–6.

Colacrai, Miryam. *El Ártico y la Antártida en las relaciones internacionales.* Porto Alegre: Ufrgs Editora, 2004.

Collor, Lindolfo. "Os antecedentes: Polo Norte." Manuscript (June 1956), The Ministry of Foreign Relations Library, Historic Collection Section, Brasília. Consulted August 10, 2020.

Dalby, Simon. "Anthropocene Geopolitics: Globalisation, Empire, Environment and Critique." *Geography Compass* 1/1 (2007): 103–118.

Dalby, Simon. *Anthropocene Geopolitics: Globalization, Security, Sustainability.* Ottawa: University of Ottawa Press, 2020.

Ferreira, Felipe Rodrigues Gomes. "O sistema do tratado da Antártica: evolução do regime e seu impacto na política externa brasileira.: MA diss., Rio Branco Institute, Ministry of Foreign Affairs, 2005.

Head, Ivan L. "Canadian Claims to Territorial Sovereignty in the Arctic Regions." *McGill Law Journal* 9, no. 3 (1963): 200–226.

Lima, Vinícius. "Um pedaço da Antártica pertence ao Brasil." *Revista da Semana*, April 30, 1955. Brazilian National Newspaper Library. Accessed November 1, 2022. http://memoria.bn.br/DocReader/docreader.aspx?bib=025909_05&pasta=ano%20195&pesq=Antártida&pagfis=16314.

Marcher, Andressa, Ronaldo T. Bernardo, Jefferson C. Simões, and Jeffrey Auger. "Water stable isotopes in snow along a traverse of the West Antarctic Ice Sheet: insights into moisture origins, air-masses distillation history, and climatic value." *An Acad Bras Cienc* 94, (Suppl. 1 2022): e20210353.

Mattos, Leonardo Faria, "O Brasil e a adesão ao Tratado da Antártica: uma Análise de Política Externa no Governo Geisel." MA diss., Fluminense Federal University, 2015.

Mattos, Leonardo Faria, and Paulo Eduardo Aguiar Saraiva Câmara. "A Ciência Antártica como Ferramenta Geopolítica para o Brasil." *Revista Marítima Brasileira* 140 (2020): 15–23.

Menezes, Eurípedes Cardoso. "Declaração da Antártica." (Speech, the Brazilian Chamber of Deputies, April 23, 1971).

O Globo. "Também temos direito à Antártica." *O Globo*, February 9, 1956. https://acervo.oglobo.globo.com/consulta-ao-acervo/?navegacaoPorData=195019560209.

Pedone, Luiz, and Gabriele Marina Molina Hernández. "A reconstrução da Estação Antártica Comandante Ferraz." *Revista Brasileira de Estudos Estratégicos* 12, no. 23 (2020): 37–55.

Poirier, Pascal (1906). "Possession of the Lands in the North of the Dominion." In *Debates of the Senate of the Dominion of Canada (1906–7)*, edited by Holland Bros (Speech, The Senate of Canada, February 20, 1906, 10th Parliament, 3rd Session: Vol. 1) https://parl.canadiana.ca/view/oop.debates_SOC1003_01.

Pierro, Bruno de. "Estação na Antártica é reaberta: nova infraestrutura, que tem capacidade para 64 pessoas e 17 laboratórios, substitui base incendiada em 2012." *Pesquisa Fapesp,* January 13, 2020. https://revistapesquisa.fapesp.br/estacao-antartica-e-reinaugurada/.

Rocha, Flávio Augusto Viana. "Sistema do Tratado da Antártica: Aspectos geopolíticos e econômicos decorrentes de uma crescente internacionalização do Continente Antártico e seus reflexos para o Brasil e para a MB." Maritime Policy and Strategy Course diss., Brazilian Naval War College, 2011.

Rosa, Luiz Henrique. "The Antarctic Science Ten Year Plan (2023–2032): perceptions as a member of the National Committee on Antarctic Research (CONAPA)." Interviewed by Guilherme Lopes da Cunha. November 30, 2022. Exchange of electronic messages.

Sánchez, Ignacio José García. "La Antártida 2050: horizontes foscos." *Cuadernos de estrategia: Instituto Español de Estudios Estratégicos Madrid* 198 (2018): 229–260.

Silva, Paulo Vecchi Ruiz Cardoso da. "Brasil, um país polar: a presença brasileira na Antártica e as perspectivas no Ártico." Higher Studies diss., Brazilian War College, 2020.

Simões, Jefferson Cardia, Carlos Alberto Eiras Garcia, Heitor Evangelista, José Goldenberg, Lucia de Siqueira Campos, Maurício Magalhães Mata, and Ulisses Franz Breme. *Antártica e as Mudanças Globais: Um Desafio para a Humanidade.* São Paulo: Editora Blucher, 2011.

Smith, Jason. "Melting the Myth of Arctic Exceptionalism." *Modern War Institute at West Point,* August 19, 2022. https://mwi.usma.edu/melting-the-myth-of-arctic-exceptionalism/.

Thorp, Arabella. "Antarctica: the treaty system and territorial claims." *House of Commons: International affairs and Defense Section*, July 18, 2012. http://researchbriefings.files.parliament.uk/documents/SN05040/SN05040.pdf.

Universidade Federal do Rio Grande do Sul. "Criosfera 2 embarca rumo à Antártica." Accessed September 29, 2022. http://www.ufrgs.br/ufrgs/noticias/criosfera-2-embarca-rumo-a-antartica-1.

Chapter 7

Antarctic Science as a Diplomatic, Conservation, Economic, and Geopolitical Tool for Brazil at the Past, Present, and Near Future

Heading to 2048

Paulo E. A. S. Câmara and Luiz Henrique Rosa

For more than forty years, Brazil has had a solid presence in Antarctica. That presence has made it indeed a polar country, even if most of its population still see themselves as citizens from a tropical country, celebrated by its luxurious forests, hot weather and warm waters, beaches, and beautiful sand dunes, rather than its presence in Antarctica. In 2021 Brazil celebrated forty years since its first expedition to Antarctica. From its humble start to present day, a long journey has led the country to a new, state-of-the-art scientific station and forty years of a successful and uninterrupted Antarctic science program. The Brazilian Antarctic Program (PROANTAR) is likely the most prolonged and oldest science program still operating in the country, an unusually successful case in Brazilian science.

One of the reasons for PROANTAR's success is that it works in close collaboration with several partners: the armed forces (especially the navy and air force), the Ministry of Science, Technology, and Innovations (MCTI), the Ministry of the Environment (MMA), and the Ministry of Foreign Affairs (MRE), as well as universities and research centers all over the country. These are the ultimate agents responsible for cutting-edge scientific research, a fundamental tool for Antarctic geopolitics, as we will discuss below. In the current chapter, we will present the importance of the Antarctic science for Brazil, directly associated with diplomatic, conservation, economic, and geopolitical aspects, which will be necessary soon, mainly in 2048, when the Antarctic Treaty will be discussed again.

1. BRAZIL AND THE ANTARCTIC TREATY: THE STRATEGIC ROLE OF SCIENCE

The Antarctic Treaty was initially signed by twelve countries in 1959 and entered into force in 1961. It is a unique instrument of governance and is currently accepted by fifty-three signatory countries. Later documents and agreements have rendered it the status of a system, usually referred to as Antarctic Treaty System (ATS). The ATS governs the entire planet area above parallel 60° S, totaling approximately 14 million square kilometers, about 8 percent of the planet. Brazil acceded to the Antarctic Treaty in 1975, within the context of the Cold War. In 1982, through Decree No. 86.830 from January 12, PROANTAR was created. In September of the same year, Brazil acquired its first polar ship,*Barão de Teffé*, an oceanographic research ship.

Furthermore, the first Antarctic Operation (OPERANTAR I) took place in the summer of 1982/1983 took place, which aimed to select a place to establish a Brazilian scientific station, the Comandante Ferraz Antarctic Station (see figure 7.1). This activity was paramount, allowing the country to become a consultative member of the treaty on September 27, 1983. However, our policy has remained unchanged after a great initial effort. Therefore, policies must be rethought and updated, conceiving the current global scenario and projections for 2048 or beyond.

It is of great importance to note that, among the fifty-three current signatory countries, only twenty-nine have the right to vote in decisions concerning Antarctic territory. They are the so-called consultative parties. Contrary to what one might think, the status of a country as a consultative member is not due to its occupation, territorial claim, or the construction of bases/stations.

Figure 7.1. The Old Brazilian Station (EACF) is Located at Admiralty Bay, King George Island, South Shetland. Personal Photographs.

It is clear from Article IX of the treaty that the status of consultative parties is due to "the promotion there of substantial scientific research activity." So, it should contemplate the vanguard of Antarctic science, meaning the publications of research results in international scientific journals, as well as in international scientific congresses and conferences (Câmara and Melo, 2018). It is noteworthy that international publications represent eternal documents proving the scientific performance of a country in the Antarctic region. Thus, a country's membership in the treaty does not confer its consultative status unless it can prove its commitment to scientific research. The other parties should still accept this proof, as in Brazil's case.

We can see that science is the tool that guarantees Brazil's (as any other country's) right to vote in parity with other world nations. Without it, we would never have been admitted as consultative members; without it, we could even lose such privileged status (Mattos and Câmara, 2020). As a consultative member of the ATS, Brazil's right to veto and vote is equal to all other countries, including world powers such as the United Statesl, Russia, China, England, and France, among others. Perhaps this is one of the few world forums in which Brazil has this high status guaranteed by its scientific activity and quality.

2. BRAZIL AND ANTARCTICA: NATURAL RESOURCES AND ECONOMIC POTENTIAL

It is estimated that Antarctica has extensive reserves of still untapped natural resources (strategic minerals, oil, gas, and others) and the largest reserve of fresh water in the world (about 70%). In addition, despite the extreme conditions, Antarctica has different wild and unexplored ecosystems. It demonstrates to shelter different life forms: plants, microorganisms, and animals able to produce biological compounds (antibiotics, enzymes, biosurfactants, antioxidant and photoprotective pigments, herbicides, and others) useful in the biotechnological process. Antarctic extremophile organisms have been shown as a comprehensive source of metabolites. Countries such as the United States, Japan, Chile, Argentina, and Brazil have already requested patents for some of those compounds or organisms' physiology, which might contribute to essential productive economic sectors in medicine, agriculture, and industry.

Brazil is the seventh country closest to Antarctica and the largest country in the South Atlantic, which is influenced by the Southern Ocean surrounding Antarctica. Climatic phenomena that occur in Antarctica profoundly affect Brazil's climate, rainfall regimes, fishing, and other activities. Thus, it is easy to imagine that the changes that occur in the Antarctic climate will also significantly affect Brazil. Similarly, human activities that generate pollution will be felt quickly in our country, much faster than in most other members-countries of the Antarctic Treaty. Therefore, effective participation in political decisions related to Antarctica is essential to Brazil because they affect the country directly. However, we stress (once again) that this participation in political decisions can only be carried out by countries that perform good scientific research there. Again, scientific research is undoubtedly a tremendous geopolitical tool in the Antarctic scenario (Mattos and Câmara, 2020).

Today, a moratorium is in effect that prohibits the exploration of mineral resources like water, oil, or gas. Also, Antarctica is recognized as a place fully dedicated to science and peace. It is important to note also that the exploration of natural resources in Antarctica is very complicated logistically and is currently not economically viable. However, as climate changes progresses and ice-free areas and the demand for new mineral resources grow larger, this scenario may change quickly. In this context, the moratorium on mineral exploration may end in 2048, bringing some other changes, and Brazil must keep that in mind when elaborating its new policies and diplomacy.

In the late 1950s, some Brazilian scholars were interested in Antarctica. In this context, a series of papers (e.g., Castro, 1956) claimed that Brazil should pose a territorial claim to parts of Antarctica like some other countries (e.g., Chile, Argentina, the United Kingdom, New Zealand, Australia, Norway, and France). Even though Brazil has never posed any territorial claim, much later in 2016, the country's National Defense Policy (BRASIL, 2016), a document approved by the country's parliament, considered Antarctica as part of the Brazilian strategic surroundings. Even facing, over the decades, several challenges in other areas (social, economic, and political), Brazil's uninterrupted presence in the frozen continent is a notorious sign of the country's determination and commitment to polar science and the future of Antarctica.

3. BRAZILIAN PRESENCE IN ANTARCTICA:
THE EARLY YEARS AND NOW

Câmara et al. (2020) recognized four phases in Brazilian Antarctic science development. However, for the purposes of this chapter, we will reduce them to two: the first was the beginning, when the country worked hard to establish itself in Antarctica, meaning acquiring a polar vessel, organizing the first expeditions, acquiring knowledge, building a station, building the three refugia and beginning the support of polar flights.

In just a few years, the first phase has led Brazil to much gains. However, in the mid-1990s, the situation came to a second phase: keeping what was accomplished thus far, with no new or ambitious steps taken. There were signs of progress as science continued to advance and papers and theses were being published; there was also the acquisition of two new polar vessels to replace the already old *Barão de Teffé*, and there were renovations and expansions at EACF, but there were also losses, as one of the three mentioned refugia was dismantled.

Other than that, no further program expansions happened for many years, and we could say that this was a phase of relatively smooth stability. PROANTAR kept doing the same activities in the same geographic region for many years. An important exception happened in 2012 with the inauguration of Cryosphere 1, an automated module located on mainland Antarctica, more than 2,000 kilometers from the Brazilian station, being the southernmost Latin American science station. This event led to an entirely new logistics for Brazil and allowed the country's presence much further south and into the mainland, an area yet unexplored for Brazil.

After more than forty years, we can summarize that Brazil currently cements its presence in Antarctica through a base (Comandante Ferraz Antarctic Station—EACF), two refuges (one on Elephant Island and the other on Nelson Island), and two polar ships, plus the Cryosphere 1 module. This data suggests that Brazilian presence in Antarctica is more modest in terms of infrastructure than several other countries, including our South American neighbors, such as Uruguay, Chile, and Argentina. However, science still needs to catch up. According to Boyadjian et al. (2020), Brazil occupies the twenty-fifth position on scientific papers published on Antarctic science, still above some of our neighboring countries like Chile, Argentina, and Uruguay, and it is the leader in scientific publications in Latin America, with solid scientific collaborations, mainly with the United States, France, Argentina, the United Kingdom, and Spain (Boyadjian et al., 2020).

4. BRAZILIAN PRESENCE IN ANTARCTICA NOW AND THE FUTURE: THE NEXT PHASE

After a period of rapid growth and the second phase of stabilization, Brazil is on the verge of a new moment: the outcome of a new horizon in 2048. This possible new phase has some new vital elements that could play an important role:

1. The elaboration and approval of a new Brazilian Polar Policy (POLANTAR). A key government document that regulates and guides

any public policies concerning Brazilian polar activities, the original POLANTAR was signed in 1987, written during the Cold War and when Brazil was still in its early years of Antarctic presence. A new and more comprehensive document paves the way for a much wider window for polar activity and policy.

2. The elaboration and approval of a new science plan. In 2013, the Ministry of Science and Technology released a critical document titled: "Antarctic Science for Brazil, an Action Plan for 2013–2022." Although it was designed to give guidance to the science performed under PROANTAR, a new plan for 2023–2032 sets the opportunity to revisit our scientific plans and gives further and updated directions.

3. Another new and essential factor in this scenario was the inauguration of the new EACF (see figure7.2). After the fire that consumed it in February 2012, the new EACF was inaugurated in 2020 and is an essential tool for Antarctic science and, therefore, of local geopolitics.

With 4,500 square miles and seventeen new and fully equipped laboratories, the new EACF is the largest research station in the entire region of the Antarctic Peninsula. Although Brazil has only a single station, the current one is state-of-the-art in all aspects, from its bold architecture and the intelligent use of renewable energies to comfort and safety. However, what draws the most attention are its seventeen research laboratories (see figure 7.3). As we have previously commented, science is a geopolitical tool. The new EACF makes this very clear with its new laboratories. EACF also has fast internet service, a conference room, a gym, and a library.

4. With the inevitable aging of Brazilian vessels, the navy is working on constructing a new polar vessel. The new vessel is not going to be an icebreaker. However, it will have a substantially higher ice resistance that will increase its range, making it possible to reach and explore further

Figure 7.2. The new Comandante Ferraz Antarctic Station is located at Admiralty Bay, King George Island, South Shetland, located on the same site as the old one, destroyed in 2012 and opened on January 16, 2020. Personal Photographs.

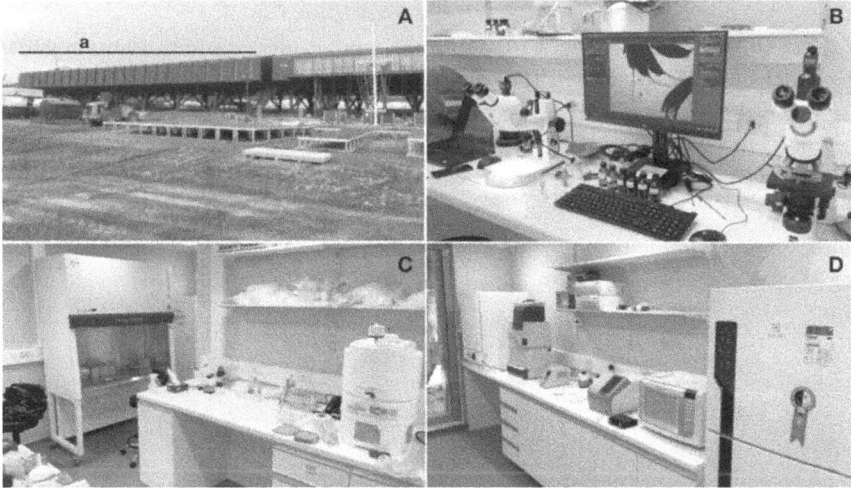

Figure 7.3. Research labs of the new Comandante Ferraz Antarctic Station. A= Station façade and lab building (a), B= Microscopy, C and D= Molecular Biology. Photos Taken by the Authors.

south, to areas now out of PROANTAR's reach and regions with more ice, like the Weddell Sea. Another advantage is increasing the time range for operations, allowing the austral polar season to start earlier and end later. The new vessel will be built in Brazil and will likely take about three to five years to be fully operational.

5. The use of the new cargo plane KC-390 *Millenium* (see figure 7.4 A). It will increase logistic capacity, saving fuel and time in the vital transit from Brazil to Antarctica and back. In addition, the new aircraft has the potential to increase logistic capacity replacing the old Lockheed C-130 Hercules, as it has higher cargo capacity.

6. New helicopters. The Navy has operated the Helibrás AS-355F2 (Aérospatiale AS355F2), known in the Brazilian Navy as UH-13, in Antarctica since 1995 when it replaced the old Westland WASP (known in the Brazilian Navy as UH-2). In addition, the navy recently acquired three new Airbus H-135 T3s (Eurocopter EC135), known in the Brazilian Navy as UH-17. In the summer of 2020/2021, it made its *debut* in Antarctica (see figure 7.4 B). These new helicopters will increase range, cargo, and personnel capacity and safety for Brazilian operations.

7. The COVID pandemic. The disease revealed our dependence on other countries, like Chile and Argentina. The closing of the Chilean borders has resulted in severe logistical challenges and even halted scientific operations in the summer of 2020/2021. However, with some lessons learned, new ideas and logistics are now in place.

8. The 2048 horizon, which should be a direction for PROANTAR. In 2048, changes can happen in the ATS governing system, including the end of the moratorium for natural resources exploration and changes in the ATS voting system.

All those aspects mentioned above, from politics to logistics, could represent a good opportunity for a new and more focused phase, so Brazil keeps track of changes and opportunities that this could bring. It is also essential to keep close contact and collaborate with other countries on their expectations for 2048.

5. THE ANTARCTIC RESEARCH: LOGISTICAL ASPECTS

The armed forces provide logistics in PROANTAR. With logistics, it is possible to carry out the necessary science in loco. In logistical terms, Antarctic research can only be carried out during the summer, usually from early November to late March. Therefore, going to Antarctica takes work. It is somehow dangerous and quite complex, involving the armed forces, especially the Brazilian Navy, as well as the use of cargo aircraft of the Brazilian Air Force, the Lockheed C-130 Hercules and, more recently, the Embraer KC-390 Millenium. Therefore, we can say that research takes place on three different logistic platforms, 1) the EACF, 2) the ships (see figure 7.5), and 3) the camping sites (see figure 7.6). The *Almirante Maximiano* polar ship (H-41), which with its five laboratories, is a trustworthy mobile research platform, enabling research in regions more distant from the EACF.

Furthermore, the ship allows for surveys otherwise impossible to be carried out from the EACF. Also, it provides a unique platform for oceanography and marine biology studies. The second (but much older) ship is the oceanographic support ship *Ary Rongel*, a ship whose main task is to provide logistic support for EACF regarding equipment, gear, fuel, and food. Nevertheless, launching the camping sites and moving scientists to different locations in the South Shetlands (one small lab only), its science capacities are more limited than the other vessel (*Maximiano*).

Important science also takes place in camps, where researchers can stay during the summer for much more extended periods in different regions of the Antarctic Peninsula far from the EACF. In general, about three to five camps occur each Antarctic summer, each lasting as many as three months. The camps' logistics are complex and provided by the Brazilian Navy, which also maintains the EACF and the ships, constituting a fundamental pillar for research.

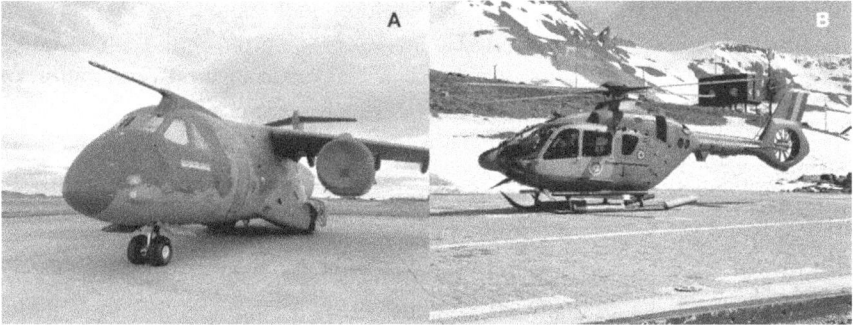

Figure 7.4. A) The new Embraer KC-390 Millenium supporting PROANTAR. B) The New Helicopter H135 (UH-17). Photos Taken by the Authors.

Figure 7.5. Polar Ship Almirante Maximiano H41 (left) and Oceanographic Support Ship Ary Rongel (H44) (right). Photos Taken by the Authors.

Figure 7.6. Camping Site Established on Deception Island. Photos Taken by the Authors.

6. THE ANTARCTIC RESEARCH: SCIENTIFIC ASPECTS

Prior to 1991, both science and logistics were provided by the navy (Câmara et al., 2020). However, since 1991, Antarctic research has been financed through the Ministry of Science, Technology, and Innovation (MCTI) and its funding agency, the National Council for Scientific and Technological Development (CNPq), and still modest participation in the Coordination of Higher Education Personnel (CAPES). The research is currently MCTI's responsibility, funded by public calls. In order to better understand how investments, funds, and project numbers supported over the years in PROANTAR work, we suggest the text of Câmara et al. (2020).

The research is currently divided into large areas: life sciences, earth sciences, and atmospheric sciences, according to Antarctic Science for Brazil, and an Action Plan for 2013–2022. Those areas are put together in five different programs: 1) the role of the cryosphere in the earth system and its interactions with South America; 2) biocomplexity of Antarctic ecosystems, their connections with South America and climate change; 3) climate change and the Southern Ocean; 4) geodynamics and geological history of Antarctica and its relations with South America; 5) dynamics of the upper Antarctic atmosphere, geospace interactions, and connections with South America. In addition, there is also an opening for new research areas, especially the ones connected to the Arctic.

There are usually twenty-two Brazilian research projects in Antarctica per call. In addition, national and international collaborations are fundamental and notorious in Antarctic Science. For a better understanding of Brazil's collaborative networks under the Antarctic treaty, see Boyadjian et al. (2020).

Unlike other countries like Chile and Argentina, Brazil does not have a polar institute, so most of its research is produced in different universities and institutes across the country and involves all mentioned areas like biology, climate, atmosphere, glaciology, geology, medicine, archaeology, basic science, and applied science.

In 2021, a new ocean on planet Earth was recognized, the Southern Ocean, which surrounds Antarctica. It is well-known that the masses of cold water of the Southern Ocean migrate through the marine currents, pass through the Confluence Brazil-Malvinas and reach the Brazilian coast with notorious physical-chemical effects on the marine biodiversity of the South Atlantic. In other words, it interferes with the Brazilian Blue Amazon (oceanic part of Brazilian sovereignty) and all its biodiversity, including fish.

The climatic dynamics that begin in the central part of Antarctica (cold fronts, for example) advance through the Antarctic Peninsula, pass through southern South America and reach Brazil. That is, the climate of Antarctica affects the climate of Brazil and, consequently, the agribusiness of Brazil. Therefore, systems for monitoring these cold air masses can help Brazilian agribusiness prevent potential losses.

Despite the extreme conditions, the different ecosystems of Antarctica are home to a high diversity of living organisms. There are animals, plants, algae, and microorganisms with the potential for biotechnological studies. It spurs the capabilities for producing enzymes, antibiotics, pigments, photoprotection, antifreeze substances, and detergents, among others of interest in medicine, agriculture, and the industrial sector of Brazil. The discovery of these substances has outstanding potential for developing bioproducts for job creation and moving the economy with high figures for agribusiness and industrial sectors in Brazil. According to Silva et al. (2022), Antarctica holds organisms with unique physiological and biochemical characteristics, with great importance as a potential source of new compounds with antimicrobial activity. Despite the legal uncertainties, there is a growing interest in the scientific community in Antarctica's biotechnological potential, and more patents have been applied to Antarctic products. According to Silva et al. (2022), China is the leading country in Antarctic antimicrobial patents, followed by the United States, South Korea, and Sweden. Brazil is not among the top five and still needs to catch up concerning antimicrobial patents. Again, according to Silva et al. (2022), universities are by far the primary source of Antarctic antimicrobial patents, demonstrating the high relevance of universities for Antarctic science.

The science projects at PROANTAR also include students from different levels, from undergraduate to graduate programs, and consequently, the training of higher-level human resources for Brazilian science, which contributes to the scientific and technological advancement of the country. In addition, by PROANTAR partnering with different countries, it increases Brazil's internationalization and exchange of knowledge and technologies.

7. THE DOWNSIDE

Despite its forty years of history and great importance to the country, both for the products generated and geopolitical aspects, Antarctic science is still poorly understood by the population and the governing segments of the country. This fact has eventually resulted in a lack of resources that may threaten our privileged status as a consultative party of ATS. It is essential to warn that, without adequate resources, both for science and logistics, Brazil will be doomed to a worrying secondary role within the Antarctic science scenario worldwide, and its permanence as a consultative member of the Antarctic Treaty is threatened.

The uncertainty of budget availability creates uncertainty. Therefore, many scientists have avoided the issue due to financial instability, which adds to the highly adverse and dangerous working conditions. In addition, the training of human resources on the subject usually needs to be improved as there is usually a lack of resources for scholarships and permanent positions in research institutions in Brazil.

Parallel to this, the formation of new Brazilian Antarctic researchers ceased. The lack of scholarships, especially at the postdoctoral level, and permanent positions, causes an exodus of highly qualified researchers to other countries or areas of knowledge. After a student becomes skilled in the subject, the loss of this researcher represents an additional cost to the country, meaning a waste of all the resources invested from the undergraduate phase through the master's degree and doctorate (ca. ten years). It is also important to note that, because PROANTAR is decentralized, universities implement most Antarctic research, including patents, so budgetary shortage in education and lack of scholarships also profoundly affect science in Antarctica.

Funding cuts have been frequent over the last four decades. Nonetheless, on the other hand, the logistic segment of PROANTAR has succeeded in keeping with the logistics and even expanding it. In contrast, the cuts have a much more significant effect in the science segment. Whether this is a matter of priority or politics should be the subject of further consideration and studies.

CONCLUSION

For forty years, Brazil has built a solid reputation in Antarctica and can proudly claim to be a polar country. Brazil is accumulating huge assets and much expertise over the decades. With fast initial growth and a somehow stagnant period, now Brazil has the opportunity to start a new period of its Antarctic presence. For this new era, it is fundamental to keep in mind the changes that may occur in 2048. We must set a goal on where we want to be, as a country, when 2048 arrives. This scenario involves diplomacy and science production. It is more critical more now than ever to be present in 2048 with a solid reputation and high-quality science. This need means overcoming budget cuts, recruiting new people for the cause, and educating the population and parliament on the importance of the ATS.

To overcome the downsides that can hamper the country's efforts to reach a more assertive position shortly, we suggest actions such as: including the polar theme in school curricula; training new generations of diplomats in polar themes; increasing investments in science and logistics, and securing its constancy; creating a high-ranking group of scientists, military, and diplomats of notorious knowledge in polar themes for advising decision-makers and government in polar themes. A road map is vital, since any new construction in Antarctica constitutes a long and painful process. For example, it took Brazil almost eight years to rebuild its only station. Ships take up to five years to be operational, and so on. It looks like 2048 is already knocking on the door.

REFERENCES

Boyadjian, A., P. E. A. S Câmara, F. A. Queiroz, and A. F. B. Platiau. "Grand challenges in Brazilian scientific research in antarctica." In *Conservação dos recursos vivos em áreas além da jurisdição nacional*, edited by Ana Flávia Barros-Platiau, and Carina Costa de Oliveira, 191–212. Rio de Janeiro: Editora Lumen Juris, 2020.

Brasil. "Petition no. 5723/2016." Law, The Brazilian Deputy Chamber (2016). Accessed November 22, 2022. https://www.camara.leg.br/proposicoesWeb/prop _mostrarintegra?codteor=1519805&filename=Despacho-REQ+5723/2016-22/12 /2016.

Câmara, P. E. A. S., Ana Flávia Barros-Platiau, Israel De Oliveira Andrade, and Giovanni R. L. Hillebrand.:Brazil in Antarctica: 40 years of science." *Antarctic Science* 33, no.1 (2020): 30–38.

Câmara, P. E. A. S., and R. B. Melo. "Brasil na antártica, os próximos 30 anos." *Revista da Escola Superior de Guerra* 33, no.68 (2018): 64–81.

Mattos, L. F., and P. E. A. S.Câmara. "A ciência antártica como ferramenta geopolítica para o Brasil." Revista Marítima Brasileira 140, no.01/03 (2020): 15–23.

Silva, Maurício B., Alexya O. Feitosa, Igor Lima, James Bispo, Ana Santos, Magna Moreira, Paulo E. A. S. Camara, Luiz Rosa, Valéria Oliveira, Alysson Duarte, and Aline Queiroz. "Antarctic organisms as a source of antimicrobial compounds: a patent review." *Anais da Academia Brasileira de Ciências* 94, no.1 (2022):1–21.

Chapter 8

Scientific Research in the Face of Antarctic Geopolitics

An Evaluation of the Fioantar Project by Fuzzy Cognitive Maps

Luiz Octávio Gavião, Adriana Marcos Vivoni,
and Maria Lucia Marques da Fonseca

The Antarctic Treaty, of which Brazil is one of the signatories, guarantees the peaceful use of the continent under the main purpose of scientific research. Brazil's interest is motivated by the geographical proximity between Antarctica and South America, which makes the polar environment and climate highly relevant to our continent. Therefore, Brazil has maintained a permanent presence in the region through the Comandante Ferraz Antarctic Station (EACF), located on the Keller Peninsula, since the 1980s. Thenceforth, the Brazilian Antarctic Program (PROANTAR) has registered an annual average of twenty research projects contemplating oceanography, biology, glaciology, geology, and meteorology. It represents a crucial Brazilian initiative in the scientific field (Andrade et al., 2018).

Despite the various research projects in the region, there are still few studies on the impact of the environment on human and animal health or the continent and South America. In this context, the Oswaldo Cruz Foundation developed a research project, Fioantar,[1] to study possible interactions or threats to public health originating in the Antarctic continent. The project is intended to study viruses, bacteria, fungi, lichens, micro bacteria, and helminths, which may be present in animals that live or circulate in the region, in water, in soil, and even permafrost, which is a type of soil found in polar regions and formed by land, ice, and rocks that are permanently frozen.

Thus, Fioantar can contribute to epidemiological surveillance, potential typing pathogens, and discovery of molecules or enzymes with biotechnological potential (Degrave, 2020).

Fiocruz installed a permanent laboratory at EACF to conduct research directly in Antarctica. Fiolab is a biosafety laboratory prepared to respond to the country's epidemiological and health surveillance needs and to support health and environmental research in Antarctica. The laboratory's performance is integrated with other Fiocruz reference laboratories in Brazil, allowing support for research that identifies microorganisms that inhabit the continent and present biotechnological potential in medicine (new drugs), environment (bioremediation), and industry (new industrial enzymes). In addition, Fiolab supports the training of researchers and future specialists in Antarctic studies applied to public health (Brazil, 2019).

The sustainability of a scientific project depends on several requirements, also called factors or variables, whose presence guarantees the longevity of its activities and impact. The requirements in table 8.1 are based on information published by Miller (2014), who analyzed the sustainability of fishing activities in Antarctica. As a general model this can be applied in other contexts, including scientific research projects. For example, fishing requires natural resources, which means the existence of species in the region; scientific research also needs to collect material for laboratory analysis. Likewise, both fishing and scientific research need human and financial resources, among others, to carry out their activities.

However, Fioantar and other scientific projects that "feed" PROANTAR may suffer, directly or indirectly, from the positive and negative effects of

Table 8.1 Research Project Requirements

Requirements	Description
C1—Natural resources	Stock of natural resources (viruses, fungi, and bacteria present in the Antarctic environment), existing in the region, which are essential inputs for scientific research.
C2—Infrastructure resources	Logistics infrastructure (Antarctic station, support points in the country, navy ships and air force aircraft, military bases in Chile and Argentina, among others) that make scientific research feasible.
C3—Human resources	Capacity, knowledge, experience, and motivation of the researchers and students who support the projects.
C4—Financial resources	Public and/or private financial resources to make scientific research viable.
C5—Scientific networking	Cooperation and networking of scientists, who leverage scientific research through the exchange of knowledge, data, information, among others.

Source: adaptad from (Miller, 2014).

Antarctic geopolitics, which involves the most diverse international interests in the region. Thus, this chapter aims to associate Fioantar's requirements with the main driving forces that involve these geopolitical dynamics. This makes it possible to assess trends and implications that affect the essential needs of the project and ensure its sustainability, helping to reassess the distribution of material, human, and financial resources over time. To simulate the interactions between the different forms and factors that involve Fioantar and Antarctic geopolitics, the methodology of fuzzy cognitive maps (FCMs) was used to model the system and produced results analyzed below.

1. ANTARCTICA GEOPOLITICS

The world is experiencing cycles of geopolitical turmoil, and Antarctica is not immune to its reflexes (Magnoli, 2013). While governance in Antarctica appears to be relatively stable compared to other regions, the circumstances surrounding interstate interests on the continent have evolved in recent decades (Ferrada, 2018; McGee et al., 2019, Liu, 2019). In this context, a series of questions can be raised: Will the region's political future remain stable? How will states balance the region's economic interests (fisheries, in particular)? Can the status quo regarding territorial claims continue? How will climate change affect the interests and actions of states in Antarctica? Will the current mining ban continue in perpetuity? Can the region remain demilitarized?

To seek answers to these questions, a group of researchers from the University of Tasmania in Australia analyzed the prospects for political stability in the Antarctic region (McGee et al., 2022). Considering geopolitics as the intersection between power, authority, and geographic space in the rivalry between states, the authors took a multidisciplinary approach to analyze the future of the Antarctic Treaty System. Thus, they established a series of geopolitical scenarios through the Oxford scenario planning approach (OSPA) method, with a particular focus on the issue of militarization of the region (Ramirez et al., 2016). The purpose of the work was to present a systematic framework capable of helping the political, scientific, academic, and media communities regarding the geopolitical future of Antarctica. In addition, the authors comprehensively analyzed the existing literature on scenarios for the region, highlighting the research by Liggett et al. (2017), Tin et al. (2013), Powell et al. (2014), Frame (2020), Frame et al. (2021), among others.

For the elaboration of scenarios, a fundamental step is the identification of driving forces. They are paramount causal factors for understanding the field under analysis, considered "the elements that animate a scenario" (Schwartz, 2012). To ensure that the most relevant dimensions of the external environment are raised, the acronym "PESTLE" was used, which indicates six categories at a macro level: political, economic, social, technological, legal, and environmental (Liggett et al., 2017). In addition, another three dimensions usually are added due to the geopolitical nature of the problem: geographic, strategic, and historical (McGee et al., 2022).

For the analysis of Antarctic geopolitics, the authors surveyed forty-nine driving forces submitted to specialists for risk assessment, considering two variables: the degree of uncertainty and the degree of importance of each driving force. A 4-point Likert scale allowed the variables to be modulated between totally uncertain (or certain) and totally important (or irrelevant). The multiplication of the values in the scale, referring to each choice, gave the final risk score of the driving forces. Then, the two most critical driving forces for generating the scenarios were selected for their elaboration: (1) the stability of the international system, from the point of view of the Antarctic Treaty, which can reduce the balance in international relations, given the eventual shifts toward multipolarity and power competition, particularly between China, Russia, and the United States, with a potential spillover effect in Antarctica; (2) the strategic advantage of militarizing Antarctica and the Southern Ocean for nonpeaceful activities such as research and activities for military purposes. The alternation in intensity for these variables gave rise to five scenarios. Figure 8.1 was constructed based on information published by McGee et al. (2022).

The "Splendid Isolation" scenario is characterized by low tension between countries, given the stability of the international system at its highest level and the consensus that the militarization of Antarctica does not bring strategic

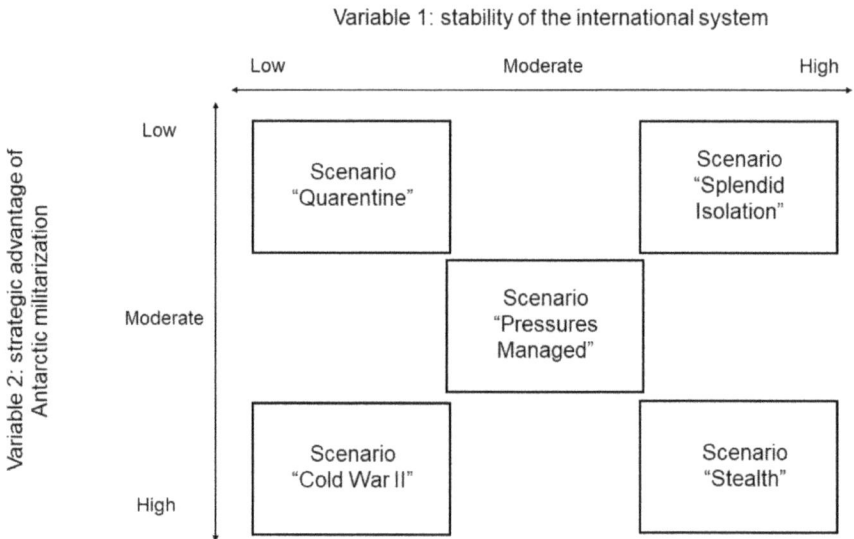

Figure 8.1.   *Scenarios.* (McGee et al., 2022).

advantages. The "Quarantine" scenario describes a future in which Antarctic geopolitics is in "quarantine" from global tensions. There is great competition for power in the international system, but the strategic value of conducting military activities in the Antarctic continent remains latent. The "Stealth" scenario illustrates a future in which Antarctica is militarized stealthily so as not to generate reactions to the expansion of military personnel and equipment in the region. Although international tension is reduced, there is a perception that using equipment and personnel for military purposes generates a high strategic advantage. The "Cold War II" scenario describes a militarization effort in Antarctica. This scenario illustrates a plausible (and alarming) future in which there is high international tension between the great powers and high strategic advantage for states that carry out military activities on the continent and in the Southern Ocean. Finally, the "Pressures Managed" scenario provides some evidence-based estimates of the militarization of Antarctica. It is based on combining the two critical uncertainties into their intermediate values. In this scenario, the various driving forces for the militarization of Antarctica are managed with some success. This scenario intends to be an anchor point for pragmatic discussions of the problem but without eclipsing the other scenarios, which remain equally plausible (McGee et al., 2022).

Other relevant studies have also analyzed Antarctic geopolitics. However, from the specific Brazilian point of view, a special mention should be made to the Report for Discussion 2425, prepared by the Institute for Applied Economic Research (IPEA) (Andrade et al., 2018). The report analyzes the different dimensions of PROANTAR, focusing on its scientific character and the geopolitical relevance of the Brazilian presence in the Antarctic continent. The preliminary route to access Antarctica is in the South Atlantic, concentrating commercial, tourist, and communication routes, in addition to vast reserves of mineral resources, such as the presalt oil reserves. Furthermore, the region is related to global water and energy security.

In addition, other driving forces related to Antarctic geopolitics were found in books and scientific articles, notably the *Handbook on the Politics of Antarctica* by Dodds et al. (2017). By analyzing the content of these texts, the central ideas were extracted and transformed into driving forces, characterizing elements in common or additional to those raised by the group of researchers at the University of Tasmania (McGee et al., 2022). Table 8.2 was constructed using data published by Andrade et al. (2018) and Hemmings (2017).

The severity of climate change impacts was considered a relevant driving force by McGee et al. (2022). However, this factor did not reach a risk score capable of replacing the two forces considered for the classification of scenarios in that research. Due to the importance of studying this topic to Fioantar, it is necessary to include it as a driving force in the system, henceforth named "EC," whose acronym means "climate stability."

Table 8.2 Driving Forces of Antarctic Geopolitics, from the Brazilian Point of View

Concepts	Direct citations
PQ1—Brazil's foreign policy—international insertion through the Antarctic Treaty	"Antarctica's importance for Brazil's foreign policy has not been much discussed in non-specialized environments and in the national media; thus, this subject is mostly unknown to the Brazilian society" (Andrade et al., 2018, 7).
	"Not by chance, the 2013 version of the National Defense Policy (PND) included Antarctica in the concept of national strategic surrounding area, together with South America, the South Atlantic and African bordering countries. The National Defense Strategy (END) considers the Brazilian participation in the decisionmaking process regarding Antarctica as a means of international insertion of Brazil. The strategic importance of Antarctica to Brazil is reaffirmed in the Brazilian Defense White Paper, which highlights the influence of the Southern Ocean on the living resources and minerals available in the Brazilian coast" (Andrade et al., 2018, 23).
PQ2—Presence of researchers in Antarctica and resulting scientific production	"With Antarctica included by the 2012 National Defense Policy in the strategic surrounding area of the country, the Brazilian performance in this continent, through its presence and scientific research, was reinforced as a strategic component. This initiative deepened the international insertion of Brazil and gave visibility to the great relevance of scientific studies developed within the Antarctic region" (Andrade et al., 2018, 7).
	"According to the Antarctic Treaty, the consultative party status, as the case of Brazil, is linked to the "promotion of substantial scientific research activity there [in Antarctica], such as the establishment of a scientific station or the dispatch of a scientific expedition." Therefore, added to the presence in the continent research quality is extremely relevant in the ATS, turning the Antarctic science into a political instrument and part of the agenda of scientific diplomacy" (Andrade et al., 2018, 22–23).

Concepts	Direct citations
PQ3—Investments in infrastructure for the Brazilian Antarctic Program (PROANTAR)—research station, expeditions, polar ships and aircraft	"Setting up scientific stations and dispatching expeditions to the Antarctic continent can be understood as essential activities, because they are provided in the Antarctic Treaty as ways of showing substantial scientific interest in the region and, therefore, achieving and maintaining the consultative party status in the treaty" (Andrade et al., 2018, 27). "In article IX, the Antarctic Treaty provides for that all countries that become members of the treaty by accession, like Brazil, must maintain a substantial scientific program in order to grant their right to participate in meetings that deliberate over the region. Therefore, the Brazilian investment in the Antarctic Science also strengthens its geopolitical interests" (Andrade et al., 2018, 32). "It is important to emphasize once again that the logistics to develop the projects approved requires the participation of the Brazilian Navy and the FAB, particularly in order to carry out research in the Southern Ocean on board of ships. They also ensured the transportation of scientific teams to different regions of Antarctica and maintained EACF" (Andrade et al., 2018, 36). "The cost of equipment and logistical activities to carry out scientific research includes, among other elements, the provision of food, drugs, camping material, and Antarctic clothing; maintenance of ships, aircrafts (such as helicopters boarded on ships), supporting vehicles, power generators, and machinery; and pre-Antarctic training. Such tasks, among others, are fundamental in the execution of research projects developed in the region" (Andrade et al., 2018, 37).

(Continued)

Concepts	Direct citations
PQ4—Territorial claims from other countries to the EACF region (Antarctic Peninsula)	"The beginning of the twentieth century brought the first deadlocks regarding sovereignty in the Antarctic territory and its jurisdiction. In 1908, the United Kingdom made the first territorial claim in the continent, followed by New Zealand (1923), France (1924), Australia (1933), Norway (1939), Chile (1940), and Argentina (1940). The main imbroglio happened between the United Kingdom, Argentina, and Chile, who claimed partially coincident areas—such as the Antarctic Peninsula. Not even the signature of a joint declaration in 1949, in which countries committed not to send warships to the continent, could prevent some incidents among these countries in the early 1950s—something that stimulated discussions about the jurisdiction that should prevail in the region" (Andrade et al., 2018, 9).
	"Territorial sovereignty is the great unresolved traditional Antarctic issue. It was the hardest nut to crack in gaining acceptance of what became the 1959 Antarctic Treaty; it was artfully contained by the language of Article IV of that treaty; and nobody has wanted to go near it since.58 So, an issue that had marginal support even in 1959—with seven states making claims, three of these overlapping and being mutually contested, and no other state on the planet publicly declaring for any of the claimants' positions—instead of being tidied away whilst some realistic reassessment of territoriality's viability in Antarctica occurred, has been embalmed. The undead still walk the corridors of Antarctic diplomacy; territorial claims are the ATS zombie.59 Too horrible to seriously contemplate, but showing no signs of finally going to their rest" (Hemmings, 2017, 516).
PQ5—Chilean logistical support to PROANTAR	"As the EACF does not have an airstrip for FAB's aircrafts, which supports Brazilian activities in Antarctica, there is a close relationship between Brazil and Chile concerning PROANTAR operation, since Brazilians use the airstrip of the Chilean Antarctic base, called Presidente Eduardo Frei Montalva Station [. . .] Besides the Frei airstrip, Brazil has used the Chilean city Punta Arenas as a supporting area for ships and FAB's aircrafts, which depart from that city to Antarctica." (Andrade et al., 2018, 29–30).

Concepts	Direct citations
PQ6—Argentina's logistical support to PROANTAR	"The airport and the port located in Ushuaia Argentina, can also be eventually used for this support. The preference for the Chilean city in Brazilian operations is mainly due to the lower cost. Moreover, Ushuaia does not have a tug, thus docking at this port depends on meteorological conditions" (Andrade et al., 2018, 30).
	"Several Antarctic programs, other than PROANTAR, use Chilean and Argentine cities as departures and supporting areas for operations. Therefore, as previously mentioned, the cooperation element is strong in the ATS" (Andrade et al., 2018, 30).
PQ7—Projetos acadêmicos e lançamento de Editais de fomento à pesquisa de temas polares	"Several Brazilian universities and research institutes develop important projects in Antarctica that positively impact pure and applied sciences and contribute to the formation of human resources, promoting scientific and technological advances in Brazil. Projects executed within PROANTAR have partnerships with several countries, resulting in the internationalization of the Brazilian science. Currently, the national Antarctic research is divided into different lines, and its progress has reflexes even in the daily life of society. Among the potential effects of biotechnological research, for example, we can underline benefits for medicine (drug formulation), agriculture (development of new pesticides and herbicides) and industry (manufacturing of products such as anticoagulants and sunscreens)" (Andrade et al., 2018, 32).
	"Considering that PROANTAR's major goal is to produce scientific knowledge about Antarctica and its relationships with other world regions, particularly with Brazil, the 2016–2022 'National Strategy for Science, Technology and Innovation' (ENCTI), elaborated by MCTIC, draws special attention to the Antarctic subject. This document particularly advocates the expansion of research in Antarctica and its adjacent área" (Andrade et al., 2018, p. 32).
	"Regarding the development of public policies for the national Antarctic science, the action plan points out the need for a joint action between CNPq (National Council for Scientific and Technological Development) and Capes (Coordination for the Improvement of Higher Education Personnel) to issue calls for research grants dedicated to studies on polar subjects" (Andrade et al., 2018, 34).

Sources: Fogarty, 2011; Andrade et al., 2018; Hemmisngs 2017.

Climate change could drive demand for electric vehicles and renewable energy technologies (wind turbines and photovoltaics, for example). This would increase demand for chemical elements used in the production of magnets and batteries, stimulating countries' interest in mining deposits of "Rare-Earth Elements."[2] in Antarctica. On the other hand, climate change makes some land and sea areas of Antarctica more accessible for human activities during most of the year. This can accelerate the possible emergence of pathogens in the Antarctic region, being of particular interest to Fiolab and Fioantar. This change in boundaries between land and sea regions can cause changes in the ecosystems of marine species in the Southern Ocean, impacting fishing activities in different areas of the globe. Furthermore, eventual global warming could lead regions of the planet to scarcity of fresh water, food insecurity, and the urgency for discovering new non-CO_2-producing energy sources. The relevance of the study of climate change is confirmed by its inclusion in the second part of COP15 on biodiversity.

2. METHODOLOGY OF FUZZY COGNITIVE MAPS

Cognitive maps (CMs) were proposed by Axelrod (1976) as a tool to analyze social systems in the real world graphically. CMs were designed to capture and analyze the causal reasoning of experts concerning a given domain. Axelrod's cognitive maps are graphic structures of nodes and edges (arcs or links). Nodes are variable concepts (like social instability, not like society), and edges are causal connections. A positive edge from node A to node B means A causally increases B. A negative edge from A to B means A causally decreases B. CMs facilitate documentary coding, constructing symbolic representations of expert documents. For instance, Kosko (1986) built Axelrod's cognitive map from Henry Kissinger's article "Starting Out in the Direction of Middle East Peace," printed in the *Los Angeles Times* (Kissinger, 1982). According to that map, Kissinger considered that religious fundamentalism decreased Soviet imperialism, which increased Syrian control of Lebanon, weakening the Lebanese government. These four concepts (i.e., fundamentalism, imperialism, military control, and governance) are only part of a complex network described by Kissinger, which includes other concepts that interact dynamically.

Over time, concepts change their state, indicating that they can remain active or lessen their influence on the system. The purely qualitative analysis of a system characterized by an imbricated web of causes and effects is practically impossible. That is why cognitive maps emerged, to emulate the dynamics of these systems through mathematical models. They allow drawing interesting conclusions about concepts that tend to expand or to be extinct, among other analyses.

Almost a decade later, Kosko (1986) introduced fuzzy cognitive maps (FCM) as a tool to model the behavior of qualitative systems. FCMs differ from CMs in that they assess the causal relationships as degrees of causality between the concepts. While CMs considers relationships as present or absent, FCMs allows the expert to modulate the intensity of the relationship with intermediate values. Thus, concept A may slightly impact concept B, for example.

CMs and FCMs are mathematically called "graphs," in which fundamental concepts of a given problem are represented as nodes. The causal connections between these nodes form arcs, also called edges or links.

FCMs have been used to quantitatively model the dynamics of complex systems and predict their behavior (Nair et al., 2020). FCMs are classified as soft-computing techniques, being explored in the most diverse areas of knowledge, such as green energy (Zare et al., 2022), sustainable development (Ameli et al., 2022), the auto industry (Rezaee et al., 2021), food waste studies (Genc et al., 2022), urban planning and management (Pluchinotta et al., 2019), medicine (Bevilacqua et al., 2018), and business intelligence (Ferreira et al., 2017), among others. In the defense sector, there are applications of FCMs in strategic scenarios (Trujillo-Cabezas, 2021), avionics systems (Ni et al., 2023), situational awareness (Munir et al., 2022), quality assessment (Bottero et al., 2018), maintenance strategy (Ahmad et al., 2022), military simulation (Yusuf et al., 2019), risk assessment (Petronijevic et al., 2022), cybersecurity (Shulha et al., 2022), and even studies including the war in Ukraine (Shahbazi, 2022; Kamali, 2022; Shams Esfandabadi et al., 2022).

As presented earlier, an FCM is formed by a set of nodes (concepts) representing the key elements of a given system, and directed arcs (links), defining the causal relationships between the nodes, form a cognitive map. Each concept is indicated by C_i, where $i = \{1, \ldots, N\}$, and N is the number of concepts. Links are labeled with weights in the range of [0, 1] or [−1, +1], showing the impact between concepts' strengths. These weights are associated with an N x N matrix called an "adjacency matrix." By mathematical convention, the cause-and-effect relationship is directed from row i to column j. For example, the relationship C_6-C_2 is represented by a weight $w_{62} = -0.3$, while the reciprocal relationship C_2-C_6 is null.

Figure 8.2 shows an example of an FCM with its corresponding adjacency matrix, which translates the causal relationships between the basic concepts of any given problem.

In general, the following steps describe the procedures for creating a cognitive map:

Step 1: select C_i concepts, which configure the cognitive map.
Step 2: define the causal relationship between the concepts.
Step 3: determine the value of the relationship between the concepts.

Example of FCM

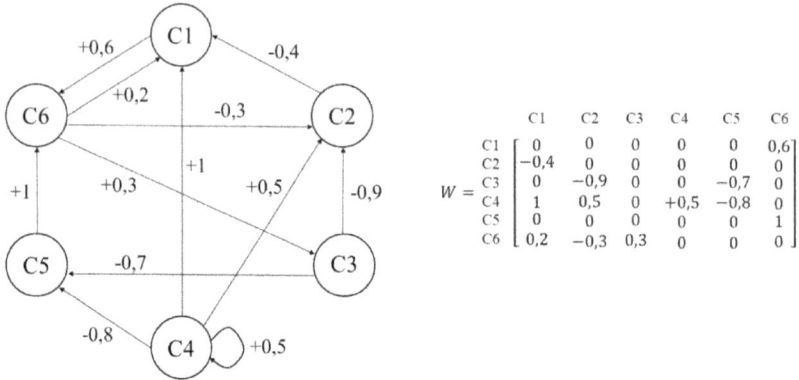

Figure 8.2. *Example of FCM.* **Konstantinos Papageorgiou et al., 2020.**

There are three categories of weights that characterize the cause-and-effect relationship between concepts:

- wij = 0: indicates that there is no causality between concepts.
- wij > 0: indicates a causal increase (C_j increases as C_i increases and C_j decreases as C_i decreases).
- wij < 0: indicates a causal decrease (C_j decreases as C_i increases, and C_j increases as C_i decreases).

Table 8.3 shows a reference for evaluating the intensity of cause-and-effect relationships between concepts.

Real-world problems are not static because constant environmental changes impact decision-makers' choices, creating a dynamic cycle (Elpiniki I Papageorgiou et al., 2014). To simulate this real-world condition, FCM models perform inferences between initial states assigned to the concepts and the weights that link them. In the initial state of the system, each concept receives a value $A_{i(k)}$, which varies in the interval [0, 1], being null when the concept is not present at the initial moment and "1" when it is complete. Inference rules calculate the following states $Ai(k+1)$, the most common of which are: (1) the Kosko inference, (2) the modified Kosko inference, and (3) the rescale inference. Figure 8.3 includes inferences used by Konstantinos Papageorgiou et al. (2020).

The notation $f(.)$ is the function for transforming the values of the states of the system, which can be: (4) bivalent (when it takes on only two values), (5) trivalent (when it takes on only three values), (6) sigmoid, or (7) hyperbolic tangent. Figure 8.4 includes functions used by Konstantinos Papageorgiou et al. (2020).

The notation λ is a positive real number ($\lambda > 0$), which determines the slope of the continuous function f, and x is the value of the concept in the initial

Table 8.3 Cause-and-Effect Relationship between Variables

Relationship intensity	Numerical values
Very strong increase (or attenuation)	0,9; 1 (-0,9; -1)
Strong increase (or attenuation)	0,7; 0,8 (-0,7; -0,8)
Moderate increase (or attenuation)	0,5; 0,6 (-0,5; -0,6)
Slight increase (or attenuation)	0,3; 0,4 (-0,3; -0,4)
Very slight increase (or attenuation)	0,1; 0,2 (-0,1; -0,2)
Null (absence of relationship)	0

Source: adaptad from Papageorgiou et al. (2020).

Equations (1) to (3)

$$A_i(k+1) = f\left(\sum_{j=1, j\neq i}^{N} w_{ij} \cdot A_j(k) \right) \qquad (1)$$

$$A_i(k+1) = f\left(A_i(k) + \sum_{j=1, j\neq i}^{N} w_{ij} \cdot A_j(k) \right) \qquad (2)$$

$$A_i(k+1) = f\left((2 \cdot A_i(k) - 1) + \sum_{j=1, j\neq i}^{N} w_{ij} \cdot (2 \cdot A_j(k) - 1) \right) \qquad (3)$$

Figure 8.3.   Equations (1) to (3). Author Contributions.

state $A_{i(k)}$. The sigmoid function guarantees that the calculated value of each concept will belong to the interval [0, 1]. When the values of the concepts are negative, receiving values in the range [–1, 1], the hyperbolic tangent function can be used instead of the sigmoid function.

Figure 8.5 illustrates the dynamics of the FCM indicated in figure 8.1, based on a rescale inference and the sigmoid function calculated from the "fcm" package of the "R" software (Dikopoulou et al., 2017). In just five stages of the dynamics in this system, it is possible to verify that concept C1 reaches the highest equilibrium value, followed by concepts C6, C4, and C3. Finally, the C5 concept loses importance, reaching the value of 0.1283. The intervals between the states are not related to the time elapsed between them, being a limitation of this dynamic with the cognitive maps.

3. APPLICATION AND RESULTS

The previous sections defined the key concepts that permeate Antarctic geopolitics and the Fioantar project. This was equivalent to Step 1 of the elaboration of a cognitive map, bringing together fourteen concepts: two

Equations (4) to (7)

$$f(x) = \begin{cases} 1, & x > 0 \\ 0, & x \le 0 \end{cases}$$

(4)

$$f(x) = \begin{cases} 1, & x > 0 \\ 0, & x = 0 \\ -1, & x < 0 \end{cases}$$

(5)

$$f(x) = \frac{1}{1 + e^{-\lambda x}}$$

(6)

$$f(x) = \tanh(\lambda . x)$$

(7)

Figure 8.4.   Equations (4) to (7). Author Contributions.

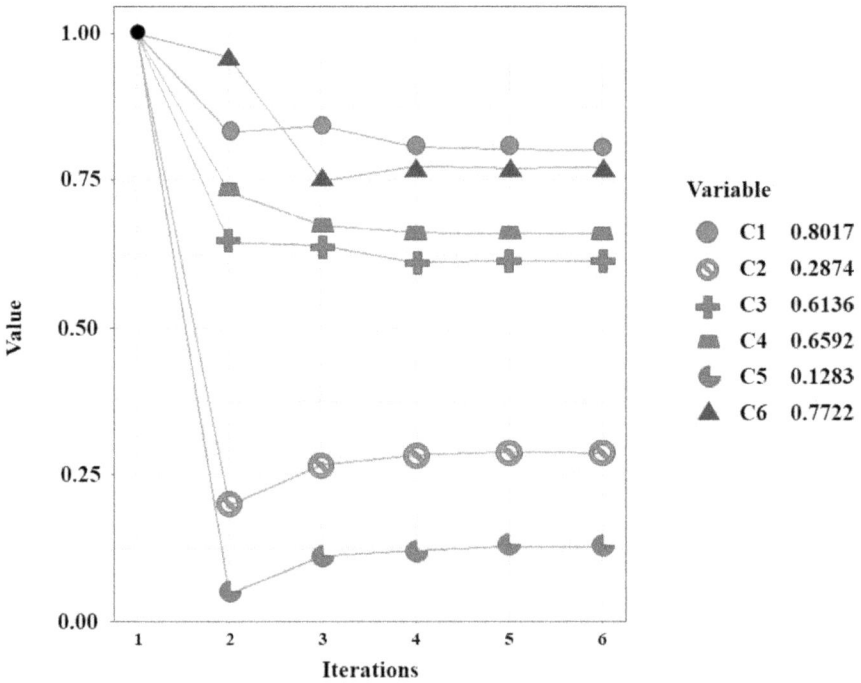

Figure 8.5.   Dynamics of a Complex System. (Dikopoulou et al., 2017.

critical uncertainties selected (McGee et al., 2022), five project requirements adapted from (Miller, 2014), and seven concepts obtained by content analysis of Andrade et al. (2018) and Hemmings (2017). Then, the causal relationship between the concepts must be evaluated, and their intensity and value determined, as indicated in table 8.4. These tasks can be carried out with the help of specialists in each sector; alternatively, through data that allow the calculation of the statistical correlation between the pairs of concepts. In this chapter, the authors analyzed the relationships in an exploratory way, reaching a consensus regarding the interactions described in the adjacency matrix (table 8.4).

To exemplify the cause-and-effect relationships between the concepts in table 8.4 it is possible to assume that the stability of the international system, relevant to the Antarctic Treaty (P1), may slightly mitigate the perception that the militarization of the region is strategically disadvantageous (S1), receiving the value (0.3). The S1 concept, for mathematical modeling of the cognitive map, indicates the strategic (dis)advantage of militarizing Antarctica. This guarantees uniformity in the definitions of concepts regarding the perception of "the bigger, the better" or "the smaller, the worse." Thus, the more significant the strategic disadvantage of militarizing Antarctica, the better for international peace and, consequently, for scientific research in the region. Likewise, the greater the stability of the international system, the better for the same research.

On the other hand, the perception that Antarctica is a strategic region for nonscientific exploration can drive an "arms race" to the region, moderately impacting peace and harmony between countries, and the value (0.6) is then indicated. Here it is possible to see that the way of describing the cause-and-effect relationship (or impact of one concept on the other), by mathematical convention, is carried out from the matrix row to the column, so the values (0.3) and (0.6) occupy the corresponding cells.

After completing the adjacency matrix, the fuzzy cognitive map model was processed in the R software, generating a series of results. First, focusing on the sustainability of Fioantar, factors C1 to C5 were prioritized for the analysis concerning the five scenarios of Antarctic geopolitics, indicated by the acronyms "IE" (Splendid Isolation), "Q" (Quarantine), "C" (Camouflage), "GF" (Cold War 2), and "PC" (Controlled Pressure), as shown in figure 8.6.

Through a linear comparison of the medians (indicated by a horizontal line in bold inside the boxes) and the position of the boxes, it appears that the "Q" and "GF" scenarios are the worst for factors C1 to C5. The boxes in the graphs represent the distribution of values assumed by C1 to C5 between the first and third quartiles, indicating the greater instability of the values in relation to the initial state of the interactions, which start with the maximum value "1." The "Q" and "GF" scenarios share the low stability of the international

Table 8.4 Adjacency Matrix

Concepts	P1	S1	EC	C1	C2	C3	C4	C5	PQ1	PQ2	PQ3	PQ4	PQ5	PQ6	PQ7
P1	0	0.3	0	0	0	0	0.3	1	0.5	0.5	0.7	-0.7	0.6	0.6	0.2
S1	0.6	0	0	0.2	-0.8	0	-0.5	0.8	0.8	0.5	-0.5	-1	0.4	0.4	0.2
EC	1	0.5	0.8	0.7	0.6	-0.3	-0.4	-0.5	-0.7	-0.7	-0.7	-1	0.5	0.3	-0.8
C1	0	0	0	0	0.8	1	1	1	1	1	1	0.6	0.4	0.4	0.7
C2	0	-0.4	0	0	0	0.8	0.4	0.7	0	1	0	0	0	0	0.5
C3	0	0	0	0	0	0	0	0.5	0	1	0	0	0	0	0.8
C4	0	0	0	0	0	0	0	0.2	0	0.8	0	0	0	0	1
C5	0	0	0	0	0	0	0	0	0	0.8	0	0	0	0	1
PQ1	0.2	0	0	0	1	0.6	1	0.7	0	1	1	-0.5	0.7	0.5	1
PQ2	0	0	0	0	0	0	0	0	1	0	0	0	0	0	0.8
PQ3	0	0	0	0	1	0.8	1	0.5	1	1	0	0	1	0.8	1
PQ4	-0.5	-0.5	0	0	-0.8	0	0	-0.7	-1	-1	-0.8	0	-1	-1	-1
PQ5	0	0	0	0	0.8	0	0	0	1	0.8	1	0	0	0	0
PQ6	0	0	0	0	0.5	0	0	0	0.8	0.6	0.8	0	0	0	0
PQ7	0	0	0	0	0	0	0	1	1	1	0.6	0	0	0	0

system, varying only in the intensity of the strategic value attributed by the leading international actors to the Antarctic continent. Both indicate a decrease in the basic requirements of scientific projects.

This behavior of factors C1 to C5 in the "GF" and "Q" scenarios is particularly interesting because it shows the coherence between the negative perception of these scenarios for the longevity of scientific projects in the Antarctic region and the results of the cognitive map. It is possible to verify in the graphs that factors C1 to C5 reach the lowest values in the interactions of the cognitive map, confirming the pessimistic evaluation of the scientific projects in the face of these scenarios. On the other hand, scenarios "IE," "PC," and "C" are the most favorable to factors C1 to C5 since the factors show the smallest decay after-system interactions. A slight preponderance of the "C" scenario over the C1, C3, and C5 factors are also visible, while the "IE" scenario is the most interesting for the C2 and C4 factors. This makes sense, considering that a context of the absence of military interests in the region and valorization of the Antarctic Treaty System tends to prioritize infrastructure resources for scientific research. On the other hand, the veiled and growing militarization activities of the continent, characteristics of the "C" scenario, can impact the scientific community in the sense of expanding efforts and engagement in favor of the projects in the region.

By analyzing each interaction separately, as shown in table 8.5, it can be seen that C1 suffers the most significant decrease in relation to the initial state, since it starts from the value "1," which characterizes the whole existence of natural resources in the different scenarios but decays to average values close to 0.5 during system interactions. It indicates that natural resources tend to be the most impacted requirement in all scenarios, affecting regional scientific

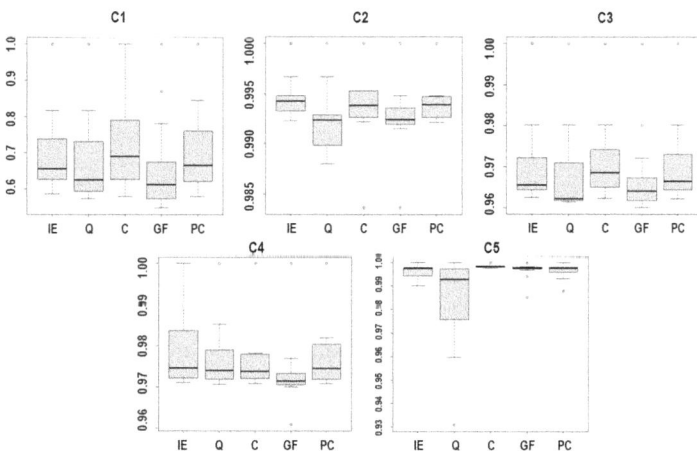

Figure 8.6.   Concepts C1 to C5 in all Scenarios. Author Contributions.

projects. This is even worse, considering that the C1 factor is the only resource not controlled by the projects. Thus, researchers from Fioantar and other projects must monitor activities in the region. In addition, it indicates the importance of preserving the Antarctic region so these resources do not become extinct.

Factor C5 decays the least during system interactions. This behavior can be associated with the resilience of the scientific community and its willingness to cooperate and work in a network to exchange knowledge, data, and information, among others, regardless of the scenario. The performance of factor C2 is like that of C5 and indicates a slight reduction in intensity concerning the initial state, with similar results. This behavior is acceptable, considering that the logistic infrastructure (represented by the support of the Antarctic station, support points in the country, navy ships and FAB aircraft, and bases in Chile and Argentina, among others) is more permanent and long term. The negative highlight for this factor remains in the "GF" scenario, as exposed, as tension in international relations can have a negative impact on cooperation in infrastructure to support EACF activities. Factors C3 and C4 behave in an intermediate way in regard to the others, with similar intensities in the interactions for different scenarios, indicating considerable resilience. This is important because human and financial resources are pillars of research projects, essential for the sustainability of scientific research in the region.

In summary, C1 is the most disturbing requirement for coordinators and members of Fioantar. Since it is an environmental variable, it cannot be controlled by the organizers and is independent of academic and governmental funding. Thus, the focus of scientific projects should prioritize factors C3 and C4 through training activities for new researchers with the potential to work on Antarctic projects and in fundraising from public and/or private sources to make scientific research viable. Furthermore, these factors are directly related to the organizational capacity and engagement of the national scientific community.

CONCLUSION

This chapter aims to associate Fioantar's requirements with the main driving forces that involve the geopolitical dynamics of the Antarctic region. The requirements corresponded to five variables, defined as "resources": natural, physical, human, financial, and social. The other driving forces were extracted from recent research and consolidated literature from relevant authors and organizations.

Modeling the interactions between the fifteen selected driving forces allowed us to assess trends and implications that affect Fioantar's essential needs and ensure its sustainability. The factors involving Fioantar and

Table 8.5 Values of First and Last Interaction

	First interaction					Last interaction				
	C1	C2	C3	C4	C5	C1	C2	C3	C4	C5
	0.8176	0.9967	0.9802	0.9918	0.99	0.5246	0.9921	0.958	0.9717	0.9951
	0.8176	0.9967	0.9802	0.9852	0.9309	0.5204	0.9919	0.9576	0.9713	0.9951
	0.8699	0.9837	0.9802	0.9781	0.998	0.5206	0.9919	0.9577	0.9714	0.9951
	0.8699	0.9837	0.9802	0.9608	0.9852	0.5058	0.9911	0.9566	0.97	0.9951
	0.8455	0.9926	0.9802	0.982	0.9879	0.5205	0.9919	0.9577	0.9713	0.9951

Percentage variation between states

	C1	C2	C3	C4	C5
IE	-0.358	-0.005	-0.023	-0.02	0.0051
Q	-0.363	-0.005	-0.023	-0.014	0.069
C	-0.402	0.0083	-0.023	-0.007	-0.003
GF	-0.419	0.0076	-0.024	0.0096	0.01
PC	-0.384	-7E-04	-0.023	-0.011	0.0074

Antarctic geopolitics interact with each other, exploring the methodology of fuzzy cognitive maps to model the system and produce results under the context of the five scenarios: "IE" (splendid isolation), "Q" (quarantine), "C" (stealth), "GF" (Cold War II), and "PC" (pressures managed).

The results indicated that Fioantar and other scientific projects that "feed" PROANTAR may suffer, directly or indirectly, from the positive and negative effects of Antarctic geopolitics, which involves the most diverse international interests in the region. Thus, from the five requirements responsible for the longevity of Fioantar, it was found that the most harmful consequence of Antarctic geopolitics falls on natural resources. Therefore, monitoring environmental conditions and natural resources is of considerable importance for Fioantar and other scientific projects.

Regarding the other variables, factors C3 and C4 directly "feed" scientific research in the short and medium term. These variables basically result from the ability to organize and engage the academic and scientific community. Continued training of new researchers and stable funding of projects and grants to support research on the Antarctic region are some interesting initiatives related to factors C3 and C4.

As to the continuity of this research, a tantalizing possibility would be to reassess interactions between various factors that constitute the system analyzed. New evaluations may bring even greater adherence to the model for the reality of Antarctic geopolitics. In addition, it is possible to add new variables to the system, expanding the adjacency matrix with new interactions and, consequently, new factor equilibrium results.

NOTES

1. The Fioantar project is divided into two research lines that aim to investigate the risks and opportunities that the microorganisms inhabiting Antarctica can offer to human health and, thus, produce relevant answers for the National Health System (SUS). The first line includes the investigation of pathogens, such as viruses, fungi, and bacteria, present in the Antarctic environment to reinforce long-term epidemiological surveillance and prevention. In order to accomplish that, Fiocruz is bringing together researchers from eight different laboratories. They are professionals engaged in production and innovation in health, international health relations, and communication. They will produce videos, unique series for social networks, interviews, and exhibitions, among other materials so that the population can follow all the results and challenges of this great project. The other important line of research is bioprospection. Extremophilic organisms, which live in extreme environments, have in their constitution molecules and present physiological and chemical competencies that are different from what we see elsewhere, which were developed throughout their evolutionary process to deal with this environment. The researchers will identify which of these

organisms have the potential to develop new technologies and health products, such as medicines and supplies (Brazil, 2019).

2. The expression "rare earth elements" (REE), for which the symbol Ln is used, corresponds to the chemical elements of lanthanum (La, Z = 57) to lutetium (Lu, Z = 71), among which are included yttrium (Y, Z = 39) and scandium (Sc, Z = 21). However, this designation is considered inappropriate because they were initially known in the form of their oxides, which resemble the materials known as "earths." In addition, the expression "rare" is also not in agreement since lanthanides are more abundant (with the exception of promethium, which does not occur in nature) than many other elements (Martins and Isolani 2005, 1).

REFERENCES

Ahmad, S., N. Kasmuri, N. A. Ismail, M. F. Miskon, and N. H. Ramli. "Maintenance Strategy Selection Using Fuzzy Delphi Method In Royal Malaysian Air Force." *Pertanika Journal of Science & Technology* 30, no. 2 (2022): 1–22.

Ameli, M., Z. S. Esfandabadi, S. Sadeghi, M. Ranjbari, and M. C. Zanetti. "COVID-19 and Sustainable Development Goals (SDGs): Scenario Analysis through Fuzzy Cognitive Map Modeling." Gondwana Research, (2022):1–19.

Andrade, I. D. O., L. F. De Mattos, A. C. da Cruz-Kaled, and G. R. L. Hillebrand. "O Brasil Na Antártica: A Importância Científica e Geopolítica Do PROANTAR No Entorno Estratégico Brasileiro." Texto Para Discussão IPEA, no. 2425, (2018): 1–62.

Axelrod, R. *Structure of Decision: The Cognitive Maps of Political Elites*. Princeton, New Jersey: Princeton University Press, 1976.

Bevilacqua, M., F. E. Ciarapica, and G. Mazzuto. "Fuzzy Cognitive Maps for Adverse Drug Event Risk Management." *Safety Science* 102 (2018): 194–210.

Bottero, M., G. Datola, and R. Monaco. "The Use of Fuzzy Cognitive Maps for Evaluating the Reuse Project of Military Barracks in Northern Italy." International Symposium on New Metropolitan Perspectives (Springer 2018): 691–99.

Brazil, Oswaldo Cruz Foundation - FIOCRUZ. Project FioAntar, 2019.

Degrave, W. M. S. Interviews Conducted with the FioAntar Project Coordinator, 2020.

Dikopoulou, Z., and Papageorgiou, E. "Inference of Fuzzy Cognitive Maps." R Package, 2017. Accessed November 20, 2022. https://cran.r-project.org/web/packages/fcm/vignettes/vignettes.html.

Dodds, K., A. D. Hemmings, and P. Roberts, *Handbook on the Politics of Antarctica.* Glos: Edward Elgar Publishing Limited, 2017.

Ferrada, L. V. "Five Factors That Will Decide the Future of Antarctica." *The Polar Journal* 8, no. 1 (2018): 84–109.

Ferreira, F. A. F., J. J. M. Ferreira, C. I. Fernandes, I. Meidutė-Kavaliauskienė, and M. S. Jalali. "Enhancing Knowledge and Strategic Planning of Bank Customer Loyalty Using Fuzzy Cognitive Maps." *Technological and Economic Development of Economy* 23, no. 6 (2017): 860–876.

Frame, B. "Towards an Antarctic Scenarios Integrated Framework." *The Polar Journal* 10, no. 1 (2020): 22–51.

Frame, B., Y. Yermakova, P. Flamm, G. Nicklin, G. De Paula, R. Badhe, and F. Tuñez. "Antarctica's Gateways and Gatekeepers: Polar Scenarios in a Polarising Anthropocene." *The Anthropocene Review* 9, no.3, (2021): 392–402.

Genc, T. O., and A. Ekici. "A New Lens to the Understanding and Reduction of Household Food Waste: A Fuzzy Cognitive Map Approach." *Sustainable Production and Consumption* 33 (2022): 389–411.

Hemmings, A. D. "Antarctic Politics in a Transforming Global Geopolitics." In *Handbook on the Politics of Antarctica*, edited by K. Dodds, A. D. Hemmings, and P. Roberts, 507–522. Cheltenham: Edward Elgar Publishing, 2017.

Kamali, A. Natural Gas-Produced Electricity as a Green Energy Resource: Consequences of the 2022 European Delegated Regulation on the Dutch Energy Transition. MA diss., University of Twente, 2022.

Kissinger, H. A. "Starting out in the Direction of Middle East Peace." *Los Angeles Times*, June 18, 1982. https://latimes.newspapers.com/search/?query=%22Starting %20out%20in%20the%20Direction%20of%20Middle%20East%20Peace%22&dr _year=1980-1989.

Kosko, B. "Fuzzy Cognitive Maps." *International Journal of Man-Machine Studies* 24, no. 1 (1986): 65–75.

Liggett, D., B. Frame, N. Gilbert, and F. Morgan. "Is It All Going South? Four Future Scenarios for Antarctica." *Polar Record* 53, no. 5 (2017): 459–7.

Liu, N. "The Rise of China and the Antarctic Treaty System?" *Australian Journal of Maritime & Ocean Affairs* 11, no. 2 (2019): 120–131.

Magnoli, D. Relaçoes Internacionais: Teoria e História, São Paulo: Saraiva Educação SA, 2013.

Martins, T. S., and P. C. Isolani. "Terras Raras: Aplicações Industriais e Biológicas." *Química Nova* 28 (2005):111–17.

McGee, J., D. Edmiston, and M. Haward. *The Future of Antarctica: Scenarios from Classical Geopolitics*, Singapore: Springer Nature, 2022.

McGee, J. and M. Haward. "Antarctic Governance in a Climate Changed World." *Australian Journal of Maritime & Ocean Affairs* 11, no. 2 (2019): 78–93.

Miller, D. G. M. "Antarctic Marine Living Resources: The Future Is Not What It Used to Be," in *Antarctic Futures: Human Engagement with the Antarctic Environment*, edited by Tina Tin, Daniela Liggett, Patrick T. Maher, Machiel Lamers, 61–95. New York: Springer, 2014.

Munir, A., A. Aved, and E. Blasch. "Situational Awareness: Techniques, Challenges, and Prospects." *AI* 3, no. 1 (2022): 55–77.

Nair, A., D. Reckien, and M. F. A. M. van Maarseveen. "Generalised Fuzzy Cognitive Maps: Considering the Time Dynamics between a Cause and an Effect." *Applied Soft Computing* 92, no. 106309 (2020):1–48.

Ni, X., M. Wang, G. Xiao, and G. Wang. "An Integrated Architecture Design Method for Multi-Platform Avionics System." In *International Conference on Aerospace System Science and Engineering*, edited by Zhongliang Jing, and Dmitry Strelets, 73–84. New York: Springer, 2023.

Papageorgiou, E. I. and J. L. Salmeron. "Methods and Algorithms for Fuzzy Cognitive Map-Based Modeling." In *Fuzzy Cognitive Maps for Applied Sciences* and Engineering: From Fundamentals to Extensions and Learning Algorithms*, edited by J. Kacprzyk, and L. C. Jain, 1–28. New York: Springer, 2014.

Papageorgiou, K., P. K. Singh, E. Papageorgiou, H. Chudasama, D. Bochtis, and G. Stamoulis. "Fuzzy Cognitive Map-Based Sustainable Socio-Economic Development Planning for Rural Communities." *Sustainability* 12, no. 1 (2020):1–31.

Petronijevic, J., A. Etienne, and A. Siadat. "Global Risk Assessment for Development Processes: From Framework to Simulation." *International Journal of Production Research* (2022):1–25.

Pluchinotta, I., D. Esposito, and D. Camarda. "Fuzzy Cognitive Mapping to Support Multi-Agent Decisions in Development of Urban Policymaking." *Sustainable Cities and Society* 46 (2019): 101402.

Powell, R. C. and K. Dodds. *Polar Geopolitics?: Knowledges, Resources and Legal Regimes*. London: Edward Elgar Publishing, 2014.

Ramirez, R. and A. Wilkinson. *Strategic Reframing: The Oxford Scenario Planning Approach*. Oxford: Oxford University Press, 2016.

Rezaee, M. J., S. Yousefi, M. Baghery, and R. K. Chakrabortty. "An Intelligent Strategy Map to Evaluate Improvement Projects of Auto Industry Using Fuzzy Cognitive Map and Fuzzy Slack-Based Efficiency Model." *Computers & Industrial Engineering* 151 (2021): 106920.

Schwartz, P. *The Art of the Long View: Planning for the future in an Uncertain World*. Currency, 2012.

Shahbazi, R. Development of a Decision Support Tool Based on Fuzzy Cognitive Mapping for Energy Transition of District Heating Systems of Leeuwarden, 2022.

Shams Esfandabadi, Z., Ranjbari, M. and Scagnelli, S. D. "The Imbalance of Food and Biofuel Markets amid Ukraine-Russia Crisis: A Systems Thinking Perspective," *Biofuel Research Journal*, vol. 9, no. 2 (2022), 1640–47.

Shulha, O., Yanenkova, I., Kuzub, M., Muda, I. and Nazarenko, V. "Banking Information Resource Cybersecurity System Modeling," *Journal of Open Innovation: Technology, Market, and Complexity*, vol. 8, no. 2 (2022), 80.

Tin, T., Liggett, D., Maher, P. T. and Lamers, M. Antarctic Futures: Human Engagement with the Antarctic Environment, Springer Science & Business Media, 2013.

Trujillo-Cabezas, R. A Hybrid Fuzzy Modeling Method to Improve the Strategic Scenarios Design.: Integrating Artificial Intelligence Algorithms and the Field of Futures Studies Methods, 2021 16th Iberian Conference on Information Systems and Technologies (CISTI), IEEE, pp. 1–6, 2021.

Yusuf, A. B., Kor, A.-L., and Tawfik, H. Development of a Simulation Experiment to Investigate In-Flight Startle Using Fuzzy Cognitive Maps and Pupillometry, 2019 International Joint Conference on Neural Networks (IJCNN), IEEE, pp. 1–10, 2019.

Zare, S. G., Alipour, M., Hafezi, M., Stewart, R. A. and Rahman, A. "Examining Wind Energy Deployment Pathways in Complex Macro-Economic and Political Settings Using a Fuzzy Cognitive Map-Based Method," *Energy*, vol. 238 (2022), 121673.

PART III

Connecting the El Dorados

Chapter 9

The Noosphere and Science Diplomacy in Brazil

Connecting the Policy Networks for the Amazon and Antarctica

Ana Flávia Barros-Platiau, Carina Costa de Oliveira, Leandra Regina Gonçalves, Andrei Polejack, and Carlos Henrique Tomé Silva

This chapter discusses key challenges related to the governance of the Amazon region and Antarctica. The Amazon region, or Amazonia, refers to a natural and political space encompassing nine countries and their diverse communities, not only the rainforest. Likewise, Antarctica refers to a natural and political space below 60 degrees latitude on the world map, encompassing a glacial ocean. The ocean is important because it is directly connected to climate change: the "primary causes of the contemporary global sea level rise are the increase in ocean thermal expansion and the melting of grounded ice (glaciers, Greenland and Antarctica)" (IOC-UNESCO, 2022, 40).

The Amazon and Antarctica are considered "El Dorados of the 21st century" (Becker 2005, 77) because they remain unexplored, although there are plenty of priceless biological and mineral resources there. However, the Amazon and Antarctica are also vital to Earth's cycles, so they can be considered what Steffen et al. (2004) calls the "Achilles' heels of the Earth system." Therefore, our main aim is to highlight the need for a new framework for social-ecological architecture and agency (Hannigan, 2015; Burch et al., 2019) on a global scale (Latour, 2015, 2018; Kotzé and Adelman, 2022) and its consequences for Brazil.

While science has enabled humanity to investigate how both the Amazon and Antarctica are connected through planetary dynamics, it has also warned how threatened they are by human activities aggravated by the Western economic acceleration since 1945, the "great acceleration" (Steffen et al., 2015; Rockström and Raworth, 2015)[1] and the "blue acceleration" (Jouffray et al., 2020), leading to the so-called Anthropocene Epoch. In this context, we discuss how science diplomacy[2] is key to responding to global environmental urgency, using the lenses of complex systems (Kavalski, 2016; Tomé, 2022) and then focusing on Brazil. Complexity thinking requires new ways of integrating institutional arrangements, economic development, and sustainable policies as parts of the same equation (Young, 2021; Boyadjian, 2021).

This chapter offers insights from international relations and international law, bringing the concepts of the noosphere and science diplomacy to connect the "El Dorados of the 21st century" to Brazil's geopolitical and scientific agendas. First, we discuss how science diplomacy is a pathway to the noosphere and for a more stable geopolitical global order. Then, we focus on Brazil as a study case, stressing the need for science-oriented institutional reform. Finally, we suggest a more sophisticated policy network in Brazil and future research agendas directly connecting the Amazon to Antarctica.

1. THE AMAZON AND ANTARCTICA CONNECTED AS LIFE-SUPPORTING SYSTEMS

The Amazon rainforest, Antarctica, and the ocean are essential life-supporting systems because of their influence in maintaining the climate dynamics and, in consequence, the biosphere. They are linked by the natural dynamics of precipitation and heat circulation and the consequences of human activities. In the case of the forest, agriculture, logging, mining, and cattle raising engender soil and water contamination and pollution, but also eutrophication (i.e., the expansion of dead zones in coastal areas due to the intense use of fertilizers and chemical nutrients [novel entities] in farming, like nitrogen and phosphorous). Antarctica remains a pristine continent, but it is threatened by global warming, future tourism, and possibly mining.

Although the Amazon and Antarctica are not usually jointly analyzed by scientists or decision-makers, several research initiatives show how they should be connected in policy-making processes. For example, Andreae et al. (2004) defended that the Amazon rainforest fires substantially affected the regional and global atmospheric circulation systems and the water cycle. They employed the term "green ocean" because "clouds over the Amazon during the rainy season are predominantly microphysically maritime." Likewise, the "green ocean Amazon" (GoAmazon2014/5) was an experiment to monitor the complex interactions of the atmospheric chemistry, vegetation, and aerosol production with aerosols, clouds, and precipitation (Martin et al., 2017). Using an intertropical convergence zone model, Zou and Xi (2014) investigated Brazil's role in heat waves in the Northern Hemisphere. Daher et al. (2015) analyzed the freshwater discharges of the Amazon River into the South Atlantic. Inoue (2018) and Pereira and Gebara (2022) highlighted the Amazonian indigenous symbolism in the context of the Anthropocene. Moreover, the International Comprehensive Ocean-Atmosphere Data Set (ICOADS) and the World Ocean Circulation Experiment database (WOCE, 2002) are two telling examples of the complexity of the recent research agenda that should be highlighted on a global scale and in Brazil.

The Amazon region is a biodiversity El Dorado, home to Indigenous and local communities (Albagli, 1998) amounting to around 13 percent of the Brazilian population, but also a vital system for Earth's cycles. The region encompasses the rainforest and transition zones, corresponding to 59 percent of the Brazilian territory, and is officially called the Legal Amazonia (Mello and Artaxo, 2017), as shown in figure 9..

Antarctica is a critical space of superlatives: the driest, highest, coldest, and windiest continent. Seven nations have territorial claims there: France, the United Kingdom, New Zealand, Norway, Australia, Chile, and Argentina. In addition, the United States, Peru, Russia, and South Africa have all reserved their right to claim territory in the future. Brazil currently has a "strategic interest" but not a claim. However, since the enforcement of the Antarctic Treaty in June 1961, Antarctica has been considered a sovereignty-free space for peace and science, with territorial claims being suspended (Hupke, 2023).

Although the first explorers arrived in Antarctica centuries ago, as Zarankin and Bezerra show in this book in chapter 10, the scientific community has recently reinforced the understanding of the interconnectedness of complex planetary dynamics and the biosphere (Miles, 1999; Gattuso and Magnan, 2022). For instance, Zhao et al. (2022) investigated how the sea surface temperature (STT) is relevant for monitoring weather events, climate, marine ecology, and straddling fish stocks. Such scientific developments have encouraged us to look at the Amazon, Antarctica, the glacial ocean, and global climate as a single dynamic system. This huge complex system must be taken seriously in multilateral agenda-setting and geopolitics.

Up to now, this enhanced understanding of planetary dynamics has yet to be followed by multilateral governance structures in general, and Brazilian in particular. In other words, existing complex connections between the Amazon, Antarctica, the ocean, and the global climate through the Atlantic Meridional Overturning Circulation (AMOC), for example, are largely absent from current Brazilian scholarship in social and human sciences (Boyadjian et al., 2021). Threats to these life-supporting systems can thwart ecosystems and biodiversity (Christiansen et al, 2022; Friedman et al., 2022) and the services they provide to humanity. Moreover, there are risks of new, unpredicted, and altered ecosystems (Stillman, 2019). Therefore, the great accelerations mentioned above correspond to "the rapid intensification of resource consumption and ecological degradation. We risk disrupting the earth's critical systems, and with them, modern civilization itself" (Rockström and Raworth, 2015, XXX). Increasing human impacts are now a matter of global public interest that multilateral decision-makers can no longer postpone. It requires a systemic approach to governance, connecting the fragmented international regulatory framework (Boutaud and Gondran, 2020; Christiansen et al., 2022). In a nutshell, the stability of the four systems is critical for life on Earth. Therefore, protecting Antarctica and the Amazon as a single set for the sake of the climate and the ocean is of utmost importance for Earth. In fact, it corresponds to the vital interest of humankind.

Nevertheless, these four agendas are only partially connected by legal and policy innovations such as the sustainable development principle, the ecosystem approach, the ecosystem services (IPBES, 2019), area-based management tools, the common heritage of humankind principle, carbon capture and storage (CCS), and the recognition of cross-cutting issues, to mention only a few concepts in recent multilateral negotiations. Therefore, the institutional system that governs them must be integrated to keep the global system functioning.

2. FRAMING THE CHALLENGES OF THE ANTHROPOCENE AND THE NOOSPHERE

We live in a "new uncertainty complex" (UNDP, 2022) in which political inaction is no longer an option. On the contrary, new economic recovery initiatives after 2021 tend to shape the future in the light of a second economic "great acceleration," including China and India as global players at the "new El Dorados." In addition, human activities in the high seas, outer space, cyberspace, and the metaverse also bear real threats (WEF, 2022). Finally, acceleration also corresponds to natural phenomena, such as forest tipping points and sea level rise (IPCC, 2019). Combined, economic and natural acceleration processes engender a plethora of scientific uncertainties (Frozel Barros, 2019; Camargo et al., 2022), represented as "tipping cascades" (Wunderling et al., 2021), as shown in figure 9.2.

In this vein, a key concept driving our research is the *Anthropocene*, guiding debates in social sciences and humanities in general (Johnson et al., 2022; Kotzé, 2022) from the standpoint of the "great acceleration" data

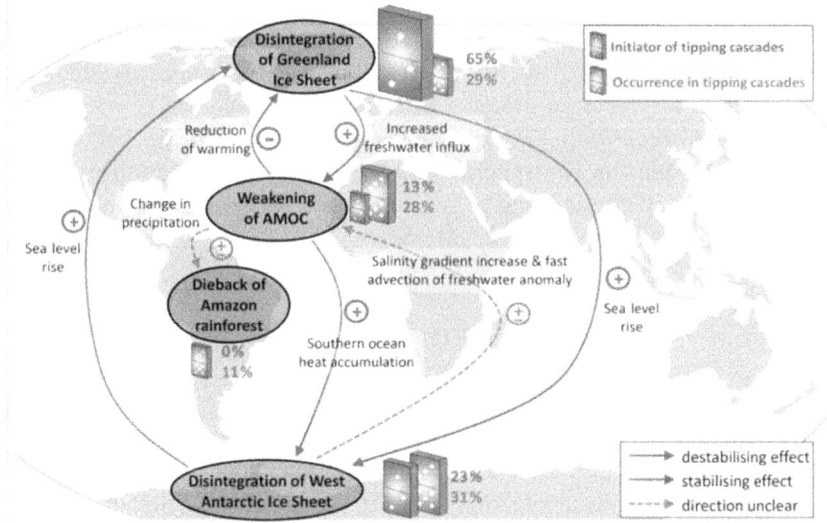

Figure 9.2. "Interactions between climate tipping elements and their roles in tipping cascades."

Source: Wunderling et al. Earth System Dynamics, vol. 12, issue 2, (2021): 601–619. https://doi.org/10.5194/esd-12-601-2021.

and the climate change agenda. The Anthropocene corresponds to a new geological epoch after the Holocene (Crutzen and Stoermer, 2000; Vidas, 2011; Viñuales, 2018). Humans have disturbed planetary dynamics and overstepped planetary thresholds to justify a new geological epoch (Rockström et al., 2009; Höfele et al., 2022). The Anthropocene hypothesis surpasses temporal and spatial limits, based on human nature dualism, urgency and irreversibility, and material complexity, described as "an intricate sequence of intended and unintended causations and consequences, overlapping subjects and goals and the coexistence and mutual intrusion of different social and natural systems" (Zelli and Pattberg, 2016, XXX). Nevertheless, there is still no scientific consensus on what the Anthropocene means or when it started.

On the one hand, geological and historical timelines taken together contribute to assessing "humanity's disruption to the Earth System" (Koster, 2022, XXX). Nevertheless, on the other hand, there were also decelerations, which would disallow the Anthropocene hypothesis as a new geological epoch (Nielsen, 2022).

As a human response to the Anthropocene alert, the noosphere is a sphere of thought, a "description of a global concentricity of interacting minds," that is, "humanity congregates to create a global culture with a global awareness or ethic," resulting from the great acceleration. Contrary to the Anthropocene, seen as an alert of disruptive changes, the noosphere is closer to what

Alexandre Kiss used to call the global consciousness (*la prise de conscience*) with the development of education and science (Kiss, 1982). It corresponds to the human capacity to react to new complex challenges humans and nature pose. That is why science-oriented policies are fundamental for the future we want. Shoshitaishvili (2021) synthesizes the comparison between the Anthropocene and the Noosphere concepts. While the Anthropocene has a temporal mode of rupture and a primary mood of crisis and warning, the noosphere is about development and hope.

3. INTERNATIONAL RELATIONS AND LAW SCHOLARSHIP

In international relations, little has been published connecting the Amazon to Antarctica, although they are both vital for the world climate and biodiversity stability. In most recent scholarship, security and trade issues prevail over sustainability and risk management in multilateral and regional agendas. Telling examples are the research agendas on the Chinese Belt and Road Initiative, the EU Global Gateway Initiative, and the EU Strategic Compass. Other concepts showing scientific contribution from different perspectives are the complex world (Cairney et al., 2019), Earth system governance, global risks (WEF, 2022), and green republicanism (Frémaux, 2019), for example.

Similarly, in international law, science-based approaches are increasingly employed. Concepts like the common interest of humanity, the common heritage of humankind, and the shared concern of humankind are not new. The concept of common interest of humanity (Oliveira et al., 2020, 2022; Oliveira; Maljean-Dubois, 2017) contributes to the understanding of the noosphere we need. The 1992 Convention on Biological Diversity (CBD) affirms in its preamble that "the conservation of biological diversity is a common concern of humankind." This is a broad concept that has minimal content. Legally speaking, the concept of the common heritage of humankind could provide a more robust framework for global life, as was the case for seabed resources. The introduction of the common heritage of humankind was also invoked for Antarctic regulation (Reid, 2011). While the signatory states of the Antarctica Treaty agreed to refer to the interest of humankind, they did not agree on a reference to the common heritage of humankind. Likewise, the preambles of the Convention on the Conservation of Antarctic Marine Living Resources, 1980 (CCAMLR) and the Protocol on Environmental Protection to the Antarctic Treaty, 1991 (the Madrid Protocol) reaffirmed the "interest of mankind" as a motivation of the parties. However, they did not refer to the notion of common heritage.

The common heritage of humanity's legal framework could design the seabed minerals regulation and has been invoked as a principle for regulating biodiversity beyond national jurisdiction (BBNJ). In this context, science diplomacy must ask for the application of this principle to strengthen the protection of ecosystems and global life.

In this vein, diplomats and other authorities have been negotiating the creation of new funding mechanisms, such as the Amazon fund, climate change, biodiversity, the envisioned BBNJ treaty, the loss and damages fund mentioned at CoP 27, and so on. However, these mechanisms need a solid scientific consensus to be adopted and political will to be adequately implemented. On top of that, when policymakers discuss forest credits, carbon credits, or blue carbon credits, building political consensus demands years of multilateral talks. Science diplomacy became a relevant topic in most recent multilateral debates concerning biodiversity, climate, ocean, and polar agendas. In the next section, we will tackle this issue broadly and it concerns Brazil. Then, we will discuss how the "policy networks" are formed and are operating in Brazil.

4. SCIENCE DIPLOMACY AND POLICY NETWORKS IN BRAZIL

The crescent influence of science in international negotiations since the twentieth century, informing about environmental and planetary thresholds, has been undermined mainly by traditional international relations and legal scholarships, mostly because these fields of knowledge avert a more transdisciplinary approach. However, science diplomacy arose as a new cognitive field of research attempting to understand the dynamics by which science and diplomacy influence one another. Moreover, as a modern social phenomenon, science diplomacy has been claimed to be critical to promote global community interests, unveiling the multiple interactions between international relations and research. From clustering geopolitically tense regions around shared research facilities to building alliances to foster research on demand from society, science diplomacy has been claimed to be the force behind better international decision-making mechanisms that can contribute to the noosphere. Examples of such include the international scientific agreements that cluster politically opposed countries, with US-Cuba relations as an example, or the implementation of research programs that combine expertise irrespective of nationality, such as the International Space Station (although scientific collaboration could not prevent Russia from stepping down the project in 2022 due to the war on Ukraine).

Research in science diplomacy requires integration of areas such as science and technology studies, philosophy of science, history, science-policy interface, and others. The general narrative on science diplomacy holds its practices around certain assumptions of science. In general, science is portrayed as apolitical, value-neutral, and international, aiding diplomacy to find balance among sectoral interests for global stewardship. However, research on science diplomacy has provided new evidence on the power play between states using science and scientists as a soft form of power (Nye, 1990) and how the blurred lines between cooperation and competition, particularly regarding technological developments, can drive international diplomatic engagements (Biermann and Möller, 2019).

From this standpoint, Antarctica has been claimed to be the ultimate example of benevolent science diplomacy (Berkman et al., 2011). However, this view seems simplistic since state parties to the treaty include only a restricted club of twenty-nine voting members who are, in fact, capable of deciding upon the future of Antarctica. Furthermore, this exclusive group of countries exposes a geopolitical tension that lies underneath the benevolent narrative of a continent dedicated to peace and science, since this elite group can use Antarctica for its geopolitical advantage. This includes setting high standards of science excellency before allowing other countries to become voting parties to the Antarctic Treaty.

The Amazon, on the other hand, is not a global common. Despite its role in regulating the weather and climate on a planetary scale, the standing forest and its riverine systems lay under the sovereignty of nine countries in South America. The international community can pressure those countries to act in favor of the protection and conservation of the Amazon. In this case, science diplomacy will tackle the international research partnerships set up to understand the region's ecological significance and the undergoing threats it faces. There are also recent international cooperation projects that contribute directly to science diplomacy. A good example is the Amazon Tall Tower Observatory, a joint initiative of Brazil and Germany, where scientific evidence fed our general comprehension of the forest and allowed authorities to claim better protection of the Amazon.

Seeing Antarctica, and its role in the planetary system as global commons in the sense of Pflieger (2015), but also recognizing the limitations of accessibility and equitable negotiation of the continent's future, exposes how grounded in elitism Antarctic science diplomacy is. In opposition, the Amazon falls under the responsibility of the member states of the Amazon Cooperation Treaty Organization (ACTO) and France (through French Guiana). However, as described in other chapters, Brazil usually stands alone for forest management. Although ACTO, with headquarters in Brasilia, was the most successful regional forest initiative ever implemented, it needs more resources to create the necessary political impact on member countries. In case of geopolitical tensions between those countries or between any foreign nation and those countries, the protection of the forest could be jeopardized. In this case, science diplomacy is a door opener for negotiations and tension alleviation. Since all Amazonian countries (except France) have limited scientific and technical capabilities, research in the Amazon will most likely require international cooperation and funding, which can trigger several venues for political pressure to sustain the standing forest.

A good example is the Amazon Fund, an international mechanism to fund research in the Amazon that European donors mainly sustain. Donors have used this mechanism to pressure Brazilian governments to favor forest conservation under the threat of cutting down the budget if specific goals were not met. So far, the Amazon Fund has financed 102 projects, with US$ 581 million disbursed, according to Brazilian official data.[3] Nevertheless, there seems to be a limit to action, since scientific partnerships can feed international pressure, but international cooperation and funding are matters of geopolitics and diplomacy. For instance, the Amazon Fund was blocked during Minister Ricardo Salles's term. However, Norway and Germany reactivated it in 2023, after President Lula signed a new decree concerning the fund. Moreover, the European Union, the United States, and the United Kingdom could become donors in the near future.

Science has always been a driving force for society. However, for decision-making processes, knowledge has been used by different variables (Littoz-Monnet, 2017). In the history of geopolitics, knowledge of geography, and the "forces of nature" were considered of paramount importance by scholars and practitioners such as Mackinder, Mahan, Sprouts, Becker, and Mattos, to mention only a few. Finally, "The current discourse about the role of science in international diplomatic negotiations promotes science as a powerful means of producing better engaged and peaceful diplomacy" (Fedoroff, 2009; Polejack, 2022, 21). Thus, if diplomats need scientific advice to negotiate the reverse of the decline of the Amazon rainforest and Antarctica, Brazilians need it even more.

5. THE POLICY NETWORKS IN BRAZIL

The "policy network" is a conceptual choice to map the most relevant actors in a specific agenda. It contributes to answering the question of which institutions oversee agenda topics (Barros-Platiau et al., 2019). Concerning the Amazon, the president of the Amazonia Council was the Brazilian vice president and army general Hamilton Mourão from 2019 to 2022. The presence of military staff in the Amazon region is largely justified by the need to control borders and the global fight against illegal activities. However, the military staff does not respond only to a geopolitical agenda since they are also necessary to fight illegal deforestation. This was the case with operations Verde Brasil, Verde Brasil 2, and Samaúma.

Moreover, national campaigns such as vaccination and voting depend directly on army support and logistics. The Ministry of Environment may also be considered one key player, connected with other ministries and agencies in Brazil, taking the legal Amazon region as reference, as shown in Figure 9.1 above. Other important ministries are the Ministry of Science, Technology, and Innovation (MCTI), Ministry of Mining and Energy (MME), Ministry of Defense (MD), and Ministry of Foreign Affairs (MRE or Itamaraty) (Barros-Platiau et al., 2019). Although they are partially connected through working groups, policies, programs, and federal or state laws, they cannot yet respond to global risks related to the Anthropocene. Also, the Amazon forest and the "Blue Amazon," the maritime zone under Brazilian jurisdiction (Carvalho, 2022), are not adequately connected from an institutional viewpoint. Neither is Antarctica connected to them. For instance, the national maritime policy dates back to 1994, when geopolitics prevailed over environmental and scientific concerns (Política Marítima Nacional, 11/10/1994, decree nº 1.265). Nevertheless, the draft of the new policy, officially

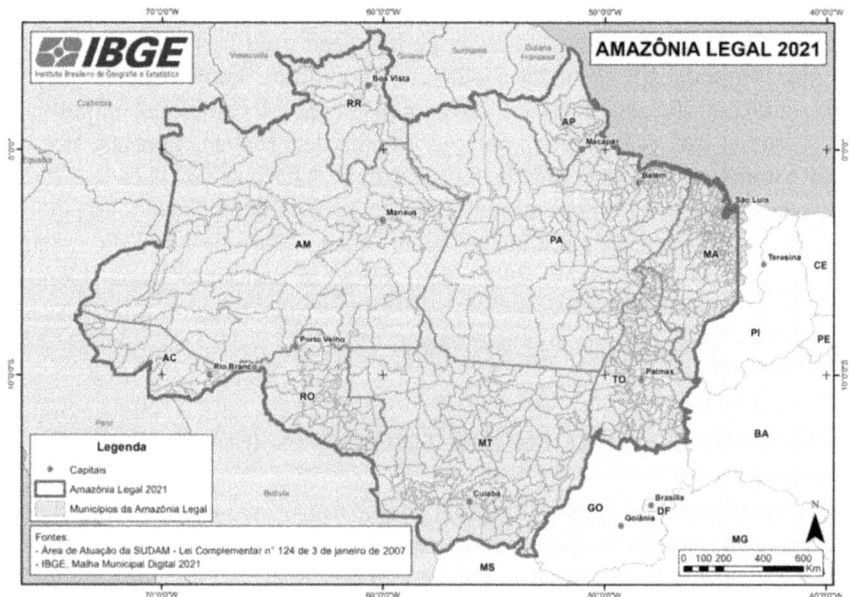

Figure 9.1.   A Brazilian Amazonia map termed Legal Amazonia.
Source: Brazilian Institute for Geography and Statistics (IBGE). Retrieved from: https://bit.ly/3TlAfJM. September 7, 2022.

presented in 2022, does not connect the Blue Amazon to Antarctica and does not even involve the related actors properly, concentrating efforts only on the governmental actors.

Myriad actors deal with the legal and Blue Amazonian agendas (Andrade et al., 2020). There are subnational authorities and interest groups, from giant corporations in agribusiness (Thives et al., 2022) to the mining sector to thousands of nongovernmental organizations, to mention only the most visible. There are also organized crime networks, notably for gold, drugs, and human trafficking (Sousa, 2022). From this perspective, the global institutional arrangement is inadequate to deal with diverse challenges, from illegal and predatory activities to the impacts of global warming, extreme weather events, and cascading effects (Chan et al., 2022). Moreover, recent technology-driven issues such as digital sequencing information (DSI) were developed "relatively independently from the international instruments on the conservation of biodiversity" (Aubry et al., 2021, XX). Likewise, Brazil must revisit the national policy network to adapt to these contemporary global challenges (Rajão et al., 2022).

On the contrary, the Antarctica Policy Network in Brazil is much better integrated than the Amazonia one through the work of the Interministerial Commission for Marine Resources (CIRM) (Barros-Platiau et al., 2019). CIRM was created in 1974 under the authority of the Brazilian Navy and reformed in 2019. Besides the Ministry of Defense, CIRM is composed of the Ministry of Foreign Affairs (MRE) and the Ministry of Science, Technology, and Innovation (MCTI), the most relevant players, plus eleven other ministries and a representative from the presidential cabinet. CIRM is responsible for the implementation of the Brazilian Antarctic Program (PROANTAR[4]) based on the national policy for Antarctica (POLANTAR, Decree 11.096 of June 15, 2022).[5] The Ministry of Environment (MMA) created a new Department of Ocean and Coastal Management (Presidential Decree 11.349 of January 1, 2023).

As Antarctica is not yet exposed to many different actors and interests in Brazil, it is reasonable to argue that the existing policy network corresponds to the preferences of the stakeholders who are holding the region as a place for peace and science rather than those who could benefit from the exploration and exploitation of its resources, such as tourism.

If there are two different policy networks in Brazil, one for the Amazon and the other for Antarctica, how are they connected? Should they be connected? Although both policy networks are composed of roughly the same ministries, the network for Antarctica is better structured and centralized under the auspices of CIRM. However, they are still poorly connected, even though army officers play a leadership role in both policy networks. The Ministry of Environment is centrally placed in the Amazonian policy network, but it operates in all sorts of themes: the urban agenda; biodiversity and climate; desertification and ozone; environmental education and citizenship; protected areas and ecotourism; environmental services, international relations, and ecosystems. Thus, the Amazonian network lacks a coordination mechanism such as CIRM, while it irradiates from the Ministry of Environment and its broad agenda.

Looking at the official websites and publications, as well as at the Brazilian legal framework, it is hard to find the concepts mentioned in the first part of this text: Anthropocene, noosphere, science diplomacy, great acceleration, blue acceleration, and others. For example, the strategic environmental assessment discussed during the IGC-5 in September 2022 for the BBNJ treaty still needs to be inserted in the agenda of the Brazilian policy networks.

Policy networks also form around issues where information plays a key role, and around issues where the value of the "commodity" is not easily measured (Keck and Sikkink, 1999), just as in Antarctica. Decision-making arenas are not only loci for making decisions but are also places where individuals in power exchange information. Thus, an arena built on science diplomacy connecting both the Amazon and Antarctica could be beneficial for Brazil. They could learn from each other's past experiences and current challenges, starting with the adaptation agenda and the carbon market discussed within the climate change regime at CoP 27 in 2022.

Antarctica policy network, for instance, could lend experiences in discussing a global issue among different countries and keeping science as its core. Furthermore, Amazon networks, on the other hand, could spirit debates on how to involve national stakeholders and keep them engaged with the local-global agenda, comprising many divergent interests in place.

Another way of connecting both agendas is through transnational networks, which can move politically usable information quickly and credibly to where it will have the most impact (Keck and Sikkink, 1999). However, even for civil society and advocacy networks, the Amazon and Antarctica still need to be connected. Probably because the Amazon and Antarctica are still distant from people, they are places in their imagination, but not places they know and are prepared to protect.

To deal with the complex challenges that are gradually deepening due to the increasing pressure on the environment of both the Amazon and Antarctica, as well as the interaction between these two global subsystems, Brazil needs to develop an institutional arrangement that would drive the actions of the various bodies involved, dully identified in the respective policy networks. The joint efforts of these bodies should seek the harmonization of principles, norms, rules, and decision-making procedures based on scientifically defined and politically supported values and goals. Hence, a forum that is based on the best available science and that includes formal representations of nongovernmental stakeholders. Naturally, Brazil has public and private scientific research capacities, entities like federal universities, the Brazilian Society for the Promotion of Science (SBPC), the Institute of Applied Economic Research (IPEA), and the Centre for Management and Strategic Studies (CGEE), whose members have traditionally interacted with public authorities concerning the policy networks.

It seems counterproductive to define this new institutional arrangement according to a principle of *subordination*, that is, creating a new administrative instance superior to the others, capable of determining the functioning of the bodies involved. Even less effective would be to assign this task to a body with the same hierarchical position as the other ministries, such as the presidential cabinet (Casa Civil). Faced with the model of presidential coalition adopted in Brazil, in which federal bodies are distributed—in the name of governability—among the political parties that support the government in Congress, either of the two solutions would give rise to power disputes and, therefore, political resistance that would undermine the effectiveness of the environmental governance framework.

A better way would be to create a coordination committee functioning as a high-level project management office (PMO) (Monteiro, Santos, and Varajão, 2016), capable of driving the action of existing ministries' bodies toward the objectives of a strategic, integrated, science-based policy for environmental sustainability. It should focus first on climate change and include the Amazon, Antarctica, and the ocean. This committee, directly linked to and under the personal leadership of the highest authority of the executive branch, would function as an innovative policy network. It would be responsible for identifying, together with all the government bodies involved, the necessary steps to achieve policy objectives, including ensuring the flow of financial resources and monitoring the execution of the tasks assigned to each body. Once the necessary steps have been defined, the heads of the executive branch and the ministries' bodies involved in policy implementation would formally assume their commitment to implementing the strategy. The committee's daily activities would be carried out by technical teams, while political leaders would meet periodically to assess the work progress and decide on strategic matters. Such a framework would guarantee the commitment and compliance of all domestic governmental actors concerned. In sum, this committee would be the airplane's pilot with two wings: Antarctica and Amazonia. Brazil has only focused on Amazonia so far.

CONCLUSION

The Amazon and Antarctica need to be protected not only because they are El Dorados; they are also Earth's vital systems. However, will humanity be able to shape the future toward the noosphere? More specifically, will Brazil be able to reform the policy networks and contribute effectively to global order stability? In this chapter, we brought some scientific and diplomatic concepts to argue that the Anthropocene alert demands more sophisticated institutional responses than we have on a global scale. Similarly, Brazil needs to take responsibility regarding humankind, not only national geopolitical interests in the short term.

In this sense, complexity is not only about connecting different issues, but also about conceptualizing the challenges emerging from their interaction (Tomé, 2023) and advancing social learning. Since Brazil can be a game changer due to the Amazon and Antarctica agendas, it seems imperative to develop a decision-making arena to resume the country's role on the global level and move forward with an integrated agenda connecting them to the global climate and the ocean agendas.

The opportunity stands for novel initiatives in which resources are optimized, ideas are shared, and a network of stakeholders promotes more effective governance toward sustainability. It is time to use the accumulated knowledge about the changes in the Anthropocene epoch to put actions in place, reinforcing the noosphere, when human beings' capacity to react to new, complex challenges triggers transformative changes.

Therefore, we suggest that the Brazilian government undertake a deep dive into scientific works and start to integrate the policy networks so that Brazil can better protect the Amazon region and contribute more effectively to the governance of Antarctica, keeping in mind that what happens in the forest has an impact on the icy continent, and vice versa. Therefore, we propose the creation of a coordination committee for the implementation of a strategic, integrated, science-based policy for environmental sustainability, with the direct involvement of all the ministries concerned and personally directed by the highest authority of the federal executive branch, as a way of guaranteeing commitment and compliance of all domestic governmental actors. Given that climate stability and sustainable use of resources are rather complex agendas, Brazil has much work ahead.

In addition to this governmental coordination, there is a need to center debates on societal participation through the inclusion of representatives of civil society, scientific academies, the private sector, and so on, in a movement usually termed "public diplomacy," where diverse stakeholders influence decision-making process toward a more comprehensive community interest defense (Gregory, 2008). By doing so, combining multistakeholder frameworks with broad participation can advance the noosphere ideas and propose a way forward to the sustainability transformations envisaged.

Finally, Brazil has jurisdiction over a significant part of the Amazon forest and the Blue Amazon. It is also a voting member of the Antarctic Treaty System. We hope that science diplomacy will be the main bridge toward the Brazilian recognition of its global responsibility within the geopolitical and research agenda, so that Brazil can successfully contribute to the establishment of the noosphere and promote its geopolitical interests.

NOTES

1. Retrieved from: http://www.igbp.net/globalchange/greatacceleration.html. October 10, 2022.

2. Science diplomacy is the resulting process that emerges from the interrelations between research and international affairs, including the provision of scientific evidence to international decision-making or the establishment of scientific collaborations for global issues of concern, among other practices (The Royal Society & AAAS, 2010).

3. Retrieved from: http://www.amazonfund.gov.br/en/home/. October 10, 2022.

4. Retrieved from: https://www.marinha.mil.br/secirm/proantar. October 10, 2022.

5. Retrieved from: https://www.marinha.mil.br/secirm/pt-br/institucional. October 10, 2022.

REFERENCES

Albagli, Sarita. *Geopolítica da Biodiversidade*. Brasília: Edições Ibama, 1998.

Andrade, Israel, Giovanni Hillebrand, Ana Flávia Barros-Platiau, Paulo Câmara, and Niels Søndergaard. "Redes políticas e governança tridimensional: Amazônia Azul, Antártica e Biodiversidade Além da Jurisdição Nacional (BBNJ)." In *Meio Ambiente Marinho, Sustentabilidade e Direito. A conservação e o uso sustentável dos recursos marinhos na zona costeira, na plataforma continental e nos fundos marinhos*, edited by Carina Costa de Oliveira, Solange Teles da Silva, Tarin Frota Mont'Alverne, Ana Flávia Barros-Platiau, George Galindo, 489–514. Rio de Janeiro: Lumen Juris, 2020.

Andreae, Meinrat, D. Rosenfeld, Paulo Artaxo, A. Costa, G. Frank, K. Longo, and M. Silva-Dias. "Smoking rain clouds over the Amazon." *Science* 303 (2004): 1337–1342.

Aubry, Sylvain, Christine Frison, Jorge Medaglia, Emile Frison, Marcel Jaspars, Muriel Rabone, Aysegul Sirakaya, Devanshi Saxena, and Esther van Zimmeren. "Bringing access and benefit sharing into the digital age."" *Plants, People, Planet.* (2021).

Barros-Platiau, Ana Flávia, Niels Søndergaard, and Jochen Prantl. "Policy Networks in Global Environmental Governance: Connecting the Blue Amazon to Antarctica and the Biodiversity Beyond National Jurisdiction (BBNJ) Agendas." *Revista Brasileira de Política Internacional* 62 (2019): 1–23.

Becker, Bertha. "Geopolítica da Amazônia." *Estudos Avançados* 19, no. 53 (2005): 71–86.

Berkman, Paul, Michael Lang, David Walton, and Oran R. Young (eds). *Science Diplomacy Antarctica, Science, and the Governance of International Spaces.* Washington: Smithsonian Institution Scholarly Press, 2011.

Biermann, Frank and Inna Möller. "Rich man's solution? Climate engineering discourses and the marginalization of the Global South." *Int Environ Agreements* 19, (2019):151–167

Boutaud, Aurélien and Natacha Gondran. *Les limites planétaires.* Paris: La Découverte, 2020.

Boyadjian, Alain, Paulo Câmara, Fábio Queiroz, and Ana Flávia Barros-Platiau. "Grand Challenges in Brazilian Scientific Research in Antarctica." *In conservation of living resources in areas beyond national jurisdiction: BBNJ and Antarctica,* edited by Ana Flávia Barros-Platiau and Carina Oliveira. Rio de Janeiro: Lumen Juris, 2020.

Boyadjian, Alain. "Complex Theory and Methods in International Relations." *Revista de Estudos Internacionais,* vol. 12, no.2 (2021): 1–26.

Burch, Sarah, Aarti Gupta, Cristina Inoue, Agni Kalfagianni, Åsa Perssone, Andrea K.Gerlakg, Atsushi Ishii, James Patterson, Jonathan Pickering, Michelle Scobiel et al. "New directions in earth system governance research." *Earth System Governance,* v. 1, 100006. (2019).

Cairney, Paul, Tanya Heikkila, and Michael Wood. *Making Policy in a Complex World.* Cambridge Elements. Public Policy. Cambridge: Cambridge University Press, 2019.

Camargo, Carolina, Riccardo Riva, Tim Hermans, and Aimée Slangen. "Trends and uncertainties of mass-driven sea-level change in the satellite altimetry era." *Earth System Dynamics,* 13, (2022): 1351–1375.

Chan Sander, Thomas Hale, Andrew Deneault, Manish Shrivastava, Kennedy Mbeva, Victoria Chengo and Joanes Atela. "Assessing the effectiveness of orchestrated climate action from five years of summits." *Nature Climate Change* 12, (2022): 628–633.

Christiansen, Sabine, Carole Durussel, Maila Guilhon, Pradeep Singh and Sebastian Unger. "Towards an Ecosystem Approach to Management in Areas Beyond National Jurisdiction: REMPs for Deep Seabed Mining and the Proposed BBNJ Instrument." *Front. Mar. Sci.* 17, no. 9 (2022): 720146.

Crutzen, Paul and Eugene Stoermer. "The Anthropocene." IGBP Global Change Newsletter 41, (2000): 17–18.

Daher, Victor, Rosa Paes, Gutemberg França, João Bosco Alvarenga, and Gregório Teixeira. "Extraction of Tide Constituents by Harmonic Analysis Using Altimetry Satellite Data in the Brazilian Coast." *Journal of Atmospheric and Oceanic Technology* 32, no. 3 (2015):614–626.

Frémaux, Anne. *After the Anthropocene: Green Republicanism in a Post-Capitalist World*. London: Palgrave MacMillan, 2019.

Friedman, Kim, Peter Bridgewater, Vera Agostini, Tundi Agardy, Alvatore Aricò, Frank Biermann, Kate Brown, Ian Cresswell, Erle Ellis, and Pierre Failler et al. "The CBD Post 2020 biodiversity framework: people's place within the rest of nature." *People and Nature* (2022).

Frozel Barros, Natália. "Un océan d'incertitudes. Problématisations et mise en forme légale des fonds marins par le travail diplomatique (1960–2016)." PhD diss., Université Paris 1 Panthéon Sorbonne, 2019.

Gattuso, Jean-Pierre and Alexandre Magnan. "L'océan, un garde-fou climatique." Polytechnique Insights, January 25, 2022. https://www.polytechnique-insights.com/tribunes/planete/locean-un-garde-fou-climatique/.

Gattuso, Jean-Pierre, Nianzhi Jiao. "Ocean-based climate actions recommended by academicians from Europe and China." *Science China Earth Sciences* 65, (2022): 1612–1614.

Gregory, Bruce. "Public diplomacy: Sunrise of an academic field." *Annals of the American Academy of Political and Social Science*, 616, no. 1 (2008): 274–290.

Hannigan, John. *The Geopolitics of Deep Oceans*. Cambridge: Polity, 2015.

Höfele, Philipp, Oliver Müller, and Lore Hühn Lore. "Introduction: The role of nature in the Anthropocene—Defining and reacting to a new geological epoch." *The Anthropocene Review* 9, no. 2 (2022): 129–138.

Inoue, Cristina. "Worlding the Study of Global Environmental Politics in the Anthropocene: Indigenous Voices from the Amazon."" *Global Environmental Politics* 18, (2018): 25–42.

IOC-UNESCO. State of the Ocean Report, pilot edition. Paris: IOC-UNESCO IOC Technical Series, 173, 2022.

IPBES. Intergovernmental Science-Policy Platform on Biodiversity and Ecosystem Services. Global assessment report on biodiversity and ecosystem services of the Intergovernmental Science-Policy Platform on Biodiversity and Ecosystem Services (Version 1). Bonn: IPBES Secretariat, 2019.

IPCC. *The Ocean and Cryosphere in a Changing Climate Report*. Cambridge: Cambridge University Press, 2019.

Johnson, Amy, Chris Hebdon, Paul Burow, Deepti Chatti, and Michael Dove. "Anthropocene." *Oxford Research Encyclopedia of Anthropology*, 2022.

Kavalski, Emilian. World Politics at the Edge of Chaos: Reflections on Complexity and Global Life. New York: SUNY series, James N. Rosenau series in Global Politics, 2016.

Keck, Margaret, Kathryn Sikkink. "Transnational advocacy networks in international and regional politics." *International Social Science Journal*, 51 (1999): 89–101.

Kiss, Alexandre. "La notion de patrimoine commun de l'humanite." *Recueil des cours* de Académie de droit international 175 (1982): 103–125.

Kotzé, Louis. "Governing Prometheans in the Anthropocene: Three Proposals to Reform International Environmental Law. Reimagining the Human-Environment Relationship." UN University and UN Environment Programme, 2022.

Koster, Emlyn. "Public-minded reflections from the Anthropocene Working Group meeting in Germany." Episodes Journal of International Geoscience, International Union of Geological Sciences (2022).

Kotzé, Louis and Sam Adelman. "Environmental Law and the Unsustainability of Sustainable Development: A Tale of Disenchantment and of Hope." *Law and Critique*, 2022.

Latour, Bruno. "Géopolitique ou Gaïapolitique?" In *L'Enjeu mondial* (2015): p. 29–36. Paris: Presses de Sciences Po.

Latour, Bruno. *Down to Earth: Politics in the New Climatic Regime.* Cambridge: Polity Press, 2018.

Littoz-Monnet, Annabelle. (ed.). *The Politics of Expertise in International Organizations: How International Bureaucracies Produce and Mobilize Knowledge.* Abingdon: Routledge, 2017.

Martin, Scot, Paulo Artaxo, Luiz Machado, Antônio Ocimar Manzi, Rodrigo Souza, Courtney Schumacher, Jian Wang, Thiago Biscaro, José Brito, Alan Calheiros, and Kolby Jardine et al. "The Green Ocean Amazon Experiment (Goamazon2014/5) Observes Pollution Affecting Gases, Aerosols, Clouds, and Rainfall Over the Rain Forest." *Bulletin of the American Meteorological Society* 98, no. 5 (2017): 981–997.

Mello, Natália, and Paulo Artaxo. "Evolução do Plano de Ação para Prevenção e Controle do Desmatamento na Amazônia Legal." *Revista do Instituto de Estudos Brasileiros*, 66 (2017): 108–129.

Oliveira, Carina, and Maljean-Dubois, Sandrine. "What is the Contribution of the Concept of Global Public Goods to Define Obligations for the Preservation of Marine Resources?" In *Protecting Forest and Marine Biodiversity*, edited by Alexander Paterson Couzens and Yanti Fristikawati Sophie Riley. London: Edward Elgar Publishing, 2017.

Martin, Scot, Paulo Artaxo, Luiz Augusto Machado, Ocimar Manzi, Rodrigo Souza, Courtney Schumacher, Jian Wang, Thiago Biscara, Joel Brito, and Alan Calheiros et al. "The green ocean amazon experiment (GOAMAZON2014/5) observes pollution affecting gases, aerosols, clouds, and rainfall over the rain forest." Repositório do INPA, 2017. Accesed November 20, 2022. https://repositorio.inpa.gov.br/handle /1/17123.

McNeill, John and Peter Engelke. *The Great Acceleration: An Environmental History of the Anthropocene since 1945.* Cambridge, MA: Harvard University Press, 2016.

Monteiro, António, Vitor Santos, and João Varajão (2016). "Project Management Office Models: A Review." In International Conference on ENTERprise Information Systems/International Conference on Project MANagement/International Conference on Health and Social Care Information Systems and Technologies, CENTERIS/ProjMAN / HCist. *Procedia Computer Science*, vol. 100 (2016): 1085–1094.

Miles, Edward. "The Concept of Ocean Governance: Evolution Toward the 21st Century and the Principle of Sustainable Ocean Use." *Coastal Management* 27, no. 1 (1999): 1–30.

Nielsen, Ron. "Anthropogenic data question the concept of the Anthropocene as a new geological Epoch." *Episodes* 45 (2022): 257–264.

Nye, Joseph S. "Soft Power." *Foreign Policy* 80 (1990): 153–171.

Oliveira, Carina, Ana Flávia Barros-Platiau, Leandra Gonçalves, Ana Paula Prates, and Larissa Suassuna. "A governança fragmentada da conservação e do uso sustentável do oceano e de seus recursos." Revista Inclusiones 9, (2022): 219–241.

Oliveira, Carina, Gabriela Moraes, and Priscila Andrade. "The Limited Contribution of Environmental Law to the Sustainable Management of Marine Resources in Brazil: The Need for an Integrated Approach." In *Sustainability and Law General and Specific Aspects*, edited by Volker Mauerhofer, Daniela Rupo, Lara Tarquinio, p. 497–519. New York: Springer, 2020.

Pereira, Joana and Maria Fernanda Gebara. "Where the material and the symbolic intertwine: Making sense of the Amazon in the Anthropocene." *Review of International Studies*, (2022) 1–20.

Pflieger, Géraldine. "Délimiter les biens communs planétaires: Le cas des océans, des fonds marins et de l'Antarctique." L'Enjeu mondial (2015):103–112.

Polejack, Andrei. Ocean science diplomacy - the All-Atlantic Ocean Research Alliance case. Ph.D. diss., World Maritime University, Sweden, 2022.

Rajão, Raoni, Antonio Nobre, Evandro Cunha, Tiago Duarte, Camilla Marcolino, Britaldo Soares-Filho, Gerd Sparovek, Ricardo R. Rodrigues, Carlos Valera, Mercedes Bustamante, Carlos Nobre, and Letícia Santos de Lima. "The risk of fake controversies for Brazilian environmental policies," *Biological Conservation* 266 (2022): 109447.

Reid, Keith. "Conserving Antarctica from the Bottom Up, Implementing UN General Assembly Resolution 61/105 in the Commission for the Conservation of Antarctic Marine Living Resources (CCAMLR)." Ocean Yearbook online, 25 (2011): 131–139.

Rockström Johan, Will Steffen, Kevin Noone, Åsa Persson, F. Stuart Chapin III, Eric Lambin, Timothy Lenton, Marten Scheffer, Carl Folke, Hans Schellnhuber, Björn Nykvist, and Cynthia Wit, et al. *Nature*, n. 461 (2009): 472–475.

Rockström, Johan and Kate Höfele. Planetary Boundaries and Human Prosperity. Project Syndicate, 2015. Accessed November 3, 2022. https://www.project-syndicate.org/commentary/environment-boundaries-human-prosperity-by-johan-rockstr-m-and-kate-raworth-2015-04.

Shoshitaishvili, Boris. "From Anthropocene to Noosphere: The Great Acceleration." *Earth's Future* 9, no. 2 (2021).

Sousa, Micheline. "Crime Organizado Transnacional na Amazônia Brasileira: O que as Forças Armadas têm a ver com isso?" MA diss., Escola de Comando e Estado-Maior do Exército.

Steffen, Will, Meinrat Andreae, Bert Bolin, Peter M. Cox, Paul J. Crutzen, Ulrich Cubasch, Hermann Held, Nebojsa Nakicenovic, Robert J. Scholes, Liana Talaue-McManus, and B. L. Turner II. "Abrupt Changes. The Achilles' Heels of the Earth System." *Environment* 46, no. 3, (2004).

Steffen, Will, Wendy Broadgate, Lisa Deutsch, Owen Gaffney, and Cornelia Ludwig. "The trajectory of the Anthropocene: The Great Acceleration." *The Anthropocene Review* (2015): 1–18.

Stillman, Jonathan. "Heat Waves, the New Normal: Summertime Temperature Extremes Will Impact Animals, Ecosystems, and Human Communities." *Physiology* (2019).

Tomé, Carlos Henrique. "Sustainability Governance in The Anthropocene: Deep Drivers and Perspectives of the Marine Biodiversity Beyond National Jurisdiction Treaty." Ph.D. diss., University of Brasilia, 2023.

Thives, Victor, Niels Søndergaard, and Cristina Inoue. "Bringing states back into commodity-centric environmental governance: the telecoupled soy trade between Brazil and China." *Third World Quarterly* 43, no. 9 (2022): 2129–2148.

UNDP. United Nations Human Development Report. Uncertain times, unsettled lives Shaping our future in a transforming world, 2022. Accessed November 22, 2022. https://hdr.undp.org/system/files/documents/global-report-document/hdr2021 -22pdf_1.pdf.

Vidas, Davor. "The Anthropocene and the international law of the sea." Philosophical *Transactions of the Royal Society. A: Mathematical, Physical and Engineering Sciences*, 369, no.1938 (2011): 909–925.

Viñuales, Jorge. "The Organisation of the Anthropocene." *Brill Research Perspectives in International Legal Theory and Practice* 1, (2018): 1–81.

Young, Oran. *Grand Challenges of Planetary Governance: Global Order in Turbulent Times*. Cheltenham: Edward Elgar Publishing, 2021.

Wunderling, Nico, Jonathan Donges, Jürgen Kurths, and Ricarda Winkelmann. "Interacting tipping elements increase risk of climate domino effects under global warming." *Earth System. Dynamics*, 12, (2021): 601–619.

Zelli, F. and Philip Pattberg. *Environmental Politics and Governance in the Anthropocene*. London: Routledge, 2016.

Zhao, Li, Tao Xie, William Perrie, Ming Ma, Jingsong Yang, Chengzu Bai, and Rick Danielson. "Detection of Sea Surface Temperature Fronts from SAR Images." *Journal of Atmospheric and Oceanic Technology*, (2022)

Zou, Youjia and Xiangying Xi. "The possible role of Brazilian promontory in Little Ice Age." *Dynamics of Atmospheres and Oceans* 67 (2014): 29–38.

WEF. World Economic Forum Global Risks Report. Accessed September 16, 2022. https://www.weforum.org/reports/global-risks-report-2022 (2022).

Chapter 10

Heritage Preservation Policies in Antarctica and the Amazon

A Comparative Approach

Andrés Zarankin and Marcia Bezerra

The critical heritage turn of the 1990s and 2000s had a meaningful impact on the emergence of new approaches, showing that treating heritage does not naturally exist in the world but is produced through power relations. Within these new proposals, heritage presents itself as a type of narrative in which international institutions usually use policy mechanisms to authoritatively set the terms of what counts as heritage, how we must take care of it, and what heritage can do. Treating heritage as a narrative allows us to examine how this rhetoric about the past evolved and how it affects the present in local and global ways; in other words, how global heritage narratives have impacted the nuances communicated across cultures and places.

For this reason, in the last decade, increasing attention has been paid to national and institutional agendas and spheres of influence. This concern has helped us understand the role of heritage in diplomatic and other political transactions and uncover the practical ways in which master narratives (or official history) are produced.

We know that heritage has the potential to perpetuate master narratives or help to criticize it and eventually change it. Archaeology, as a disciplined focus on the study of material culture, has great potential to analyze heritage narratives, contributing to the apprehension of meanings and ideologies behind the places and objects chosen to be representatives of cultural values.

This chapter discusses the similarities and differences between the heritage narratives of the two spaces. They are generally represented as similar (predominantly natural and wild) and at the same time opposed (glacial versus tropical), Antarctica and Amazon. Therefore, we will begin by presenting a brief discussion on the history of heritage construction policies in Antarctica and the Amazon within their respective sociopolitical contexts, and subsequently cross-reference this information.

1. ANTARCTICA HERITAGE

Antarctica is the only continent on Earth that is not divided into countries. It does not have cities or stable human populations, no activity of economic exploitation is allowed, and it is recognized by the Antarctic Treaty as an international territory, with scientific research being the only permitted activity. It is also the last great space to be incorporated into the human domain circuit at the beginning of the nineteenth century.

The history of Antarctica comprises three general periods. The earliest, associated with the arrival of companies that sent hunters of marine mammals (seals and whales), was during the first half of the nineteenth century. In a few years, the continent's animal population was almost exterminated: preservation policies were lacking, and the savage competition of several international companies raged on. During the second period a change occurred during which exploitation decreased as the predominant activity in Antarctica, exploration, became predominant. This moment is known as the "heroic era." which lasted from the mid-nineteenth century to the beginning of the twentieth and had prominent figures such as Robert Falcon Scott, Roald Amundsen, Otto Nordenskjöld, and Ernest Henry Shackleton, among others, as protagonists. They were the heroes from whom hegemonic historiography was built, centered on adventures and explorations. Finally, the third and last period is related to the signature of the Antarctic Treaty,[1] which transformed Antarctica into a protected international space dedicated to scientific research.

Although Antarctica is an international territory, that does not mean there are no sovereignty claims (they are temporarily blocked as long as the Antarctic Treaty is in force—currently until 2041). Because of these nationalist claims, Antarctic historical and heritage narratives have become a complex political arena. Narratives about Antarctica's discovery have more than one version, especially regarding dates and protagonists (see Miers, 1920; Ossoinak Garibaldi, 1950). For example, some state that British trader William Smith was the discoverer (see Fitte, 1959, 1962, 1974), whereas others mention survivors of a Spanish shipwreck (Pinochet de la Barra, 1992). Some even propose members of a crew of whale- or seal-hunting vessels from South America or North America as the first human beings to have landed there (see Berguno, 1993a and b; Bertrand, 1971; Hodge, 1976; Martin, 1940; O'Gorman, 1963; Slaney, 1921; Stackpole, 1955).

This political influence of nationalist characters also conditioned the decisions on the nominations of historical sites and monuments in Antarctica. In the 1970s, there was an awareness of the need to preserve historical sites. Therefore, in 1972, a list of Antarctic Historic Sites and Monuments (HSMs) was created, allowing any party to the Antarctic Treaty to propose the inclusion of a historic site. HSMs are a kind of material expression of the dominant narratives of Antarctic history (Senatore and Zarankin, 2014). As Senatore states, "Mmaterial culture has played an active role in constructing heritage discourses that have significant cultural and political consequences in the present" ((2019: 756; see Avango 2016, 2017; Leane et al. 2016; Roura 2017; Senatore 2018; Senatore and Zarankin 2014).

The monuments under the Antarctic Treaty are fully compliant with this, intending to identify, protect, and preserve Antarctica's historical and cultural values. Adopted measures, decisions, and resolutions must have the consensus of the signatory states at the Antarctic Treaty Consultative Meetings. As a result of this situation, it is no surprise that the first sites were considered critical to protect those associated with the heroic era (Wellington, 1972). The number of listed sites and the criteria to designate and manage them gradually changed after agreements under the Antarctic Treaty System (Barr, 2018; Pearson, 2004, 2011). However, the designation process reinforces national interests (Evans, 2011; Senatore, 2019).

Successive Antarctic Treaty Consultative Meetings have developed guidelines to ensure the process for designating historic sites. So far, ninety-five HSMs have been listed. They are monuments—human artifacts rather than areas—and many are near scientific stations and cannot be damaged, removed, or destroyed. The 2009 guideline established that:

> Parties who wish to nominate a particular Historic Site and/or Monument should address in the proposal one or more of the following: A) a particular event of importance in the history of science or exploration of Antarctica occurred at the place; B) a particular association with a person who played an essential role in the history of science or exploration in Antarctica; C) a particular association with a notable feat of endurance or achievement; D) be representative of, or forming part of, some wide-ranging activity that has been important in the development and knowledge of Antarctica; E) bear particular technical, historical, cultural or architectural value in its materials, design or method of construction; F) have the potential, through study, to reveal information or to educate people about significant human activities in Antarctica; G) bear symbolic or commemorative value for people of many nations. (Senatore and Zarankin, 2011)

When analyzing which countries proposed each monument, what objects or places they are, and their meaning and relevance, it is clear that there is a wide diversity of monuments far from a single register. In general, they have in common the reinforcement of the identity of these spaces with nationalist narratives. In a paper with Ximena Senatore (Senatore and Zarankin, 2011), we discuss the number of sites, looking at their official designation as monuments over time (eighty-four sites in 2009). The analysis shows that most sites were designated to commemorate a period between 1900 and 1920. However, we observed a distinctive representation of the different moments, and there was great emphasis in the early twentieth century.

In a group of thirty-five sites, thirty commemorate events taken place during the heroic era (Senatore and Zarankin, 2011). Only five of them celebrate previous exploratory expeditions during the nineteenth century (No. 36, 37, 57, 59, 81). None of these sites are related to or mention the seal hunters' presence; only two refer to whalers' activities during that period. One of them marks Henryk Bull and Captain Leonard Kristensen's whaling expedition in the Antarctic in 1895 (No. 65), and the other, the whaling station on Deception Island (No. 71). This site also monumentalizes the longest settlement on Antarctic lands, extending from 1912 to 1931 (Senatore and Zarankin, 2011).

Roura (2017) also carried out an analysis of the profile of these sites. The author concluded that only fifty-six HSMs were listed between 1819–1969, giving a somewhat partial view of the past, a severe problem if the objective is helping to reconstruct Antarctic history (Engel et al., 2019).

Since 2009, eleven more sites have been incorporated into the Antarctic HSM list. Again, all of them commemorated specific places or objects. Among others, we can mention HSM-85, a plaque commemorating the

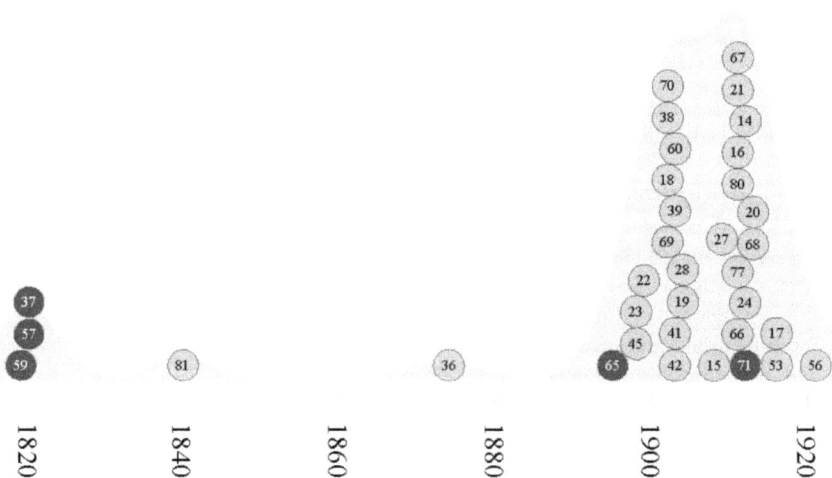

Figure 10.1. **Distribution of Nominated Antarctic Historic Sites and Monuments According to the Date of the Events Commemorated by Them (from 1820 to 1920).** Senatore and Zarankin 2011.

PM-3A nuclear power plant at McMurdo Station, or HSM-87, the location of the first permanently occupied German Antarctic research station "Georg Forster" at the Schirmacher Oasis, Dronning Maud Land, HSM-92. In addition, the oversnow heavy tractor "Kharkovchanka," used in Antarctica from 1959 to 2010, and one of the most famous HSM-93, Endurance, wreck of the vessel owned and used by Sir Ernest Shackleton during his 1914–1915 Imperial Trans-Antarctic Expedition. Finally, only the last two HSM sites have something to do with thenineteenth-century HSM-94, Carl Anton Larsen Multiexpedition cairn (1892), and HSM-95, wreck of San Telmo.

2. NEW ACTORS AND THE TRANSFORMATION
OF THEIR REMAINS INTO HERITAGE

Recent archaeological studies have been fundamental to understanding human history in Antarctica and introducing new actors in the heritage narratives (Harrowfield 2005; Zarankin and Senatore 2007). Attention is mainly focused on the early occupation and exploitation of the territory. Since its discovery at the beginning of the nineteenth century, the South Shetland Islands were visited by sealing vessels. Hunters were interested in obtaining large quantities of oil and furs to be sold in different markets. In contrast to written documents, archaeological fieldwork in the South Shetlands has primarily dealt with nineteenth-century sealers' camps. The material analysis of these places (including structures and objects) provides not only insight into sealers' daily life in previously unknown territory, but also the basis to include a subaltern group, previously excluded from master narratives and official heritage and now beginning to be incorporated into discussions of the early history of this place (Zarankin and Senatore 1996, 1997, 1999, 2000).

Even though sealing has always been an integral part of the subsistence economy, modern sealing was closely connected to developing a market economy. Throughout the nineteenth century, exploitation depended on supply and demand of skins and oil. However, animal resources were obtained and sold on a global scale. Sealing companies were critical to this process.

Modern hunting areas were first located in the northern hemisphere, particularly in the Arctic and the subarctic regions. In the late eighteenth century, demand for seal products increased, and so did the number of sealing companies. North American enterprises were not the only ones participating in the exploitation: British and South American companies, among others, were part of it as well. Competition and growing pressure on natural resources forced sealing vessels to find new hunting areas. In this context, sealers reached the coasts of Patagonia and the subantarctic islands. It was just a matter of time before they got to Antarctica.

The South Shetland Islands, 120 kilometers away from the Antarctic Peninsula, and approximately 1,200 kilometers south of Cape Horn, were the first region of the new continent to become known. They were officially discovered in 1819 by Captain Smith, a British merchant who deviated from his route to Valparaiso because of a storm. According to historical sources, several species inhabited this region, such as seals (along with sea elephants, sea lions, and other pinnipeds), which did not consider humans a menace. Therefore, sealing vessels started visiting the islands during the summer, when the ice sheet did not prevent them from reaching the shore.

Documentary sources indicate that sealing companies landed a series of gangs on different points of the South Shetland Islands. Each gang brought together various huntsmen (in command of one or more officers) who established their camps on the coast: sealing evolved with different intensities throughout the nineteenth century. As the activity ended, the camps' location and the stories connected to these spaces were gradually forgotten. A group of British geographers in the 1950s eventually rediscovered the remains of a sealing structure on Livingston Island. From that moment on, several groups of archaeologists surveyed the area. In the 1980s, the Chilean project started researching Desolation and Livingston Islands. The Argentinean project worked on Livingston Island from the mid-1990s to the beginning of the twenty-first century. Finally, the Brazilian project, which was a continuation of the Argentinian's in 2009, gathered all the other teams in an international study to share information (location of historical sites, lists of archaeological findings, management proposals), logistics, and publications.

Our Brazilian project, "Landscape in White," is interested in discussing the relationship between humans and Antarctica from its earliest occupation (the nineteenth century) until the present (Zarankin et al., 2011; Zarankin and Salerno, 2017; Zarankin et al., 2021). That includes the first attempts of the modern world to incorporate a hostile region, utterly unknown until the nineteenth century, into its economic and political boundaries. On the one hand, the project worked at a macro level, seeking to understand the nationalist and capitalist network of interests, which involved the South Shetlands at the beginning of the century.

Conversely, the project started to study the region's incorporation at a micro level, involving the life of the people who occupied and exploited Antarctica for the first time. The reconstruction of sealers' daily practices finally became relevant. The project follows the guidelines of archaeology (generally) and historical archaeology (specificly). Therefore, it assumes that it is possible to learn about the life of people if we study their material world and interpret the role it plays in the definition of social relationships. In the case of historical archaeology, this can imply studying archaeological (the

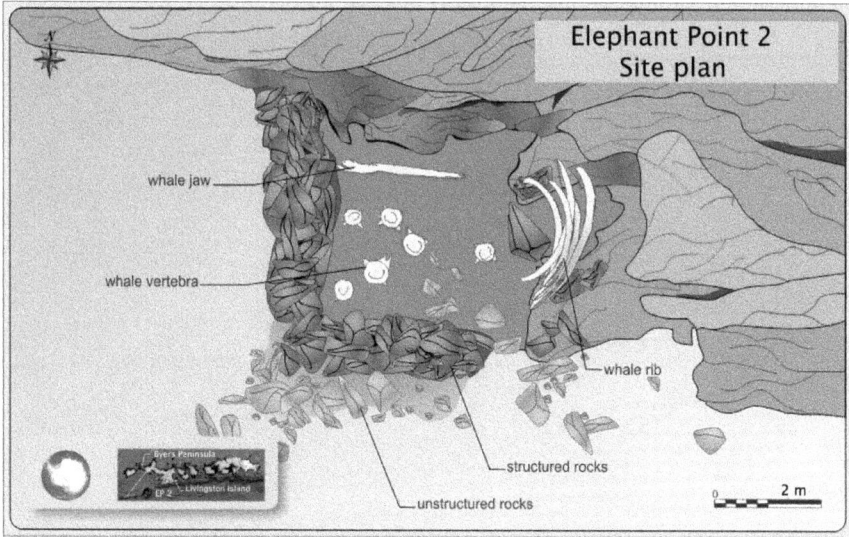

Figure 10.2.   Archaeological Site Punta Elefante 2. LEACH 2014.

material traces that people left behind) and historical evidence (the information provided in written documents).

Archaeological and historical sources have provided information on different aspects of sealers' first steps in the South Shetlands. While archaeological evidence proves helpful in understanding sealers' life on land, historical evidence primarily deals with their existence on board the vessels. Archaeological studies in Livingston Island (62° 30' Lat. S / 60° 30' Long. O) show that this island was frequently visited by sealers during the nineteenth century, and—at least until today—it has shown the highest concentrations of sealing camps in the South Shetlands. On the island's western side is Byers Peninsula: archaeological activities combined the survey of the area and the excavation of specific locations. This strategy allowed the identification of twenty-seven archaeological sites and the recovery of an essential collection of sealers' objects.

Those remains (sites and artifacts) were fundamental to creating awareness about preserving this heritage, allowing us to value alternative narratives that show the importance of these subaltern groups for Antarctic history. In addition, this heritage is contributing to new publications on Antarctic history, including new protagonists other than captains and adventurers, who have always been the heroes and well-known names of Antarctic history.

Although the future looks quite promising, and these sealed sites and objects take part in protected areas in Antarctica, they have yet to be officially included in the Antarctic HSM list. However, as Senatore shows in her study

Figure 10.3. Excavations Under Way at Punta Elefante 2 Shelter Site, Showing the Whale Rrib Roof Frames and Vertebrae Furniture in Situ. Stone Walls to Lower Right and Left Foreground. LEACH 2014.

of tourist experiences of visiting historical sites and remains, the interest in this dark side of Antarctic history is growing (Senatore et al., 2019; Senatore, 2019). We can say that heritage-making in Antarctica is slowly starting to change, but at least it is good news.

3. AMAZON HERITAGE

The biome constitutes the Amazon with the most extensive biodiversity in the world. Its territory comprises nine countries (Bolivia, Brazil, Colombia, Ecuador, French Guiana (France), Guyana, Peru, Suriname, and Venezuela), all having distinct historical legacies of colonization and development. For example, the Legal Amazon region in Brazil comprises nine states (Acre, Amapá, Amazonas, Maranhão, Mato Grosso, Pará, Rondônia, Roraima, and Tocantins) that share the Amazon basin's ecosystems and face similar socio-environmental challenges.

The Amazon was envisioned and invented by travelers in the sixteenth century and had a significant role in Western thought for a long time. It has influenced science's perspective of the environment and the ways of life of Indigenous populations. From the eighteenth century onward, several expeditions aimed to observe and document nature and Indigenous peoples. They gathered explorers searching for a place where they might encounter men and nature "in its purest form" (Barreto, 1999–2000, 35). The "pre-Edenic primitivism" and the "primordial hell" visions alternated, according to Gondim (1994, 10), as potential explanations of a new and unknown world. The European imagination of the forest, and its human and nonhuman inhabitants, continually attracted foreigners and, later, Brazilians who perceived the region as an immense laboratory to support their theories about the world.

The myth of El Dorado provides the imagination of an unexplored world. Castro (2010, 106) notes that "as a result, at the imaginary level, the relationship between man and nature is built." She observes that the "invention of modern myths as the myth of the untouched nature," allied with European colonial domination, has implications for the recent Amazonian history (see chapter 5). These ideas, which further support the erroneous premise of inexhaustible resources, have also influenced common sense and the failure of the current public policies for the Amazon region. The inadequate exploitation of natural resources goes hand in hand with the threat to human populations, both having marked the long-term history of the Amazon. Nevertheless, this history is also written by the human agency that has transformed and preserved the Amazonian landscapes.

The Amazonian territory is a mosaic of past and present histories intertwined in many aspects. Their similarities have indicated the establishment of extensive exchange networks in the precolonial period. Their differences point to the extraordinary cultural diversity that persists (Barreto, Lima, and Betancourt, 2016). Consequently, heritage in the Amazon incorporates archaeological, colonial, modern, and contemporary assets. The tangible and intangible dimensions of Amazonian heritage are blurred in part of the "natural" and "cultural" dimensions. Even the rainforest cannot be reduced to natural heritage, and the same is true for "cultural" heritage. For more specific methods and policies of heritage management, however, the distinction of categories has driven the identification, registration, and preservation of heritage resources.

The National, Historical, and Artistic Heritage Institute (IPHAN) (the Brazilian agency responsible for heritage protection), recognizes diverse heritage in the Amazon region. The categories of material, immaterial, and natural heritage include: 1) archaeological sites, such as mounds, geoglyphs, megaliths, shell mounds, anthropogenic dark earth sites, rock art paintings, caves, underwater sites; 2) historical sites, such as church ruins, fortresses, mills, fish traps; and 3) traditional knowledge, such as cultural expressions, places, besides agriculture systems, music, dance, handicraft, festivals, Catholic processions, falls. Moreover, it contains natural sites, such as parks, conservation units, and ecosystems.

Four are on the World Heritage List (WHL/UNESCO). They comprise: 1) oral and graphic expressions of the Wajãpi, produced by an Indigenous group; 2) the procession of the Círio de Nazaré, an annual and historic Catholic event; 3) the cultural complex of Bumba-meu-boi, a ritualistic expression involving music and performance; and 4) the Central Amazon Conservation Complex, a national park.

There are five Amazonian properties on the Tentative List of UNESCO. There are three national parks, two theaters, and the Acre Geoglyphs (large-scale archaeological sites constituted by excavating ditches arranged in geometric forms; see Schaan, 2012). Although undeniably rich, the Amazonian heritage located in northern Brazilian states represents only 4 percent of the cultural resources that are *tombados* (formally recognized by a particular type of registration procedure) by IPHAN in Brazil (Lima, 2018a). Many valuable natural and cultural assets are not even officially designated as heritage sites. In this sense, Lima (2018a, 21) admits that the identification and recognition process are two of the region's main challenges for heritage management.

Over the last decade, different expressions of heritage have been claimed by local communities and studied by scholars from multiple fields (see Lima, 2018b). The interaction between these two modes of thought has brought

Figure 10.4. Archaeological Site - Megaliths, Calçoene, Amapá. Photo: M. Bezerra.

Figure 10.5. The Círio de Nazaré, Belém, Pará. Brazilian Intangible Heritage Included in the WHL—UNESCO. Photo: A. Garcia

visibility to historically excluded pasts, knowledge, and marginalized communities of the Amazon. It has also broadened our understanding of heritage and drawn attention to how closely bound the people and the environmental history in the Amazon are. Likewise, it became clear that temporality has a unique meaning in the Amazon heritage's constitution. Through daily interactions with things and other presences, people experience both the past and the present; they dwell in the landscapes (Ingold, 1993). The archaeological investigations have offered valuable and potential data to these debates.

4. ARCHAEOLOGICAL HERITAGE IN THE AMAZON

The Amazon became the "paradise of naturalists" (Bates, 1944, 84) in the nineteenth century and soon began to welcome several scientific expeditions composed of "more specialized naturalists" (Meirelles Filho, 2009, 19). These missions were crucial in recognizing and reporting several archaeological sites and artifacts as they traveled to different parts of the Amazonian territory.

Many naturalist travelers have recorded and examined archaeological findings and provided theories to explain the occurrence and origins of the sites and artifacts (Barreto, 1999–2000). According to Sanjad (2011) and Linhares

(2017), archaeological materiality was pivotal in nation formation debates. Thus, discoveries and explorations enhanced their relevance in contemporary Brazil. Consequently, the history of archaeology in the Amazon contributes to the institutionalization of science in the country.

The ideas arising from these intense exploratory activities sustained the permanence of a stereotyped vision of the indigenous populations that lingers in the neoevolutionism debates that dominated Amazonian archaeology for decades (Schaan, 2012). The premise of a scarcity of resources as a limiting factor for the settlement of fully developed societies in the Amazon was the basis of the interpretive model accepted from the second half of the twentieth century onwards (Meggers, 1971). This perspective proposed that populations with high social complexity would have experienced a process of degeneration as they had been incapable of maintaining their agricultural activities perennially.

However, archaeological research conducted at the turn of the twentieth century has demonstrated that the conception of agriculture, as conceived in the Old World's prehistory, does not fit the Amazonian context properly. Furthermore, archaeobotanical studies (Neves et al., 2021) have confirmed the existence of an abundance of resources. That would have relieved "the populations from the burden of laborious agriculture" (Moraes, 2015, 38). Therefore, Neves suggests that we approach the history of the ancient Amazon based on the "management of the abundance" (Lima, 2020), as practiced by the populations that occupied the region in the precolonial period.

Archaeological data show that past management strategies transformed landscapes and contributed to the formation of the Amazon ecosystem. From the perspective of historical ecology (Balée, 1998), archaeological knowledge has deconstructed the idea of untouched nature and demographic void. Research offers some premises. First, the Amazon rainforest has an anthropogenic origin (at least 11.8%, according to Balée (1989)). Second, dense populations occupied the region during the precolonial period. Finally, environmental management strategies employed by Indigenous populations ensured the survival of the Amazonian environment. This long-lasting Indigenous history began twelve thousand years ago (Neves et al., 2021) and left marks that form a vast and rich array of heritage assets.

Brazil has over twenty-six thousand registered archaeological sites (IPHAN, 2022). More than 20 percent are in the Amazon, upward of five thousand sites. In 2003, the United Nations Educational, Scientific and Cultural Organization (UNESCO) designated a set of four conservation units (UC)—the Central Amazon Conservation Complex—as a Natural World Heritage (NWH) site (UNESCO 2022). There is impressive archaeological heritage in the area covered by the UCs. Some sites are under investigation by teams of archaeologists, such as those in the Mamirauá Institute for Sustainable Development (IDSM) (Lima et al., 2021).

During fieldwork, the researchers noticed that people identified traces of the past in the landscape. Plants were often associated with human presence in the past since they are not necessarily sharing the same "natural" places. According to the local people, it implies that ancient societies cultivated them. As previously argued by Cabral (2016 and 2022), the team of archaeologists questioned the conventional notion of the archaeological site (Lima et al., 2021, 6).

The ancient vestiges were perceived as physically constituted by landscapes. Bezerra (2017), while studying a group of ancient fish traps on Marajó Island in the Amazon, has suggested that river water is a fluid component of these structures and therefore a part of the archaeological heritage. How do we define the boundaries of an archaeological site in the Amazon? Moreover, who sets these boundaries?

In 2019, IPHAN announced a definition of an archaeological site through Ordinance No. 316. According to its attributions, the institute is the coordinator for Brazil's archaeological research permissions and heritage protection. On November 4, 2019, IPHAN specified the procedures for identifying and recognizing archaeological sites. However, the normative approach of this space excludes the ancient human agency over the landscapes. Human activities determine the archaeological matter, forming traces, artifacts, and other archaeological record components. Sometimes disconnected, landscape elements may also be considered vestiges of the past, such as trees

Figure 10.6.   Archaeological Site - Fish Trap, Marajó Island, Pará. Photo: A. Garcia.

(Limaet al., 2021), birds (Cabral, forthcoming), and the Amazonian Rivers (Bezerra, 2017).

According to Orton (2000, 67), when asked to define a site, archaeologists would allegedly reply, "I cannot define precisely, but I recognize one when I see it." This assumption suggests that the indication of a site occurs through technical expertise, prior experience, and visual perception. Communities in the Amazon perceive indicators of old human presence in the landscapes like we archaeologists recognize a site when we find one. Western categories of site, heritage, and the authority of archaeology are subverted, thus influencing other modes of knowing the past and its traces (Cabral, 2016; Bezerra, 2018). Beyond the normative state boundaries, archaeological heritage is active and merges with the ordinary landscapes of the people who live near the sites.

Andrade (2018, 22) suggests using the cultural landscape seal instrument to broaden the scope of the public policies for archaeological preservation. She argues for a "landscape heritage network" that encompasses the past, the local people, and knowledge of the present. In the Amazon, this "heritage network" weaves past and present landscapes in a myriad of unique and complex dimensions.

5. ANCIENT AMAZONIAN LANDSCAPES

Indigenous peoples have transformed Amazonian geographies over millennia. Provided that in Amerindian ontologies, the strict dualism of nature and culture is not sustained, it is plausible that the anthropogenic forest is composed of a source of ancestors' stories and experiences, which also incorporate archaeological assets. In this sense, the Amazonian archaeological heritage comprises a multitude of humans and nonhumans who lived, and still live, in its landscapes. According to Neves et al. (2021, 27), the Amazon "has been shaped by an archive of human action," reinforcing the assumption that the natural/cultural, material/immaterial, and human/nonhuman dichotomies concerning the archaeological heritage are untenable.

Indigenous perspectives on archaeological remains have transformed the field of archaeology and challenged the concept of heritage in the Amazon. Virtanen (2019, 336–331) points out that Amazonian cultural heritage is "not only produced by humans; it is also produced with non-humans through interactions and avoidances (. . .) [and] materialized in various cultural heritage forms." These reflections rely on her fieldwork with the Apurinã—an Indigenous Amazonian people—whose territories in the western Amazon include a group of geoglyphs dating from 1000 to 3000 years BP (Schaan, 2012). According to Virtanen, the ancient geoglyphs are still in the Apurinã's memories.

As Cabral (2014, 326) describes, for the Wajãpi—an indigenous Amazonian people—the archaeological remains found in their territory come to have meaning if they recognize their interconnection with the Wajãpi's knowledge, places, and people. They associate a living bird with traces of ancient times. The past inscribed into the Wajãpi landscapes refreshes the sense of archaeological vestiges (Cabral, 2022). The "archaeological" dimension embraces much more than the materiality of objects and sites. To the indigenous archaeologist Jaime Xamen Wai Wai, "Archaeology is everything" (Rodrigues, Kater, and XamenWai Wai, 2020, 117), and not just restricted to the things recovered from the sites and classified as archaeological heritage by Western science.

Amazon forest peoples (Indigenous, riverine, quilombolas) create special bonds with archaeological things. The proximity to the sites intensifies the engagement with the past. Houses and gardens are built over anthropogenic dark earth sites or in areas where archaeological places remain scattered on the surface. Artifact collecting is a common practice in the region (Bezerra and Ferreira, 2022; Cabral, Pereira, and Bezerra, 2018; Lima, 2019; Lima et al., 2021). Daily experience with the material culture of the past fuels the Amazonian imagination, as the archaeological finds and sites are related to haunting narratives (Bezerra and Ferreira, 2022). These elements—artifacts, sites, environment, imaginary—are tangled up and form archaeological heritage. Ongoing environmental destruction threatens these long-term landscapes.

6. ARCHAEOLOGY AND ENVIRONMENTAL POLICIES

Due to the impact of development activities and the failure of the current government's environmental policy, people who fight for the Amazon's preservation have been even more active in recent years. The anti-indigenous ideology benefits groups who illegally exploit Indigenous territories in the Amazon. The Amazonian ecosystems are being destroyed at an increasing rate, and the violence against forest peoples and those striving to prevent human rights violations in the region has worsened. At the time of this writing, we were baffled by the murders of Brazilian Indigenous supporter Bruno Pereira and English journalist Dom Philips (Lakhani, 2022) in Vale do Javari, State of Amazonas. Moreover, the statue of the rubber tapper and environmental activist Chico Mendes, killed in 1988, was vandalized and toppled a month after the homicides of Bruno Pereira and Dom Phillips (Nascimento, 2022). These episodes materialize the violence exacerbated since the beginning of this government.

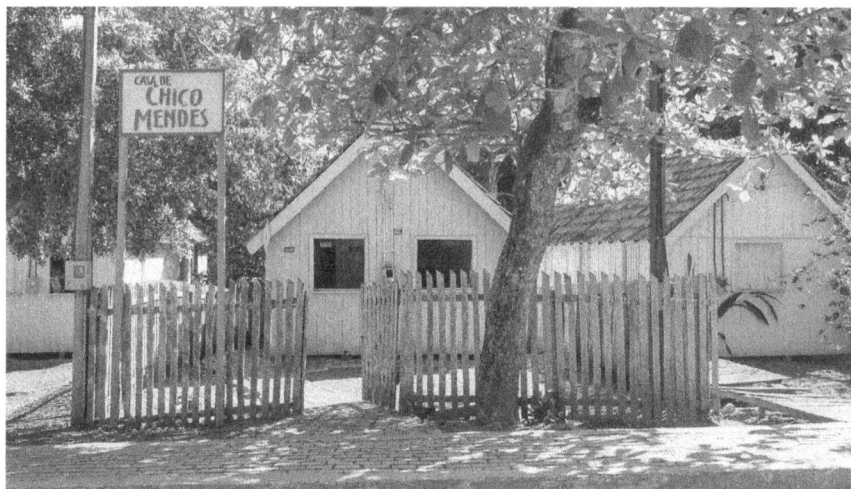

Figure 10.7. The Chico Mendes´House, Xapuri, Acre. Recognized as Brazilian Historical Heritage Since 2011. Photo: M. Bezerra.

Development projects have a disastrous and irreversible effect on populations and archaeological sites. The forest's devastation, aggravated by a change in environmental licensing procedures, impacts "humanized landscapes and, consequently, the forest peoples' heritage" (Rocha, 2020, 169). The loss of the forest means the loss of millennia of history and human experiences with this ecosystem. Archaeological site damage, likewise, annihilates a plethora of ancient knowledge preserved by time.

Environmental public policies should consider the long-term process of local knowledge production. Ancient knowledge preserved in archaeological sites is valuable for implementing sustainable development models. In tandem with the palaeoecological approach, the study of archaeology offers relevant answers for ancient strategies: it indicates a pivotal role in making today's biodiversity (Neves et al., 2021). For twelve thousand years, human agency over the landscape has ensured the existence and survival of the Amazon rainforest. Today, resistance movements from the local communities have also been decisive in conserving biodiversity and archaeological assets. Abdenur et al. (2020) emphasize that climate diplomacy could also play a vital role in the preservation of the archaeological heritage in the Amazon, as the global community would indeed benefit from the ancestral "lessons" of environmental management revealed by archaeology.

By including past and present people in the environmental history of the Amazon, archaeology takes a position against the technology and bureaucratic model applied to addressing environmental issues. According to Zhouri (2008, 98), this pragmatic vision "attributes to the environment the status of an autonomous reality external to social relations." It alienates from environmental governance the collectives that are, in fact, active in the struggles against destructive development policies.

These criticisms echo in the field of archaeology, especially in debates regarding its involvement in development projects and the implications for the archaeological heritage and the local populations (Zarankin and Pellini, 2012; Bezerra, 2015; Rocha et al., 2013; Rocha, 2020). Until recently, 98 percent of archaeological research in the country was carried out within the scope of the environmental licensing process (Bezerra, 2015). Over the last twenty years, almost 90 percent of the projects undertaken in the northern states that comprise the Brazilian Amazon have been related to preventive archaeology (Cabral, Pereira, and Bezerra, 2018).

This scenario has eventually led to growing activism among archaeologists working in the region. They have been engaging with local people and transforming the discipline's knowledge to change people's lives (Rocha et al., 2013; Hartemann and Moraes, 2018; Lima, 2019; Rocha, 2020, among others). Traditional communities activate the archaeological heritage as a political and identity tool in these contexts and are associated with a network of places, knowledge, and affections. This broadens the meanings of heritage beyond archaeology and situates archaeology in people's daily lives in the present.

7. SOME THOUGHTS ON ANTARCTIC AND AMAZON HERITAGE

If we understand heritage as a culturally and politically complex process of negotiation, creating memories that involve a variety of discourses and practices that create meanings with relevance and usefulness in the present, the construction of particular heritage standards through time in Antarctica and the Amazon starts to make sense.

In the case of Antarctica, it is clear how the construction of the heritage thought within an international territory reflects aspirations of national sovereignty. Thus, despite the heterogeneity of elements included in the lists of HSMs, most respond to the interests of different nations. Tractors, bases, shipwrecks, expeditionary campsites, and monoliths are part of a narrative heritage. Similarly, there are discourses reflecting nationalistic, androcentric, and elitist meanings.

At the same time, within a context in which nature preservation and human occupation are the primary concern, stories about the extreme commercial exploitation of Antarctica, the destruction of its fauna, and the use of underpaid labor, are memories that the system chooses to hide and make invisible.

Unsurprisingly, there are no HSMs related to the early sealer exploitation of the continent.

In opposition to the silencing of subaltern groups and their stories, which is the key to understanding the arrival of human beings to Antarctica, archaeology has been working to include them as part of the official narratives, in order to build antihegemonic heritages with new protagonists. This is the only way to understand the transformation processes and the relationship between humans and Antarctica.

The Amazon presents its logic as being closer to the case of the Arctic, a vast territory, which is not a continent, and each country it encompasses has sovereignty over its territory. It is crucial to mention this since existing accounts circulate the idea that both territories are world domains. On the one hand, narratives support exploitation and internationalization; on the other, movements embracing ecosystem defense recognize its vital role in the planet's climate. The internal narratives also alternate between these two directions, with increased reliance on the first, which has been the cornerstone of the current government's environmental policies.

However, archaeological heritage studies demonstrated the Amazon's relevance for Brazil and the global community, stressing that biodiversity conservation is not the only factor. Indeed, biodiversity is the result of thousands of years of human intervention. In this sense, debates about Amazon heritage must transcend the natural versus cultural and past versus present dichotomies. Humanized landscapes are the Amazon's heritage. They convey a historical and symbolic meaning informed by the knowledge and experiences of thousands of generations who have been writing this history and who, through their environmental management lessons, will be paramount in safeguarding the future of the Amazon's heritage.

Antarctica and the Amazon share the primacy of dominated narratives about heritage, centered on concepts such as wilderness and pristine and untouched nature. In other words, for most people, the prominent heritage of these territories is their nature (fauna, flora, and drinking water—rivers and glaciers). However, differences become evident when associating these spaces with human action. In the case of Antarctica, as we saw in this chapter, this relationship is fundamentally built on nationalist and elitist perspectives, emphasizing the heritage of white explorers. The remains of their expeditions have been the central focus of heritage policies on this continent since the beginning. In the case of the Amazon, notwithstanding the burden of the colonial period, indigenous peoples and traditional communities have been rendered invisible. This is why archaeology continues to be crucial for favoring other antihegemonic heritages that allow the construction of more diverse narratives about influential and essential territories.

ACKNOWLEDGMENT

We would like to thank Fábio Albergaria Queiroz, Ana Flávia Barros-Platiau, and Guilherme Lopes da Cunha for the invitation to take part in this publication, and our universities, UFMG and UFPA for the support, as well as the funding from the CNPq, CONICET, and FAPEMIG.

NOTE

1. The Antarctic Treaty is a document signed on December 1, 1959, by the countries that claim possession of continental parts of Antarctica, in which they agree to suspend their claims indefinitely, allowing for the freedom of scientific exploration of the continent under the regime of international cooperation.

REFERENCES

Abdenur, A. E., C. P. Moraes, E. K. Tamanaha, F. O. Almeida; B.P. Maximo. "Protecting archaeological sites in the Amazon is essential for environmental well-being." *Latin America and Caribbean Forests and Biodiversity*, December 15, 2020, https://climate-diplomacy.org/magazine/environment/protecting -archaeological-sites-amazon-essential-environmental-wellbeing.

Andrade, M. N. "Os Olhares Sobre o Patrimônio Arqueológico de Itaipu (Niterói/RJ) e sua Ressignificação como Paisagem Cultural." PhD Diss., Universidade Federal do Rio de Janeiro, 2018..

Avango, D. "Acting artifacts: on the meaning of material culture in Antarctica." In *Antarctica and the Humanities*, edited by P. Roberts, A. Hawkins, and L.-M. Van der Watt, 159–179. London: Palgrave Macmillan, 2016.

Avango, D. "Remains of industry in the Polar Regions: histories, processes, heritage." *Entreprises et Histoire* 87: (2017):133–149.

Avango, D. and Hacquebord, L. "The history and heritage of natural resource exploitation in the Arctic and Antarctic: The LASHIPA project." *Patrimoine de l'industrie* 19 (2008): 7–16.

Balée, W. "The Culture of Amazonian forests." In *Resource Management in Amazonia: Indigenous and folk strategies*, edited by D. A. Posey, and W. Balée, 1–21. New York: New York Botanical Garden, 1989.

Balée, W. *Advances in Historical Ecology*. New York: Columbia University Press, 1998.

Darr, S. "Twenty years of protection of historic values in Antarctica under the Madrid Protocol." *Polar Journal* 8 (2018): 241–264

Barreto, C. "A construção de um passado pré-colonial: uma breve história da arqueologia no Brasil." *Revista USP* 44 (1999–2000): 32–51.

Barreto, C., H. P. Lima, and C. J. Betancourt. *Cerâmicas Arqueológicas da Amazônia: rumo a uma nova síntese.* Belém: Iphan: MPEG, 2016.

Bates, H. W. *O naturalista do rio Amazonas.* São Paulo: Companhia Editora Nacional, 1944. 2 v. (Brasiliana, 237).

Berguño, J. "Las Shetland del Sur: El ciclo lobero." Primera parte. *Boletín Antártico Chileno* 12, (Abril 1993a): 5–13.

Berguño, J. (1993b). "Las Shetland del Sur: El ciclo lobero. Segunda parte. *Boletín Antártico Chileno* 12 (October 1993): 2–9.

Bertrand, K. J. *Americans in Antarctica, 1775–1948.* New York: American Geographical Society, 1971.

Bezerra, M. "At that Edge: Archaeology, Heritage Education, and Human Rights in the Brazilian Amazon." *International Journal of Historical Archaeology*, 19 (2015): 822–831.

Bezerra, M. *Teto e Afeto: sobre as pessoas, as coisas e a arqueologia na Amazônia.* Belém: GK Noronha, 2017.

Bezerra, M. "O machado que vaza ou algumas notas sobre as pessoas e as superfícies do passado presente na Amazônia." *Vestígios - Revista Latino-Americana de Arqueologia Histórica* 12, no.2 (2018): 51–58.

Bezerra, M., and G. L. Ferreira. "Affective Museums: The practice of Collecting Archaeological Artefacts in the Brazilian Amazon." In *The Oxford Handbook of Museum Archaeology*, edited by A. Stevenson. London: Oxford University Press, 2022.

Cabral, M. "De cacos, pedras moles e outras marcas: percursos de uma Arqueologia não-qualificada." *Amazônica - Revista de Antropologia* 6, no. 2, (2014): 314–331.

Cabral, M. P. "Cuando un pájaro viviente es un vestigio arqueológico: considerando la arqueología desde una perspectiva de conocimiento diferente." In *Otros pasados: ontologias alternativas en el estudio de lo que ha sido*, edited by F. Rojas, B. Hamann, and B. Anderson. Bogotá: Universidad de Los Andes Press /El Fondo de Promoción de la Cultura, 2022.

Cabral, M. P. Pereira, D., and Bezerra, M. "Patrimônio arqueológico na Amazônia: a pesquisa, a gestão e as pessoas." *Revista do Patrimônio Histórico e Artístico Nacional*, 38 (2018): 247–268.

Engel, K., S. Mc Bride, R. Vijayaraghavan, and C. Ziemke-Dickens. "Antarctic Heritage Revisited." Syndicate Report (ANTA604), University of Canterbury, 2019. Accessed November 20, 2022. https://ir.canterbury.ac.nz

Evans, S. L. "Icy heritage: managing historic sites in the Antarctic: pristine wilderness, anthropogenic degradation, or cultural landscape." *Polar Journal* 1, no.1, (2011): 87–100.

Fitte, E. *El descubrimiento de la Antártida: crónica de los hombres y barcos que exploraron las aguas de las Shetland del Sur.* Buenos Aires: Emecé, 1962.

Fitte, E. *Crónicas del Atlántico Sur: Patagonia, Malvinas y Antártida.* Buenos Aires: Emecé, 1974.

Gondim, N. *A invenção da Amazônia.* São Paulo, SP: Marco Zero, 1994.

Harrowfield, D. L. "Archaeology in Antarctica." *New Zealand Journal of Archaeology* 26 (2005): 5–28.

Hartemann, G., and I. P. de Moraes. "Contar histórias e caminhar com ancestrais: por perspectivas afrocentradas e decoloniais na arqueologia." *Vestígios - Revista Latino-Americana de Arqueologia Histórica* 12, no. 2 (2018): 9–34.

Hodge, J. "El Extremo Sur de América." *América* 28, no. 8 (1976): 7–16.

IPHAN. "Portaria nº 316." Law, procedures for archeological sites (November 4, 2019). https://www.in.gov.br/web/dou/-/portaria-n-316-de-4-de-novembro-de-2019-225612769.

IPHAN. "Patrimônio Arqueológico." Accessed November 16, 2022. http://portal.iphan.gov.br/pagina/detalhes/1376.

Lakhani, N. "Brazil's weak response to Phillips–Pereira murders threatens Indigenous people, lawyer says." *The Guardian*, July 16, 2022. https://www.theguardian.com/world/2022/jul/15/dom-philips-bruno-pereira-murders-brazil-indigenous.

Leane, E., Winter, T., and Salazar, J. "Caught between nationalism and internationalism: replicating histories of Antarctica in Hobart." *International Journal of Heritage Studies* 22, no.3 (2016): 214–227.

Lima, H. P. "Patrimônio Para Quem? Por Uma Arqueologia Sensível." *Habitus* 17, no. 1 (2019): 25–38.

Lima, M., M. A. da Silva, S. C. Lima, M. F. Cassino, E. Tamanaha. "Desafios das práticas arqueológicas e da preservação: dinâmicas socioculturais sobre e nos entornos dos sítios arqueológicos na Amazônia." *Boletim do Museu Paraense Emilio Goeldi. Ciências Humanas* 16, no. 2, (2021): e20190153.

Lima, I. M. "Eduardo Góes Neves: 'O Brasil não tem ideia do que é a Amazônia." *Gama Revista,* October 10, 2020. https://gamarevista.com.br.

Linhares, A. M. A. *Um Grego Agora Nu: índios marajoara e identidade nacional brasileira.* Curitiba: CRV, 2017.

Martin, L. "Antarctica Discovered by a Connecticut Yankee, Captain Nathiel Brown Palmer." *The Geographical Review* 30, no. 4, (1940): 529–562.

Meggers, B. J. *Amazonia: man and culture in a counterfeit paradise.* Chicago: Aldine; Atherton, 1971.

Meirelles Filho, J. *Grandes Expedições à Amazônia Brasileira - 1500–1930.* São Paulo: Metalivros, 2009.

Miers, J. "Account of Discovery of New South Shetland, with Observations on its Importance in Geographical, Commercial and Political Point of View: with Two Plates." *Edinburgh Philosophical Review* 3 (1920): 367–380.

Moraes, C. de P. O determinismo agrícola na arqueologia amazônica. *Estudos Avançados* 29, no. 83 (2015): 25–43.

Nascimento, A. "Estátua de Chico Mendes é arrancada por vândalos em praça no Acre e filha aponta descaso: 'falta de respeito.'" O Globo, July 3, 2022. https://g1.globo.com/ac/acre/natureza/amazonia/noticia/2022/07/03/estatua-de-chico-mendes-e-arrancada-por-vandalos-em-praca-no-acre-e-filha-aponta-descaso-falta-de-respeito.ghtml.

Neves, E. G., L. P. Furquim, C. Levis, B. C. Rocha, J. G. Waitling, F. O. de Almeida, C. J. Betancourt, A. B. Junqueira, C.P. Moraes, G. Morcote-Rios, M.P. Shock, E. K. Tamanaha. "Peoples of the Amazon before European Colonization." In *Amazon Assessment Report 2021*, 3–40, Science Panel for the Amazon, 2021. Accessed

November 21, 2022. https://www.theamazonwewant.org/wp-content/uploads/2022/05/Chapter-8-Bound-May-9.pdf.

O'Gorman, F. "The Return to the Antarctic Fur Seal." *New Scientist* 20 (1963): 6–374.

Ossoinak Garibaldi, E. *Cronología de los Viajes a las Regiones Australes. Antecedentes Argentinos.* Buenos Aires: Universidad de Buenos Aires, Instituto de la Producción. Publicación 12, 1950.

Pearson, M. "Artifacts or rubbish: a dilemma for Antarctic managers." In *Cultural Heritage in Antarctic and Antarctic Regions*, edited by S. Barr and P. Chaplin, 39–43, Lorenskog: IPHC-ICOMOS, 2004.

Pearson, M. "Polar heritage conservation and archaeology." In *Polar settlements—Location, techniques and conservation*, edited by S. Barr and P. Chaplin, 24–34. Fjellhamar: International Council on Monuments and Sites ICOMOS, S. Barr & P. Chaplin, 2011.

Pinochet de la Barra, O. "El misterio del San Telmo ¿Náufragos españoles pisaron por primera vez la Antártida?" *Boletín Antártico Chileno* (abril 1992): 2–5.

Rocha, B. C. "'Rescuing' the ground from under their feet? Contract archaeology and human rights violations in the Brazilian Amazon." In *Critical Perspectives on Cultural Memory and Heritage: Construction, Transformation, and Destruction* edited by V. Apaydin, 169–188. London: UCL Press, 2020.

Rocha, B. C., C. Jácome, F. F. Stuchi, G. Z. Mongeló, and R. Valle. "Arqueologia pelas gentes: um manifesto. constatações e posicionamentos críticos cobre a arqueologia brasileira em tempos de PAC." *Revista de Arqueologia* 26, no. 1 (2013): 130–140.

Rodrigues, I. M. M., T. Kater, and J. Xamen Wai Wai. "Arqueologia indígena dos povos do rio Mapuera: entrevista com Jaime Xamen Wai Wai." *Revista do Museu de Arqueologia e Etnologia* 35 (2020): 114–121.

Roura, R. M. "Antarctic cultural heritage: Geopolitics and management." In *Handbook of Antarctic Politics*, edited by K. Dodds, A. Hemmings, and P. Edward Roberts, 468–484. Cheltenham: Elgar Press, 2017

Schaan, D. P. *Sacred Geographies of Ancient Amazonia: Historical Ecology of Social Complexity.* Walnut Creek: Left Coast Press, 2012.

Sanjad, N. "Ciência dos potes quebrados: nação e região na arqueologia brasileira do século XIX." *Anais do Museu Paulista: História e Cultura Material* 19, no. 1 (2011): 134–164.

Senatore, M. X. "Antarctic historical sealing industry and material things." In *Historical Antarctic Sealing Industry*, edited by R. Headland, 61–71. Cambridge: Scott Polar Research Institute, Cambridge University, 2018.

Senatore, M. X. *Assessing tourism patterns in the South Shetland Islands for the conservation of 19th-century archaeological sites in Antarctica.* London: Polar Record, 2019.

Senatore, M. X., and A. Zarankin. "Widening the scope of the Antarcticheritage archaeology and the ugly, the dirty, and the evil in Antarctic history." In *Polar settlements—Location, techniques and conservation,* edited by S. Barr & P. Chaplin, 51–59. Fjellhamar: International Council on Monuments and Sites ICOMOS, 2011.

Senatore, M. X., and A. Zarankin. "Against the domain of master narratives: archaeology and history in Antarctica." In *Against the Typological Tyranny in Archaeology:*

A View from South America, edited by Gnecco, C. and Langebaek, C., 121–132. New York: Springer.

Slaney, H. "Notice of the voyage of Edward Barnsfield, Master of his Majesty's Ship Andromache, to New South Shetland." *Edinburgh Philosophical Journal* 4 (1921): 345–348.

Stackpole, E. *The Voyages of the Huron and the Huntress: The American Sealers and the Discovery of the Continent of Antarctica*. Mystic, CT: Marine Historical Association, 1955.

UNESCO, United Nations Educational. "Central Amazon Conservation Complex." Accessed November 24, 2022. https://whc.unesco.org/en/list/998.

Virtanen, P. K. "Ancestors' times and protection of Amazonian Indigenous biocultural heritage." *AlterNative* 15, no. 4 (2019): 330–339.

Zarankin, A., and M. X. Senatore. "Ocupación Humana en Tierras Antárticas: una aproximación arqueológica. Soplando el viento." *Actas de las Terceras Jornadas de Arqueología de la Patagonia 3* (1996): 629–644.

Zarankin, A., and M. X. Senatore. "Arqueología en Antártida. Primeras Estrategias Humanas de Ocupación y Explotación en Península Byers, Isla Livingston, Shetland del Sur." *Actas de las Cuartas Jornadas de Investigaciones Antárticas - Instituto Antártico Argentino 4* (1997): 7–10.

Zarankin, A., and M. X. Senatore. *Arqueología en Antártida, Estrategias, Tácticas y los paisajes del capitalismo. En prensa en Desde el país de los gigantes. Perspectivas Arqueológicas en Patagonia*. Río Gallegos: Universidad Nacional de la Patagonia Austral, 1999.

Zarankin, A., and M. X. Senatore. "Hasta el fin del Mundo. Arqueología en las Islas Shetland del Sur. El caso de Península Byers, Isla Livingston." *Praehistoria* 3 (2000): 219–236.

Zarankin, A. and M. X. Senatore. *Historias de un Pasado en Blanco: Arqueología Histórica Antártica*. Belo Horizonte: Argumentum, 2007.

Zarankin, A., S. Hissa, M. Salerno, Y-A. Froner, G. Alkmim, L. Assis, and A. Batista. "Paisagens em branco: Arqueologia e antropologia antárticas - Avanços e desafios. Vestígios." *Revista Latino-Americana de Arqueología Histórica* 5, no. 2 (2011): 9–52.

Zarankin, A. and J. R. Pellini. "Arqueologia e Companhia: Reflexões Sobre a introdução de uma lógica de Mercado na prática arqueológica brasileira." *Revista de Arqueologia* 25, no. 2, (2012): 44–60.

Zarankin, A., and M. Salerno. "Antarctic archaeology: Discovering the history of the southernmost end of the world." In *The Oxford Handbook of Historical Archaeology*, edited by James Symonds and Vesa-Pekka Herva. New York: Oxford University Press, 2017.

Zarankin, A., F. Codevilla, M. Salerno, M. J. Cruz, G. Radicchi, A. Martire, L. Stollmeier, and A. Oliveira. "Paisagens em Branco, balanço após 10 anos de existência no Brasil." In *Antartica em Minas, Avanços científicos nas áreas de medicina/fisiologia, microbiologia e arqueologia do polo sul e sua importância para o Brasil*, edited by Andres Zarankin, Luiz H. Rosa, Rosa M. Esteves Arantes e Fernanda Codevilla Soares, 5–22. Belo Horizonte: Imprensa UFMG, 2021.

Andrés Zarankin and Marcia Bezerra

Zhouri, A. "Justiça Ambiental, Diversidade Cultural e *Accountability* Desafios para a governança ambiental." *Revista Brasileira de Ciências Sociais* 23, no. 68 (2008): 97–194.

Index

Pages references for figures are italicized.

About the Contributors

Adriana Marcos Vivoni holds a BA in microbiology and immunology from the Federal University of Rio de Janeiro (1999), a MSc (2001) and a PhD (2005) in science (microbiology), from the same institution. She is currently a researcher at the Oswaldo Cruz Institute at Rio de Janeiro and works as coordinator of the National Reference Laboratory for anthrax and as curator of the *Bacillus* genus and related genera culture collection of Fiocruz. Her field of expertise is microbiology with an emphasis in medical microbiology. Her current research is mainly focused on typing and molecular epidemiology of *Bacillus* bacteria and related genera with particular interest in isolation, identification, and molecular typing of *B. anthracis*. In 2018, she joined the multidisciplinary team of FIOANTAR, the FIOCRUZ scientific program for Antarctic research.

Ana Flávia Barros-Platiau is an associate professor at the University of Brasilia (UnB) at the International Relations Institute and associate researcher at the Brazilian Defense College (ESD) in Brasilia. She has a PhD (2001) in international relations from the Université de Paris I (Panthéon-Sorbonne). Her postdoctoral research was conducted at the CERIC (Centre d' Études et de Recherches Internationales et Communautaires) in the University of Aix Marseille (France). She is the director of the Brasilia Research Centre for the scientific network Earth System Governance. Her research areas include global sustainability governance, ocean and polar diplomacy, and Brazilian foreign policy.

Andrei Polejack holds a master's degree in ecology from the University of Brasilia, where he was trained as a natural scientist. After twenty years working for the Brazilian science and technology governmental sector, he is now transitioning to social sciences after getting a PhD from the World Maritime University. His research on ocean science diplomacy and its role in progressing ocean sustainability and governance was based on a Global South perspective. Andrei chaired many ocean and Antarctic-related international fora and acted as a delegate from Brazil in several international negotiations.

Andrés Zarankin is a professor of archaeology at the Department of Anthropology and Sociology, Faculty of Philosophy and Human Sciences, in the Federal University of Minas Gerais. He holds a PhD from the University of Campinas, Brazil (2001), and a BA in anthropology from the Universidad de Buenos Aires, UBA, Argentina (1994). Hi postdoctoral research was conducted at Consejo Nacional de Investigaciones Cientificas y Tecnicas, CONICET, Argentina (2003) and the Institute of Philosophy and Human Sciences / UNICAMP, IFCH-UNICAMP, Brazil (2006). His focus is on developing new ways of studying the Antarctic continent from an archaeological approach with an emphasis on the first human occupations in Antarctica for more than two decades. Since 2007, he has coordinated the Laboratory of Antarctic Studies in Human Sciences, located in the Federal University of Minas Gerais (Brazil). In recent years, he has been researching new approaches and theoretical frameworks to address new ways of understanding Antarctica from the human sciences perspective.

Carina Costa de Oliveira is an associate professor of international and environmental law at the Faculty of Law, University of Brasilia, Brazil. She was a visiting scholar at the C-EENRG, University of Cambridge, the University of Adelaide, Australia, and the CERIC (Centre d' Études et de Recherches Internationales et Communautaires) at the University of Aix-Marseille (France). She earned a PhD in international law, from Panthéon-Assas, France. She is the coordinator of the research group on law, natural resources and sustainability (Gern-UnB: https://sites.google.com/ccom.unb.br/ndsr -gern). She was the organizer of books on marine environment and law on topics such as exploration and exploitation on the coastal zone, the continental shelf, and the deep seabed (2015–2021). Research areas include public and private international law, environmental law, conservation and sustainable use of marine resources.

Carlos Alfredo Lazary Teixeira is executive director of the Amazon Cooperation Treaty Organization (ACTO) as well as a lawyer and diplomat. He was the ambassador of Brazil in Ecuador (2015–2018) and in Lima (2011–2015). During his career as a diplomat, he was deputy chief of mission in Washington, DC, consul general in Atlanta, and deputy consul general in Miami (United States), consul general in Ciudad del Este (Paraguay), and head of the political sector of the embassy of Brazil in Buenos Aires (Argentina). He was also the substitute representative in the Coordinating Intergovernmental Committee of the River Plate Basin and a member of the Brazilian Delegation for the Negotiations of the Paraguay—Paraná Waterway. In Brazil, he worked at the General Secretariat of the National Security Council (Amazon Issues: Calha Norte and Nossa Natureza programs), was special advisor to the president's chief of staff (biofuels program, atomic energy program, health industrial complex program, representative at COFIG and CAMEX), a member of the president's protocol team, and head of the Trade Promotion Division of the Ministry of Foreign Affairs.

Carlos Henrique Tomé Silva is a legislative consultant of the Brazilian Federal Senate for the environment and urban development. He is a civil engineer (1995) and a lawyer (2006). He holds a master's degree (2011) and a PhD degree (2023) in international relations at the University of Brasilia, developing research on complexity theory and global ocean and polar governance.

Everton Vieira Vargas: Ambassador Vargas graduated from the Brazilian Diplomatic Academy (1977). He earned his MA in international relations at Boston University (1984) and his PhD in Sociology at the University of Brasilia, with honors (2001). He served as ambassador to Germany (2009–2013), Argentina (2013–2016), and the European Union (2016–2018). He was previously posted to the embassy of Brazil in Bonn (1981–1985), to the Mission of Brazil to the UN in New York (1988–1992), and to the embassy in Tokyo (1992–1995). His positions at the Brazilian Ministry of Foreign Affairs include under-secretary general for political affairs (2007–2009), special advisor and chief of staff to the secretary-general of the ministry (2005–2007), director-general of the Department for Environment and Special Affairs (2001–2005), head of the environment division (1998–2001) and of the Division for Science and Technology (1987–1988). He was chief negotiator of climate change (2001–2007). He is the author of several articles on the environment and sustainable development, on sociology and international law. He was a professor of diplomatic language at Instituto Rio Branco between 2002 and 2007. He was also international relations coordinator for the government of the State of Pará (2019–2023).

Fábio Albergaria de Queiroz is an adjunct professor of international relations and geopolitics at the Brazilian Defense College (ESD). He holds a BA in international relations (2000), an MA in sustainable development (2003), a PhD in international relations (2011), postdoctoral studies in international relations (2014–2015), and comparative studies on the Americas (2020–2022) from the University of Brasilia/Brazil. He is the winner of the Federal Coordination for the Improvement of Higher Education Personnel's (CAPES/ Ministry of Education) Thesis Award (2012)—the most distinguished academic prize in Brazil—in Political Science and International Relations with a thesis on "Security and Hydropolitics: The Amazon and la Plata Basins in a comparative perspective."

Flávio Helmold Macieira holds a law degree from the Federal Fluminense University (1974). He graduated from the Brazilian Diplomatic Academy, course for diplomatic formation (1977), as well as in the course for diplomats' professional development with the dissertation, "Brazil and the MTCR (Missile Technology Control Regime). The initial period of Brazilian participation in the regime: observation and analysis" (1998). He earned his MA in international relations at Dublin City University with the dissertation, "Dependency Theory and the relationship between Brazil and the USA" (2002), and a postgraduate degree from the Advanced Defense Studies Program at the Brazilian War College (2020) with a dissertation on "Central America and the Caribbean as a macro-region strategically relevant for Brazil: analysis and propositions aiming at a new regional Brazilian agenda." As a Brazilian career diplomat, Flávio Macieira has been posted to the embassies of Brazil in Sofia (1979–1982), Baghdad (1986–1988), Paris (1994–1998), Dublin (1998–2003), Bern (2003–2006), to the General Consulate in Barcelona (1982–1986), and as an ambassador to Managua (2008–2012), Oslo and Reykjavik (2012–2016), and Panama City (2016–2018). In January 2023, Ambassador Macieira was appointed coordinator for the reopening of the Brazilian embassy in Caracas.

Gilberto Fernando Fisch holds a BA in meteorology from the University of São Paulo (1981), a master's degree in meteorology from the University of São Paulo (1986), a PhD in meteorology from the National Institute for Space Research - INPE (1995), and conducted postdoctoral studies at the Institute of Hydrology (1994). He is a senior researcher at the Institute of Aeronautics and Space (IAE) from the Brazilian Department of Aerospace Science and Technology (DCTA), professor of planetary boundary layer and micrometeorology at INPE, professor of atmospheric processes and climate variability and monitoring at the University of Taubaté (UNITAU), and senior visiting professor at Pennsylvania State University (2018–2019). He has more than 150 articles published in specialized journals from Brazil and abroad. He has developed research in geosciences, with an emphasis on meteorology, and has published on issues related to the following topics: Amazonia, planetary boundary layer, climate, forest and pasture, radiosonde, micrometeorology, water cycle atmospheric modeling, wind profile, and aerospace weather. He has participated in the Intergovernmental Panel on Climate Change (IPCC) as an expert reviewer for the 5th Report (AR5) and as a collaborating author of the Brazilian Panel on Climate Change on the issue of future regional climate changes.

Guilherme Lopes da Cunha is an adjunct professor at the Brazilian War College (ESG), and a collaborating professor at the Brazilian Defense College (ESD) from the Brazilian Ministry of Defense. He is associate researcher for the projects "Critical Analysis of Judicial Decisions Relating to Environmental Crimes in the Amazon: the case of Apuí and Lábrea" and "Prospective for Security and Defense" (PROCAD-DEFESA), supported by the Brazilian Ministries of Defense and Education. His postdoctoral research was conducted at the Institute of International Relations (IREL) in the University of Brasilia (UnB). His PhD (2017) and MA (2013) in international political economy is from the Federal University of Rio de Janeiro, and Bachelor of Laws (2005). His is an executive committee member and section program chair of the Interdisciplinary Studies Section (IDSS) at the International Studies Association (ISA).

José Antonio Marengo Orsini holds a BA in physics and meteorology (1981) and a master's degree in water resources engineering (1987) from Universidad Nacional Agraria, Lima, Peru, and a PhD in meteorology from University of Wisconsin - Madison (1991). He has postdoctoral studies at NASA-GISS, Columbia University in New York and at Florida State University in climate modeling. He is currently a professor at the postgraduate program from the Brazilian National Institute for Space Research (INPE) and the State University of São Paulo (UNESP), and R&D general director at the National Center for Monitoring and Early Warning of Natural Disasters (CEMADEN) from the Brazilian Ministry of Science, Technology, and Innovation (MCTI). He is a member of several international panels of the Organization of the United Nations (IPCC, WMO). He is a consultant in environmental studies on global changes, impacts, vulnerability, and adaptation to climate change. He researches climatology, the Amazon, climate modeling, climate change, extreme events, hydrology and natural disasters, and disaster risk reduction. He is a Fellow of the World Academy of Sciences.

Leandra Regina Gonçalves is a professor at the Federal University of São Paulo (UNIFESP). She is an interdisciplinary researcher who navigates between social and natural sciences trying to discuss and find solutions for ocean sustainability. With a background in biology and a PhD in international relations, Leandra was a postdoctoral researcher at the Oceanographic Institute at the University of São Paulo (Brazil). She was at the University of California - Santa Barbara as a visiting researcher working on her project about the institutional interplay perspective on multilevel governance, the case of the São Paulo coastal region. She has also been involved with NGOs such as Greenpeace, Fundação SOS Mata Atlântica, and others, working mostly with marine policy. Recently, she has been a lead author (policy effectiveness) for the United Nations Environment Programme's (UNEP) Global Environment Outlook 6. Since 2012, she has been a Research Fellow in the Earth System Governance Project.

Luiz Henrique Rosa holds a PhD in microbiology (with emphasis on mycology) and a postdoctorate at the Natural Products Utilization Research Unit of the United States Department of Agriculture (NPURU-USDA-USA). He is a titular professor in the Department of Microbiology at the Federal University of Minas Gerais (UFMG) and chief editor of the *Brazilian Journal of Microbiology*. Professor Rosa has 164 peer-reviewed scientific articles, 38 book chapters, and has published 2 books. He works in the Brazilian Antarctic Program (PROANTAR) investigating taxonomy, diversity, and ecology of Antarctic fungi and their use in biotechnological processes. Luiz Rosa is the coordinator of the polar microbiology thematic laboratory of the Cryostat INCT and is head of the Laboratory of Polar Microbiology and Tropical Connections (MicroPolar) of the Department of Microbiology at UFMG.

Luiz Octávio Gavião is an adjunct professor in defense and logistics at the Brazilian War College (ESG). He has authored two books, sixteen book chapters, and more than ninety articles published in high-ranking journals, congresses, and symposiums. He holds a master's degree in military studies from the United States Marine Corps University (2003), an MBA in business management from Rio de Janeiro Federal University (2006), as well as an MA (2014) and PhD (2017) in production engineering from the Federal Fluminense University (UFF). He served as commanding officer of the 16th Navy Contingent in the United Nations Stabilization Mission in Haiti (MINUSTAH) in 2012.

Marcia Bezerra is a professor at the Federal University of Pará, in Amazon, where she teaches archaeology to the undergraduate program in museology/FAV/ICA and the MA/DSc program in anthropology/PPGA. She holds a BA in archaeology (FINES/RJ), an MA in ancient and medieval history (UFRJ), and a DSc in archaeology (University of São Paulo/USP). She is the former president (2013–2016) of the Society of Brazilian Archaeology (SAB) and South American representative of the World Archaeological Congress/WAC (2008–2016). She has conducted research in the Brazilian Amazon since 2008. Her interests include material culture studies, collecting practices, ethnography of heritage, Amazonian archaeology, archaeology in popular culture, museum archaeology, heritage education, and the teaching of archaeology.

Maria Lucia Marques da Fonseca holds a BA in social communication from Centro Universitário da Cidade (1998) and in architecture and urbanism from the Santa Ursula University (1981), an MA in policy and management in science, technology, and innovation in health from the National School of Public Health (2011). She is currently a public health management analyst at the Oswaldo Cruz Foundation (FIOCRUZ) coordinating cooperation with Asia, Oceania, and the Middle East. She is a researcher of the Global Health and Health Diplomacy Observatory of Fiocruz and member of several work groups, such as: 1) Fiocruz-China; 2) FioLab - Fiocruz Biosafety Laboratory in Antarctica - Brazilian Station (Comandante Ferraz Antarctic Station); 3) FioAntar—Fiocruz Antártica, under the Brazilian Antarctic Program (PROANTAR). She is also a member of the Technical Chamber for International Cooperation of Fiocruz.

Paulo E. A. S. Câmara is a biologist, holding an MA in botany and in sciences and a PhD in plant evolution and systematics from the University of Missouri, Saint Louis. With nine years of experience on polar scientific projects, he is currently a PI on a project aiming to study vegetation connections between Arctic and Antarctic environments under the Brazilian Antarctic Program (PROANTAR). Professor Câmara has 120 peer-reviewed scientific papers and 23 book chapters published. He is currently a professor at graduate programs at the University of Brasilia and the Federal University of Santa Catarina. He worked as a botanist for four years in the Brazilian Amazon rainforest. He is also a graduate from the Brazilian War College (ESG) and has published papers on geopolitical aspects of Antarctica.

Rodrigo Augusto Lima de Medeiros is Full Professor at Centro Universitário de Brasilia (UniCEUB) and an analyst at the Brazilian Ministry of Environment (MMA). Holds a BA in anthropology (2000), a BA in law (2020), an MBA in advanced studies in defense (2019), an MA and PhD in social sciences (2007 and 2012, respectively). During his PhD he was a visiting scholar at the University of North Carolina University(2010).

Milton Keynes UK
Ingram Content Group UK Ltd.
UKHW050053070923
428074UK00005BA/229

9 781666 902686